K

Countertransference
AND THE
Treatment of Trauma

Countertransference
AND THE
Treatment of Trauma

Constance J. Dalenberg

AMERICAN PSYCHOLOGICAL ASSOCIATION

WASHINGTON, DC

Published by
American Psychological Association
750 First Street, NE
Washington, DC 20002

Copies may be ordered from
APA Order Department
P.O. Box 92984
Washington, DC 20090-2984

In the U.K., Europe, Africa, and the Middle East, copies may be ordered from
American Psychological Association
3 Henrietta Street
Covent Garden, London
WC2E 8LU England

Typeset in Palatino by EPS Group Inc., Easton, MD

Printer: United Book Press, Baltimore, MD
Cover Designer: Ed Atkeson, Berg Design
Production Editor: Kristine Enderle

The opinions and statements published are the responsibility of the authors, and such opinions and statements do not necessarily represent the policies of the APA.

Library of Congress Cataloging-in-Publication Data
Dalenberg, Constance J.
    Countertransference and the treatment of trauma/Constance J. Dalenberg.
        p. cm.
    Includes bibliographical references and index.
    ISBN 1-55798-687-8 (alk. paper)
        1. Countertransference (Psychology).   2. Psychic trauma—Treatment.
3. Psychoanalysis.   I. Title.

    RC489.C68 D37 2000
    616.85'210651—dc21   00-024634

British Library Cataloguing-in-Publication Data
A CIP record is available from the British Library.

Printed in the United States of America
First Edition

Dedicated to Paul Nelson Dalenberg
(1920–1999)

Contents

Preface

Writing about the science of psychotherapy has given me great pleasure. I love the process of writing itself and the enhanced clarity of thought it often brings. There is also the chance in the written communication of ideas to practice and thus to hone one's scientific integrity—a critical feature of psychotherapy. One practices a way of thinking that physicist Richard Feynman called "a kind of utter honesty," a leaning over backwards to see clearly and fairly that which is real.

In trying to do so, I endeavored to find examples in my practice and in my research in which I or other clinicians worked under severe countertransferential strain. I found it valuable to examine those cases and those instances that sat on the border of my capacity for empathy, those clinical situations most likely to generate responses I would later regret. I hope that the patterns discovered and lessons learned can be used to expand my own and others' potential for empathy, and perhaps to prevent or mitigate some of the more painful therapeutic ruptures. To the extent that I can, I wish to help place the study of countertransference more clearly in the group of psychological topics most appropriate for scientific as well as more clinically based study.

I extend my gratitude to the clients and research participants who spent so many hours working to teach me the foundations of traumatic transference and the central dimensions of my own and other therapists' trauma countertransference. My friends, students, and research colleagues at the Trauma Research Institute and at San Diego's California School of Professional Psychology also have helped to deepen my understanding. I am particularly grateful to Judy Epstein and Stephen H. Gould, the first readers of this book, and to Tom Smith, my constant object. Further, the administrators and scholars of Doctors for Sexual Abuse Care (DSAC) in New Zealand sponsored the first extensive presentations of the theoretical ideas of this book. Thanks to Claire Hurst and Juliet Broadmore and to the wonderfully responsive New Zealand audiences for their help in refining these ideas.

Finally, I am indebted to those whose work provides the core theory, research, and clinical thought on which my own writings are based. These scholars include Lucy Berliner, John Briere, Laura Brown, Eve Carlson, Christine Courtois, David Finkelhor, Glen Gabbard, Judith Herman, Laurie Pearlman, Kenneth Pope (who originally encouraged me to write this book), and Bessel van der Kolk.

Countertransference
AND THE
Treatment of Trauma

1

Countertransference in Psychotherapy: Definitional Issues

The first strong emotion I recall feeling in the room with my traumatized clients was terror. I was 22 and facing 55-year-old Mr. B, who had recently been banned from his profession due to misconduct. I felt 17. The other two trauma clients I recall from that first year were a 6-year-old boy (who was recovering from an accident that broke his legs and left both parents with paraplegia) and a 32-year-old battered woman. I could not have articulated it at the time, but I felt a duty not only to them, but also to the magnitude of their pain, and I was very afraid that I would fail them. I needed the expertise of my supervisors desperately, and in response to my nervous questions, they freely offered it.

Gently but firmly, and with ample citations to support their positions, my early supervisors suggested that I must not let my clients know my feelings, positive or negative, about working with them. Knowledge of a therapist's feelings is "burdensome," one noted. And because most clients are capable of some intuitive knowledge of their therapists' emotional reactions, it was important to internally monitor and short-circuit these feelings. I had informed Mr. B of my nervousness, which several of my supervisors believed to be a major and perhaps irreversible error.

Obediently, I began nodding sagely at my first clients, hoping to think of a brilliant and transformative interpretation or a sophisticated cognitive–behavioral analysis to offer. It was during this period that my supervisors introduced my colleagues and me to the term "countertransference."

The label countertransference was selectively applied to some of our strong positive and negative feelings about our clients, and it appeared to provide the theoretical underpinnings for the advice that I had been given. Depending on the supervisor, *countertransference* meant either the therapist's conflict-based emotional reactions to the client or all emotional reactions and related behaviors by the therapist. This controversy in definitions is discussed below. However, it was interesting that, independent of their theoretical orientation, experienced clinicians felt the need to discuss this concept.

As a group, my colleagues and I were intrigued by the new topic of countertransference but were not entirely grateful. Typically, if countertransference reactions were to be a major focus of discussion, the general supervision session would be more threatening than usual. Not only would we be told that we were making the wrong interventions in the wrong places, we also would learn that the thoughts and feelings that accompanied our actions were probably linked to our own neuroses. We were told that we were not controlling, containing, suppressing, or even sufficiently monitoring our countertransference; instead we were "acting it out." Defects in our characters and hidden desires to punish or to be punished were typically presented as the source of our mistakes by the analytic supervisors; the cognitive–behavioral professors concentrated more on our more consciously felt wish to rescue and to be admired and on our lack of attention to clients' spoken needs. In general, countertransference was presented as the enemy of neutrality—a crack or bubble in the mirror we were to hold before our clients to reflect their own behaviors, conflicts, desires, and deficits.

My analytic supervisors were presenting the mainstream view of countertransference at the time, best illustrated by one of Sigmund Freud's most commonly quoted statements on the subject:

> We have become aware of the "counter-transference," which arises in [the therapist] as a result of the patient's

influence on his unconscious feelings, and we are almost inclined to insist that he shall recognize this counter-transference in himself and overcome it (S. Freud, 1910/1957, pp. 144–145).

Countertransference must be "overcome," it is argued—mastered, controlled, or eliminated—because it can interfere with the neutral and objective operations of the psychotherapist. And certainly this describes one plausible outcome. Countertransference can be a source of enormous problems. At the time of his writing, Freud was deeply entangled in a number of countertransference-based debacles—often they were erotic relationships between his colleagues and protegés and their current or former patients. Breuer, Freud's coauthor in *Studies on Hysteria* (1895/1955), fled in panic from the sexual transference of the first patient of psychoanalysis, Bertha Pappenheim (Anna O); others engaged in sexual affairs that were embarrassing to the young science.

Freud's disciple, Sandor Ferenczi, became involved with analysand Gizella Palos and then with her daughter Elma. Eventually, Ferenczi convinced Freud to step into the middle of this scenario to see whether Elma's love for Ferenczi would stand up to the analysis. Carl Jung also consulted Freud regarding his sexual involvement with his adolescent patient Sabina Speilrein (Carotenuto, 1982). Freud refused to see Speilrein, but consoled Jung that "such experiences, though painful, are necessary and hard to avoid" (cited in McGuire, 1974, p. 230). Speilrein eventually became a psychoanalyst, herself writing to Freud about Jung's role in her life as "a faithless lover and a cad" (cited in Baur, 1997, p. 39).

We can well imagine Freud's fears for psychoanalysis, as he continued to hear accusations against Jones, Fromm-Reichman (who had married her patient Erich Fromm), Otto Rank, and Fritz Perls. It is not surprising, in this historical context, that Freud considered countertransference itself to be dangerous. Freud counseled Jung that the latter had not yet achieved "the necessary objectivity in [his] practice," noting that Jung still became involved emotionally with his patients. "I believe an article on 'countertransference' is sorely needed," he wrote in 1911. "Of course we could not publish it, we should have to circulate copies among ourselves" (cited in McGuire, 1974, p. 476). Early cognitive or behavioral texts were similarly silent on the subject.

Modern texts on treatment in general and trauma treatment in particular now more commonly suggest at least some more positive roles for countertransference (see Chapter 2). Most frequently they note that countertransference can be a critical source of information, although the sharing of this information with the patient is still controversial. The importance of boundaries in practice remains and becomes increasingly clear, and the examination of countertransference itself has taken a much more respected place within the field. There are now few arenas within this domain that are treated in the secretive manner that Freud advocated. Yet, countertransference continues to be a source of much shame and discomfort among therapists (cf. Davies & Frawley, 1994; Pearlman & Saakvitne, 1995; Pope & Tabachnick, 1993). Unfortunately, even the definition of the concept is unclear.

Definitions of Countertransference

A case example from my more recent clinical past can be used to illustrate the problems of defining countertransference:

> When I walked to the waiting room to meet Mr. C and stood holding the door, he came abruptly to his feet and strode past me, bumping my shoulder as he went by. I directed him to my office, which he entered before me. Standing in the center of the room with his arms crossed, he said that he had been to six [expletive deleted] psychologists before me, all of whom had falsely accused him of threatening them with violence. Although he had an arrest record and admitted to previous violence, he continued, these accusations by previous psychologists were lies. He suspected that they stemmed from a con-

spiracy between the psychologists and his ex-wife, all of whom were trying to keep him from his sons. His wife was accusing him of sexual molestation of his children, which also was a lie. He had filed suit against her already for defamation and planned to sue the psychotherapists. His meeting with me was a court-ordered evaluation.

In our initial 90-minute meeting, he spoke angrily about his abuse-ridden childhood, drug history, previous assaults on others, and corruption in the mental health profession. He spoke in a loud and angry voice, sprinkling his monologues with obscenities, threats of litigation, and reminders that he was a very violent man who had been wronged by psychologists before. The results of his Minnesota Multiphasic Personality Inventory (MMPI) had been forwarded, and it showed elevations on the Psychopathic Deviancy, Paranoia, and Mania scales. He frightened me.

Was my fear countertransference? It depends, naturally, on the choice of definitions. The broadest or most inclusive definitions are called "totalistic" views. Here my fear obviously qualifies: Countertransference is defined as "the entirety of the analyst's emotional reactions to the patient within the treatment situation" (Bouchard, Normandin, & Seguin, 1995, p. 719). Another example of a totalist definition is Christopher Bollas's (1983) statement that countertransference is "a continuous internal response to the presence of an analysand" (p. 1). My own definition of trauma countertransference, detailed below, is in the totalist camp.

More "particularist" views carve out specific classes of the psychotherapist's emotional response to define as "countertransference" (M. Cohen, 1952; Gitelson, 1952; Grotstein, 1995). The focus could be on whether the psychotherapist's response is a hindrance to the treatment (if so, it is countertransference) or a help. Alternatively, the question could be whether a response is "objective" or the result of preexisting biases and conflicts of the therapist (objective responses not being countertransferential), or whether the response is related directly to the client's transference or is independent of it (countertransference being defined as counter to the client's transference). Briere (1989), for instance, defined counter-transference in the treatment of victims of sexually abuse as "biased therapist behaviors that are based on earlier life experiences or learning" (p. 73). Cohen (1952), another particularist, wrote, "when, in the patient–analyst relationship, anxiety is aroused in the analyst with the effect that communication between the two is interfered with by some alteration in the analyst's behavior, verbal or otherwise, then countertransference is present" (p. 235).

The "classical" view, most in keeping with the original definition as it has been understood by Freud's many critics and followers, is that "countertransference is equated with the [therapist's] transference, or with other conflict-laden reactions to the patient" (Gorkin, 1987, p. 3), and that it is distinct from the "real" relationship. A modern example is Grotstein's (1995) particularist definition of countertransference as the therapist's "own unforced reemergence of his or her own infantile transference neurosis/psychosis that constitutes subjective feelings toward the patient" (p. 491). Some (e.g., Bird, 1972) have argued that "countertransference" and "transference" are not meaningfully different concepts. Countertransference is merely the therapist's transference to the client.

The problem with most of these dichotomies is that almost all reactions of the therapist contain both objective and subjective features, both reactions that are dependent on the patient and reactions independent of him or her, both realistic reactions and fantastic–magical–conflict-ridden beliefs, wishes, and emotions. My fear of Mr. C made me uncomfortable, and interfered with my ability to give him the deepest level of my attentive concentration. On the other hand, Mr. C's hostile engagement pattern was in part unconscious, and his discovery and understanding of the way in which he invoked fear in me, through my disclosure of the countertransference, appeared to be valuable to him. My own and Mr. C's awareness of my fear was both helpful to the later treatment (in that he learned something of his effect on others) and a hindrance to it (because it was distracting to me).

Similarly, having spoken to a few of Mr. C's previous psychotherapists, I found universal agreement on the subject that

Mr. C was a frightening man, particularly for those who became more closely involved with him. I therefore could claim evidence that my reaction was objective. Yet I was reared in a sheltered family enclave in a violent and riot-torn area, where one family rule for dividing the bad guys from the good guys was their use or nonuse of profanity. My parents' daughter disapproved strongly of Mr. C and was frightened by his sexually explicit and primitively violent speech. My fear thus was both objective, in Winnocott's (1949) sense of being a reality-based reaction to the patient's material and presentation, and subjective, because of my classification of Mr. C based on my own prejudicial (at least in part) reactions to his use of language. To make the matter more complicated, as I came to know him, Mr. C admitted that his language was in part a conscious intimidation tactic.

If we were to use the transference–countertransference models in the literature, we might also say that this is an example of an aggressor–victim pattern (Davies & Frawley, 1994). Mr. C identified with his violent parents, playing the aggressor, and I countertransferentially played his prior role, that of victim. Thus he let me know his feelings through a repetition within the relationship. In this formulation, I reacted directly to the transference with my own countertransference. But, as the author of this narrative, I have free rein to claim that the first irrational emotional reaction came from Mr. C, not from me. After all, Mr. C was a labeled perpetrator with a history of harassing therapists before he walked into my office. Then again, I knew that before he came to me. Perhaps mine was the opening invitation to play aggressor to my victim. Perhaps my transference led to his counter-reaction. If we reserve the label countertransference for reactions that are "counter," or reactions to the client's transference, it thus is extremely difficult to classify a given response.

I do not find objectionable, and in fact I applaud, the attempts by other theorists to differentiate the objective from the nonobjective and the neurotic from the healthy within the therapist's reactions. I also agree that the disentanglement of the causal threads (who pulled what reaction out of whom) is a worthy endeavor in a therapeutic hour. What I challenge is the assumption—even for theory's sake—that there are pure cases of these types: purely objective emotional reactions to the client, for instance, entirely free from the influence of the therapist's prior history, conflicts, and biases. I disagree that it is typically useful to say that one emotional reaction is "objective" and another is "countertransference." Even in the largely objective case, such a dichotomy can blind the therapist to the client's claim that he or she too has a piece of the truth.

It is important to acknowledge that the totalistic view of countertransference I advocate—including all of the therapist's feelings and emotion-related behavior toward the client —has been subjected to criticism from the time that Heimann (1950) introduced it. "Such a sweeping definition of countertransference," wrote Gorkin (1987, p. 13), "[has] obvious problems, for unless one is prepared to categorize all of the patient's feelings and fantasies toward the therapist as transference, it would seem to make little linguistic sense to subsume all of the therapist's reactions under the rubric of countertransference." True enough, but I would take a different lesson from the statement than Gorkin wished to imply. Specifically, I would argue that, with the exception of purely physiological or biologically based reactions of one individual to the presence of another, all human interactions are based on interactions that come before and the conflicts and rewards that are associated with these relationships. This is a basic principle of learning. However, given our varied human experiences, some of the transferences we bring into the therapeutic hour—those to a given personality presentation or to a specific situation—will be consensual (shared by many or most in our culture) whereas others will be (relatively) unique.

I believe that, when most therapists speak of countertransference that is "objective" (cf. Winnicott, 1949) or part of the "real relationship" and not countertransference at all, they typically mean that the feeling would be expected to occur in most people confronted by the same stimulus. Winnicott's discussion, for example, centered on the internal acknowledgment and possible disclosure of countertransference hate, most specifically when it is "objective and justified hate" (p. 72), that is, a consensually agreed-on occasion for hate. Of course, a consensual occasion for hostility also can serve a purpose for a therapist or client with a uniquely determined or conflict-based ax to grind. However, in making the crucial decisions of whether the countertransference response in question is a good source of information for the patient about his or her own extratherapy relationships and therefore appropriate for disclosure, it is the consensual–unique rather than the conflictual–nonconflictual dimension that is likely to be of most use. If most individuals will react to the client (consensually) with fear, this will no doubt be an interpersonal problem independent of why this is so. If a countertransference reaction is consensual rather than unique to the psychotherapist, it is thus more likely to constitute valuable information for the client.

Thus, it is my goal in this book to discuss the common (consensual) countertransference responses to traumatized patients. I hope to make them more recognizable, easier to integrate into a treatment process, and less personally disruptive to the therapist. Furthermore, as a practical aid to the clinician, I hope to provide a somewhat more sophisticated lexicon for disclosure of countertransference when necessary. I also hope to speak in a language that is equally applicable to the psychodynamic, humanistic, and cognitive therapist—a goal more easily met when countertransference is divorced from its connection to infantile conflict.

I will consider as part of my definition of *traumatic countertransference* the following types of responses:

- □ the characteristic attachment that the therapist feels and displays toward the traumatized patient
- □ the characteristic emotional reaction in the therapist to common trauma transference dynamics
- □ the actions taken by the therapist in trauma treatment that have emotional significance to the client and to the therapist in defining their relationship
- □ the unique and conflict-based responses of the therapist to trauma material.

Countertransference and Trauma

Although the literature on countertransference is broad, the writings that are specific to the trauma therapist are much more limited. Of great value have been *Treating the Adult Survivor of Childhood Sexual Abuse: A Psychoanalytic Perspective*, (M. Davies & Frawley, 1994), *Trauma and the Therapist: Countertransference and Vicarious Traumatization in Psychotherapy with Incest Survivors* (Pearlman & Saakvitne, 1995), and *Countertransference in the Treatment of PTSD* (Wilson & Lindy, 1994). These texts are helpful, although they focus largely on victims of sexual abuse or incest and not (with the partial exception of Wilson and Lindy) on the broader issues of trauma.

But why *should* one focus on trauma victims in a book on countertransference? The most obvious answer is that trauma victims figure prominently in virtually every well-known therapeutic dilemma or disaster associated with strong countertransference reactions. They appear to be overrepresented among those who self-mutilate or commit suicide (Briere & Runtz, 1988; Himber, 1994)—at times for reasons that are later tied to countertransference errors (Modestin, 1987). Trauma victims, particularly those who have received a borderline-personality diagnosis or who were abused as children, also show heightened tendencies to terminate therapy early, to fail to attach to the therapist, or to act aggressively in therapy (Briere, 1989; Gabbard & Wilkinson, 1994). Similarly, their success rates in well-proven treatments for other mental illnesses are lower than is found for clients who have no history of trauma, leading to frustration and confusion in the treating professional (Baider, Peretz, & De-Nour, 1997). Trauma victims also are clearly overrepresented among clients who become involved in erotic attachments with their therapists that end poorly—either in termination or in enactment (Bates & Brodsky, 1989; Collins, 1989). Mismanagement of these transferences can put client and therapist alike in psychic or physical danger (see chapters 6, 7, and 8).

The litany of difficult situations above suggests that the trauma victim, by virtue of other symptoms that tend to occur along with trauma history, will present the clinician with more than the usual number of opportunities to sort through difficult transference–countertransference interactions. There is reason to believe that the traumatic transference often differs in form and character from the transference of other clients. This in itself is an important finding to explore (and could well be related to the undesirable psychotherapy outcomes cited above).

It is not surprising that, given the complexities we are beginning to touch on, traumatized patients report that their therapists often disappoint or even betray them. One-quarter of interview participants (patients with histories of child abuse) in the Dale, Allen, & Measor (1996) study had experienced episodes of therapy that they rated as "making things worse." In the Trauma Countertransference Study described on page 19 and in Appendix, 48 of 84 respondents stated that they had experienced a "serious betrayal" in psychotherapy from one or more therapists. These "betrayals" were frequent both in successful and in unsuccessful therapies (as defined in this case by client report). It was illuminating to me to hear these descriptions of therapist failures, as well as the descriptions of the therapists' efforts, again with varying success, to repair the breaches. I am deeply grateful to these individuals for their generous contribution to my education.

Finally, as is discussed more deeply in chapter 3, there is good clinical and experimental evidence to suggest that therapists often have countertransferential reactions to the *fact* of trauma that are distinct from their feelings about the traumatized patient. The therapist's pre-existing thoughts and beliefs about the trauma itself may affect the course of therapy greatly.

Organization of the Text

To provide information that is valuable to the trauma therapist, this text is organized along the lines of relational difficulties common to traumatized populations and their intimate others (including their therapists). The text begins with a general argument in favor of countertransference disclosure as a useful tool within trauma therapy (chapter 2). Chapter 3 focuses on countertransference as a facilitator and hindrance to client disclosures of trauma memories and therefore to their evaluations of those memories. In subsequent chapters, major themes within the literature on traumatic transference are tied to the parallel literature on traumatic countertransference, as defined earlier.

The themes in traumatic transference include the following:

☐ By definition, and given its unassimilable nature, trauma attacks the coherence, reality-testing, and worldview of the victim. As the therapist attempts to fight the dissociation and to "inhabit partially the patient's inner world" (Briere, 1992, p. 85), he or she too feels the threat to self-coherence. Anxiety is a frequent reported response to other groups (e.g., psychotics) whose reality-testing wavers under stress (e.g., Brody & Farber, 1996). The client's struggle to determine what is true and to live with uncertainty is examined in chapter 4, as is the countertransference response to the client's unconscious and conscious press for belief or disbelief.

☐ The intensity of the traumatic transference, and thus, in many cases, of the traumatic countertransference, can overwhelm both participants. Herman (1992) referred to traumatic transference as possessing a "life or death quality [that is] unparalleled in ordinary therapeutic experience" (p. 136). I certainly agree. Further, the intensity of the transference often feels coercive to the therapist. He or she might blame the client (unfairly) for this felt coercion, when it is less a conscious manipulation than an outgrowth of the meeting of intense unmet need with the human capacity for empathy.

The client's and therapist's desires to maintain a safe and benevolent world lead them to wrestle jointly with blame, shame, and responsibility in the relationship (cf. Dalenberg & Jacobs, 1994). Therapy itself can be a source of shame for the client, because it encourages disclosure of unpleasant truths, and for the therapist, who can feel as if he or she is placed in the role of prosecutor or character assassin for someone who came for help and compassion (Josephs, 1995). Such issues are discussed in chapter 5.

□ The likelihood that a client will accuse his or her therapist of malfeasance is highlighted in virtually every text on treatment of trauma. Spiegel and Spiegel (1978) defined traumatic transference as occurring when "the patient unconsciously expects that the therapist, despite overt helpfulness and concern, will covertly exploit the patient for his or her own narcissistic gratification" (p. 72). For self-protection, the client often attacks or accuses, provoking understandably defensive responses in the clinician. Thus, the therapist is confronted with two emotionally difficult dilemmas. First, the therapist must manage his or her own countertransference anger and counterhostility. Second, the therapist must somehow retain a hold on his or her own true self in the face of continued relational information that he or she is evil, dangerous, or a potential abuser.

The accusations of malfeasance and incompetence at times strike home to a therapist who is frightened and frustrated by the propensity for self-endangerment in the traumatized client. The phenomenon of "repetition compulsion," although I believe it to be misunderstood in the scholarly literature on trauma, still represents a pattern that is familiar and upsetting to any trauma therapist. Continuing to care for an individual who is constantly at risk of physical or psychic destruction is enormously taxing and places the therapist at risk for "compassion fatigue" and emotional exhaustion (Stamm, 1995). Exhaustion and psychic disequilibrium encourage acting out countertransference to protect the self against these changes. These themes are addressed in chapters 6 and 7.

□ Client ambivalence about attachment can be extremely confusing and disheartening to the therapist, who is unaccustomed to client experience of attachment as dangerous and yet necessary for survival (cf. Waites, 1993). This quality, which often looks as though it were a combination of an addiction and an allergy to closeness, leads to rapid fluctuation in transference dynamics. The therapist might find himself or herself in repeated boundary negotiations, feeling besieged by requests for intimacy one moment and accused of intrusion the next. The issue of boundaries and the additional specific issue of sexual transference and countertransference are discussed in chapter 8.

□ Chapter 9 addresses the resolution of trauma and issues regarding termination in trauma therapy. What does it mean, in the long run, to "learn to live with" trauma and tragedy?

Data Sources for the Present Discussion of Countertransference

Case Studies

The data, theory, and clinical examples I offer in the chapters that follow integrate a number of very distinct sources, some of which have been underutilized. As is true for most texts I have read and admired, I use the accounts of my clients and case studies provided by my colleagues. Verbatim dialogue is offered when it is available. I suspect that many readers will see much complexity in the therapist and client exchanges.

Other case examples are taken from the hundreds of individual stories of physical, emotional, and sexual trauma offered by research participants at the Trauma Research Institute (TRI) in La Jolla, CA. The similarities in the clients' accounts (in their understanding, in their affective reactions and transference, in the transference–countertransference patterns) are explored here. The patterns are evidence for the possibility of building a scientific framework for predicting the consequences of trauma and the manifestations of those consequences in psychotherapy.

As a scientist, I welcome the discovery of similarities, hoping that they will line up neatly into theorems and "laws" that simplify our lives. The task of the therapist would be less arduous if there were some regularity to the problematic transference patterns, and the resultant countertransference patterns, that traumatized patients bring to therapy. If, in the broadest sense, it could be discovered that the meaning assigned to trauma and the emotional responses to it are not infinite, then a more fruitful and focused discussion of responses and patterns would be likely to emerge over time.

But then there are differences—error variance, the enemy of statistical significance and hardworking researchers. Yet differences *between* individuals highlight the potential of differences that can take place *within* individuals. They give emotional ammunition (perhaps faith) to the therapist in his or her fight against the common client belief in the inevitability of his or her own brand of pain. "But anyone with my background would feel suicidal/worthless/violent," we hear clients say. "I cannot erase my past, so I cannot change my emotional present." But this version of the adage "as the twig is bent, so grows the tree" is as false for people as it is for trees. Once the splint is removed, the twig bends and grows toward the sun. Interpretations and conclusions drawn from traumatic transference thus can change when the cognitive and emotional environment changes. I hope that the client and therapist accounts here will present the therapist with more variability, and thus more flexibility, in response to common trauma dynamics.

I also should mention that I have deeply considered the issues related to confidentiality in this text. With few exceptions, my own clients have seen the transcripts and summaries used here. Many times, they commented in the text on their histories or their views of our interactions. For client protection, little demographic information is offered about clients or TRI study participants other than the nature of the trauma and the gender, age, and race of the client. A demographic summary is given in Table 1.1. The clinical sample consisted of 22 clients whom I have treated, and the research sample (from the Trauma Countertransference Study) included 84 participants in an in-depth survey study of client assessment of therapist countertransference during trauma treatment. Table 1.1 also suggests my interest in providing a range of patient traumas and related countertransference dilemmas for thoughtful examination. In the text, my clients

Table 1.1

Demographic Description and Source of Trauma: Clinical and TRI Countertransference Study Samples

	Research Sample	
Race/Gender/Trauma	Clinical Sample	Trauma Countertransference Study
Black	3	9
White	15	62
Hispanic	4	13
Male	10	22
Female	12	62
Abuse	10	41
Rape–Assault	3	13
Traumatic loss	5	16
War	2	7
Other	2	7

are identified by letters (e.g., Client M); research study participants have been given fictitious names.

Empirical Literature

Abstraction of general principles on the basis of clinical case histories from a limited sample of psychologists is subject to well-known (if frequently ignored) sources of error. If ever the "ideal observer" were postulated to exist, certainly there now is adequate evidence that he or she does not. Instead, the picture has emerged of the personal historian (clinicians included) as motivated by social desirability—inappropriately confident and often misled. The specific research arena of countertransference is further complicated by the fact that theory would suggest that the person telling the tale (often the therapist) might be the individual least competent to do so. That is, because countertransference is by definition often unconscious, it is difficult to justify the assumption that the dynamics will be well explained by the clinician who generated the experience.

In response to this challenge, at TRI we have attempted to develop research paradigms and strategies that would supplement the knowledge gained from clinician reports. These include studies of the clinician and studies that use clients as the historians of therapy progress. In clinician studies, we often try to present the therapist with situations to which they might react naturally in their therapist role, rather than asking them what they might or might not do in a given situation. For example, we might present the clinician with realistic tapes of clients speaking to them, stopping the tape at various points and asking for an immediate response. In client studies, we have conducted in-depth analysis of the client's view of the therapist, with particular attention to the client's view of hindrances and obstacles produced by therapist countertransference. Additional samples provide examples of client disclosure style within differing trauma types. A brief list of our research paradigms is given here.

Trauma Countertransference Study. Eighty-four clients, who were participants in a larger questionnaire study, were surveyed about experiences in therapy. Each person had sought therapy for perceived trauma-related symptoms. Interviews focused on client perceptions of therapists' countertransference reactions to the clients' trauma as a help or hindrance to therapy. Further description of the methods of this study is given in the Appendix, including a list of interview questions. Results are discussed throughout this text.

Child Disclosure Study. More than 3000 tapes were available for random selection from the vast library of the Center for Child Protection in San Diego, California. In these tapes, children are questioned by expert forensic interviewers regarding their memories and feelings about recent experiences of sexual or physical abuse. This research sample is a source of examples of interviewer countertransference responses to traumatic material. Ma-

jor results of this project are discussed in chapter 3 and
4.

Sexual Countertransference Study. Experienced and in-
experienced therapists listened to professional actors express sexual feelings toward therapists and responded to
the "clients" on tape. The therapists' responses were then
rated by a client sample along perceived countertransference dimensions. A follow-up sample of clients who
had resolved or who had not resolved sexual transference or countertransference issues was collected through
the Internet. Results and excerpts are discussed in chapter 8.

Holocaust Remembrance Study. Survivors of the Holocaust participated in one of two interviews, one focusing
on societal and interpersonal reactions they had experienced in telling their stories, the other centered on
decision-making in communicating the story to their
children. Thirty participants have completed one of these
2- to 4-hour interviews. Excerpts from these interviews
are included in chapter 3 and chapter 9.

Standards-of-Care Study. A series of surveys of professionals in the San Diego area assessed complex ethical
and treatment standards regarding clinical and boundary
issues and dilemmas. Topics covered included touch,
self-disclosure, and use of informed consent. Participants
were interviewed for 1–2 hours. The findings of the Standard of Care interview on touch are presented in chapter
8.

Participant-as-Teacher Study. This experimental paradigm was used to investigate the predictors of punitive
behavior toward children, particularly in those with
abuse history. Participants believe they are rewarding or
punishing a child in a nearby room (actually a tape)
through a computer as the child learns to spell. As the
"child" becomes increasingly provocative, the effect of
participant anger, shame, dissociation, and abuse history
on subsequent angry and punitive behavior by an authority figure is measured. Results are discussed in chapter 6.

The empirical literature as it now exists is a mass of conflicting, largely atheoretical studies with differing and often poorly articulated definitions of trauma and the damage it breeds. Yet patterns emerge in careful examination of these hundreds of books and articles. The distributions of findings form an image, much as the clients' stories create an image, of reality. It is hoped that these pictures, taken from many angles, might combine to create a hologram that is more accurate, more comprehensive, and more helpful than the information provided using a single method. This book is written to educate researcher and clinician to one another's discoveries and to encourage each to gain a bit more respect for the difficulties inherent in the achievement of the other's professional goals. In moving back and forth between the examinations of the empirical and theoretical literature on signs and patterns in countertransference, theoretical understanding of these reactions, and case examples of successful and unsuccessful resolution, I am mindful of Latts and Gelson's (1995) empirical demonstration that both theory and countertransference awareness are necessary to develop skills for the management of countertransference.

A Final Word on Words

To conclude this section, it is important to comment on the use of the words "victim" and "survivor" throughout this book. The "Survivor Psalm," written and used by trauma victims at the Dimondale Clinic in Chicago, ends with the words "I was a victim; I am a survivor."

Word choice is a matter of controversy in therapeutic circles. "Victim" implies lack of control, helplessness, and lack of power; "survivor" calls to mind strength, courage, and invulnerability. The issues raised by those who challenge the use of "victim" are fair, but I argue that the usage is appropriate. It is crucial to "empower" victims of trauma, allowing them to recognize their infinite options. But this excellent point—too long in coming to the trauma literature—should not overshadow the reality of exploitation and harm.

I remember an abusive father who also was uncomfortable with the word and the concept of "victim." Disdainfully, he spoke to his weeping son, whom he had humiliated in front of family and therapist: "You'll survive," he said. "We all survive." The father meant, and later said, that he believed his own abusive actions were justified and should not generate distress in his son or censure from his community. But his son *was* his victim, and "victim" and "survivor" are not incompatible terms. Both capture a part of the picture, and I use both of these important and accurate words.

2

The Argument for Highlighting, Examining, and Disclosing Countertransference in Trauma Therapy

My cognitive psychology professor at the University of Denver, Al Schacter, told a story about a mother and daughter who were preparing a Christmas roast from an old family recipe. As Mrs. X explained the process—timing, seasoning, cooking temperature—she demonstrated each step to her daughter. Before placing the roast in the oven, Mrs. X cut off a large portion of the corner of the roast at an angle and reapplied the seasoning, discarding a portion of the meat. Her daughter asked why this step was necessary. Mrs. X, after offering several possibilities that both women disregarded as implausible, finally stated that she did not know. She only knew that her mother had been clear as to the importance of this step.

Intrigued by her daughter's question, Mrs. X called her own mother, who, to Mrs. X's surprise, also was at a loss. She knew only that the step in question was important, crucially important, to the proper outcome. Grandmother X eventually passed the question up the generational chain to her mother, the oldest living member of her family. Fortunately, Great-Grandmother X knew the answer. Great-Grandmother X had a small kitchen and a very small, irregularly shaped oven. To cook a roast large enough to feed her family, she had to carve it into this particular shape.

The most interesting part of this story is that the recipe might have included preparation for an irregular oven for a dozen generations or more before the precipitous entry of the wise child with the reasonable question. In many alternative endings that we could imagine, Mrs. X would have said to her daughter, "I don't know, dear. That's just how it's done." And that would have been sufficient to leave the recipe intact for another generation.

How much more complicated are the recipes we are given by our parents for the negotiation of human relationships. ("Handle others' anger this way." "Display your emotion only under the following circumstances and with these display rules.") And how much less likely it is that we will say (or even think) "Dad, is this part of your interpersonal behavior, Step A, necessary to getting what you want? What function does that part of the emotional display serve?" If we did ask, in our own way ("Mom, why do you have to cry every time anyone gets a little angry?"), is it not also likely that in many cases our teachers (parents) will not know the answer? In this way, our complex interpersonal strategies evolve, fitted (a) to today's needs, (b) to environments we no longer fully remember from our own past, and (c) to models of our parents' environments, mixed in with (d) triggered evolutionary tendencies to prepare for those events that might endanger anyone.

So in this multidetermined interpersonal strategy, how is each child to determine which "steps" or features of his or her own emotional repertoire are necessary to today's requirements? One clue in the story above is the historical hunt for the matching environment to the questioned function. That is, Mrs. X did not dare give up the wasteful and unnecessary step in her recipe until she knew the function it used to serve, and she knew that her environment had changed in relevant ways, enabling the desired outcome (a perfect roast) in the absence of the questioned activity.

Thus, in the equivalent of the first step above, traumatized clients are helped by the therapist to understand the functionality of symptoms as matched to a former acutely or chronically traumatic environment. Normalizing the presence of "symptoms" is one key to allowing change; otherwise, one is dominated by the amorphous sense that some actions are not optional, although one cannot explain why. This viewpoint is beautifully articulated in descriptions of trauma-focused therapy by Briere (1992, 1996), Courtois (1988), Ochberg (1988), or Herman (1992). Briere (1992) suggested that the message in trauma-focused therapy might be offered this way:

> You have spent much of your life struggling to survive what was done to you as a child. The solutions you've found for the fear, emptiness, and memories you carry represent the best you could do in the face of the abuse you experienced. Although some others, perhaps even you, see your coping behaviors as sick or "dysfunctional," your actions have been the reverse: healthy accommodations to a toxic environment (p. 83).

Most clients react in powerfully positive ways to this facet of therapy, and they come to believe with the therapist that their worldviews were shaped by the trauma (understandably) in ways that primarily protect against future comparable trauma. Such discoveries feed the human need for a comprehensible past (Spence, 1982) and generally do not threaten the self-image greatly. With varying specific exceptions, clients also will agree, after some consideration of alternatives within therapy, that some adaptations are no longer logically necessary, and that they have enormous cost. So far, so good.

But believing intellectually that it is likely that the world has changed and knowing emotionally that different behaviors are preferable are two entirely separate conclusions—especially when the stakes are high. The interpersonal choices made by the survivor in the past may have saved his or her life. This fits with the life-or-death quality of the traumatic transference (e.g., Herman, 1992, p. 136) referenced in chapter 1. How does one help a traumatized client to convince himself or herself that it is "safe" to walk into a new interpersonal furnace and risk (or even ask) to be emotionally re-formed? How does one help the client to try a new recipe for interpersonal functioning?

The Provision of Safety

The trauma treatment literature is virtually unanimous in supporting the necessity of providing a safe therapeutic environment (Briere, 1992; Pearlman & Saakvitne, 1995; Salter, 1995). But what is meant, in the deepest sense, by the word "safe"? Safe from what? Safe from sexual exploitation and physical harm? This is certainly a minimum standard and one that most therapists can meet. (See chapter 8 for the hidden difficulties in accomplishing this goal.) But when we move to Briere's (1992) admonition to create an environment for the trauma patient in which it is safe to "go back to frightening thoughts and images of . . . childhood" (p. 83) or Pearlman and Saakvitne's (1995) request that we maintain a safety zone for the client "to express . . . private feelings and needs" (p. 83), the therapist's wish to comply can be easily compromised. For what feels "unsafe" about therapy to the traumatized client is in large measure the potential triggering of the therapist's countertransference behaviors—disapproval, disgust, dominance, rejection—by the client's behavior and history. That is, the client fears disruption, either in communication or in closeness, in the felt relationship. Safety is promoted by the therapist's "never [changing the] interpersonal distance with the client" or by "never demand[ing] anything emotionally in exchange"· (Salter, 1995, p. 261), by showing in his or her behavior "that vulnerability is possible without injury, criticism, or rejection" (Briere, 1996, p. 123), and by not giving the client "evidence that the clinician is prone to potentially abusive, neglectful or boundary-violating behavior." (Briere, 1996, p. 123). These authors and others (e.g., Courtois, 1988; Pearlman & Saakvitne, 1995) acknowledged that complete safety is an unachievable goal, but they highlighted countertransference errors as the central stumbling block to good-enough therapeutic settings. Creating a safe environment *mandates* attention to the actual countertransference of the therapist and to the expected countertransference from the client's perspective.

The traumatized client has reason to fear countertransference behaviors. The countertransference, if it is detected by

the client, declares the separate existence of the therapist—
announces otherness and the possibility of contradiction, censure, and betrayal. Countertransference also presents the
danger of confirming the patient's trauma-related beliefs.
("You are right that I am ashamed and disgusted by your
behavior; I no longer wish to be with you.") Moreover, because clients typically are actually desperate for disconfir-
mation of such beliefs (cf. Weiss, 1993), these therapist mistakes can lead to a profound despair and hopelessness in the
client. The question persists: How can the therapist represent
a "safe haven" to the client but still remain a separate person
capable of providing an alternative worldview?

The most obvious solution, and one implicit in many discussions of safety, is to withhold or greatly mute the emotional expression of the countertransference. The client learns
that anger, shame, and terror will not overwhelm the therapist, who serves as a "container" (cf. Bion, 1984), "detoxify-
ing" or "metabolizing" the emotions and helping the client
to reintegrate them in tolerable forms. It is noncontroversial
that this is a needed function within many trauma therapies.
I do not believe that it is constructive to spend time critiquing
the extreme versions of countertransference nondisclosure or
disclosure that some therapists (but very few) present.
Rather, I would like first to make a more general argument
for the value of countertransference disclosure and to point
out that there are dangers to choosing the blank-screen position as an ideal.

Dangers of Countertransference
Nondisclosure in Trauma Therapy

The most salient dangers to a policy of general countertransference nondisclosure fall into two distinct classes. The first
consists of those dangers that flow from the inevitable "leaking" of therapist affect within a relationship in which the
client knows that the therapist will not disclose his or her
true state. The second class follows from the therapist's more

successful suppression (or dissociation or repression) of his or her emotional display.

Danger Associated With Therapist "Leaks" Within a Nondisclosing Relationship

Therapists who take a position favoring nondisclosure (the more classical position) do not claim that the visible display of countertransference can be totally eliminated. Reich (1951, 1960), for instance, stated that the therapist should apologize for clear errors (e.g., misstatements, forgetting appointments), but should not explain the reasons for the mistake. Client assumptions or fears about possible reasons for therapist behavior or emotion typically are explored by therapists in this school, many of whom believe that disclosure would foreclose the fantasy process and preclude discovery of deeper material.

In the TRI Trauma Countertransference Study, 31 (37%) of 84 participants stated that their therapists generally took the nondisclosure route. The study used in-depth interviews to assess client views of trauma therapy. The relevant interview item is as follows:

> Some therapists [Type 1] have a policy of trying to withhold any expression of their own emotions, sometimes because they are trying not to burden you with their emotional reactions. Other therapists [Type 2] frequently share their emotions, thinking that therapy must be genuine and honest. Most therapists are not perfect examples of one extreme or the other, but which type would you say describes your therapist in general?

Twenty-seven of the 31 clients who stated that they had Type 1 therapists also stated that the clinicians did show emotional reactions at times. It is interesting that this group of therapists were more likely, according to their clients, to engage in an emotional display that was classified by the client as a "trauma" or a "betrayal." (These subclasses of countertransference display are discussed throughout this text in the content sections.) Examples were shaming the client, becoming angry at the client, or rejecting the client (as assessed by client self-report). Twenty-two of the 31 Type 1 therapists (71%) reportedly engaged in one or more of these countertransference betrayals as did 26 of the 53 (49%) Type 2 therapists. How might this have happened, given the benevolent motives and reasonable training that we can assume is present for most of these therapists? Why is the countertransference display of the nondisclosing therapist seen as dangerous by the trauma client?

Danger of Unpredictable Emotions in an Attachment Figure

The first pattern that emerges in the context of nondisclosure-based therapies is developmental. Here, both client and therapist go through a "honeymoon period," in which the client believes that the therapist is the perfect answer to a desperate need. Many of us, particularly at the beginning of our careers as therapists, try the route of benevolent tolerance of behaviors that ordinarily are emotionally difficult, basking in the glow of the client's positive comparisons between the therapist and those who respond to provocation with less saintly behaviors. However, in the case of provocative behavior (see chapter 7), persistent boundary violation (see chapter 8), self-endangerment, and suicidality (see chapter 6), traumatized clients are notoriously likely to press the therapist to his or her breaking point. At some point, the therapist often decides (quite precipitously) that the client should be "confronted."

Dozens of examples are offered in the literature of sudden shifts by the therapist from tolerance to confrontation, and usually they are reported to have positive effects. Zerbe (1995), for instance, wrote of his spontaneous response to a critical assault on his competence by a difficult, multiply hospitalized patient with whom he had been stalemated:

> I'm tired of how you are trying to devalue and destroy your treatment and that of the other patients who are also here. You bludgeon the staff with your criticisms,

but you don't do anything about yourself! When is it
going to stop? (p. 161)

Meissner (1996) cited this quotation as an example of an "effective and reasonable . . . confrontation" (p. 40) that should
not be called countertransference. Ehrenberg (1992) discussed
the positive effect of yawning and confessing a sense of boredom with a patient. Similarly, L. Epstein (1977) outlined the
benefits of shifting his view of a client from "love-starved
child" to "nasty, withholding, contemptuous, uncooperative
bitch" and reacting accordingly. The client improved greatly
after he changed his behavior, Epstein notes finding her first
job and an apartment. After several years, she surprised him
by suggesting that, because she had never liked him, and did
not expect that to change, she might be better off with another therapist. Epstein made the referral.

In most examples taken from the literature, therapists presented anecdotes in which they perceived the outcome of the
confrontation to be positive. It is possible, though, that extreme negative responses from the therapist after a history of
benevolence will shock the client into silence and obedience,
which can be indistinguishable from a positive outcome from
the therapist's point of view. A participant in the TRI Trauma
Countertransference Study (a male victim of physical abuse
and assault) described his therapy experience this way:

> *Andrew:* One day I was just talking, you know, talking
> about my neighbor, and he says, like out of nowhere he
> says, "Do you have to make everyone your enemy?"
>
> *Interviewer:* It was in that voice? Were you imitating him?
>
> *Andrew:* Yes. It was totally annoyed, angry, like I was this
> worthless shit who was antagonizing everyone. Now I
> know this sounds like no big deal, but you have to un-
> derstand that we had talked about this guy [the neigh-
> bor] so often and he had agreed with me, agreed with
> me. He never said *anything* that let me know that he felt
> that way about me. (Andrew shakes his head in disbe-
> lief.)

Interviewer: So what did you do?

Andrew: What could I do? I just agreed with him, and then I got out of there, permanently.

Interviewer: You mean you left therapy?

Andrew: Yep.

Interviewer: Right then?

Andrew: Well, no, I think maybe two, three months later. I just told him I thought I had learned enough about myself, and I left. I thanked him. Nice guy, really. It's just that I couldn't really get that [incident] out of my mind.

Over and over, TRI study participants who discussed disturbing or self-labeled traumatic incidents from therapy stressed the unpredictability of the perceived change in therapist behavior. Unpredictability is a hallmark of trauma in general (see Carlson, 1997), so it is not surprising that this feature made the events more disturbing. Brewin, Dalgleish, & Joseph (1996) stated that chronic processing of trauma without resolution is particularly common when there is a large discrepancy between the prior assumptions (e.g., this therapist is different and will not hurt me) and the traumatic information (e.g., this therapist injured me just as I have previously been injured.). The events that participants placed in the category of therapeutic trauma or therapeutic betrayal in the Trauma Countertransference Study were rated by them as (a) more surprising to them than were other therapist behaviors, (b) more out of character for the therapist, and (c) less likely to be resolved if the clinician was a nondisclosing (Type 1) therapist rather than a disclosing (Type 2) therapist.

Although the incidents described would most likely be upsetting to clients of any background, the traumatized client is likely to find attachment-related surprise (unexpected rejection, intolerance, or punishment) more frightening than others might. Going back to the question about the meaning of "safety," the traumatized client could need a more reliable emotional environment than other clients would—again, a statement made by most trauma treatment specialists. Having had the experience of fundamental betrayal by the world (and in some cases, by their parents), trauma clients find that trustworthiness and predictability of attachment figures is crucial to the negotiation of settings that contain expectations of the acknowledgment of vulnerabilities (Briere, 1996; Salter, 1995; see chapter 8 in this volume).

Danger of Hypervigilant Discovery of Therapist Emotions

One hypothesized advantage of the nondisclosing strategy is that clients will be more free to focus on themselves. Early in treatment, however, traumatized clients cannot risk dropping the vigilant analysis of their therapists' potential emotional state. Attachment is a dangerous process for the trauma victim, and it cannot be entered blindly. As such, trauma treatment experts unanimously cite client hypervigilance as a problem and a fact of therapy with this population. Clients "may become expert at reading the slightest nuance in the abuser" given that correct assessment of a perpetrator is so important to preserve personal safety (Briere, 1996, p. 53). The therapist is watched constantly: "Transferentially the [therapist] is always on the brink of becoming an abusing or abused other" (Davies & Frawley, 1994, p. 50).

According to the participants in the Trauma Countertransference Study, when a therapist has a policy of nondisclosure, traumatized clients focus on possible therapist emotions *more* often rather than less often (compared with clients of Type 2 therapists). In fact, three of the four participants who claimed that their therapists never showed or acknowledged emotion were unable to tolerate this experience. Marie, a rape survivor, put it this way:

> *Marie:* I was obsessed with what he was thinking, just obsessed. And I would talk about it and think about it endlessly. I really think it pleased him, made him think we were really doing therapy. But I just got more and more focused on did he really like me, what did he want, was he sick of me yet.

Interviewer: Did you talk to him about it?

Marie: Oh, sure, yeah. It was humiliating after a while. I started calling him a lot, calling his answering machine mostly. But I'd say "I need to know what you think about this," and he'd say "What do you think I think?" And on and on, you know.

Interviewer: So I take it he was trying to help you understand that way that you read your own fears into other people's behavior, you know what I mean? Was he trying to help you understand that you were frightened about people liking you or that you were afraid of people abandoning you?

Marie: Yes, but how . . . what . . . I never knew if it was true or not. How does that help?

Given the compulsive compliance characterized by many abused, traumatized, or otherwise frightened persons (cf. Crittendon, 1997), the client might attempt to cooperate with the therapy by molding the self to the perceived needs of the therapist. If the rules of therapy appear to imply that therapist emotion or countertransference (that is, what the therapist *is* thinking and feeling as opposed to what he or she *might be* thinking and feeling) is off-limits for honest discussion, the client might not wish put the therapist on the spot and might engage in a humiliating entreaty to achieve the comfort of knowledge that the therapist is not angry, disgusted, or about to choose abandonment.

That said, the more common pattern within the pairing of the hypervigilant client and the Type 1 therapist in the Trauma Countertransference Study data was the client's report of eventual "discovery" of the therapist's ill-intent, which no amount of therapist attention appeared to mitigate. Fifty of the 84 participants believed that they were more reactive to the therapist than most patients would be within psychotherapy. This was equally true for Type 1 and Type 2 therapists' clients, but the Type 2 therapists appeared better able to move the client through the reactivity to an integrated understanding and capacity to self-soothe. It could be that other personality characteristics or theoretical strategies associated with emotional self-disclosure in a therapist were important, and causality cannot be assumed. However, the clients' reports of the mechanism of successful mitigation of therapists' unintentional betrayal was overwhelmingly said to be disclosure of countertransference.

Hypervigilance often is associated with hypersensitivity in the trauma survivor, particularly in the chronic trauma survivor. Therefore, some "discoveries" of therapist malevolence are made based on evidence that is flimsy at best, leading to understandably exasperated reactions in the therapist (see chapters 6, 7, and 8). Regardless of the level of disclosure chosen by the trauma therapist, some method of encouragement of client processing of the discoveries made during the hypervigilant search is necessary to productive therapy for many survivors. In an authority figure, distress that is unnamed (cf. Pearlman & Saakvitne, 1995) is typically too frightening for a trauma victim to be tolerated alone.

Danger Associated With Successful Therapist Suppression of Affective Display

It has long been unacceptable within therapeutic literature, and especially in the trauma therapy literature, to claim that one is "objective" and able to provide a "blank screen." The most typical arguments here center on the impossibility of suppressing the personality of the therapist, evident to the patient to some extent within any long-term therapy. "Self-revelation," argued Aron (1991), "is not a choice for the therapist; it is an inevitable and continuous aspect of the analytic process" (p. 47). Another important meaning of the rejection of the blank-screen concept, however, is that nonresponse *is* response, especially in situations that call for great emotion.

A powerful description from Greenson (1967, pp. 219–220) seems relevant as an example of the potential cruelty in nonresponse by a "young analyst" treating a mother who had recently experienced a health crisis with her infant son. (I place "young analyst" in quotes, by the way, to emphasize how often this epithet is used in our descriptions of counter-

transference errors. Perhaps this is one way of distancing ourselves from the acknowledgement of the frequency of our
harm-producing actions.) Greenson's young analyst was silent during his patient's outpouring of her panic about her
child. Afterward, she too became silent, and her analyst told
her that she was resisting. He hypothesized to himself that
her resistance might have been related to her death wishes
toward her son and her subsequent guilt.

The patient said nothing during the next hour, although
tears streamed down her cheeks. The session ended in silence. The next week, she quit therapy, claiming that her therapist "was sicker than she was." The analyst never did learn
what happened to the baby. Greenson felt that some compassion and open concern was needed to maintain the alliance. I agree, and would add that compassion in this instance
includes a shared anxiety and sadness for the child, the disclosure of which might have normalized the patient's emotions and contained them.

Greenson's example also brings to mind a story I once
heard of a child's act of kindness:

> When a little girl was late arriving home from school,
> her concerned mother began to scold her. Her daughter
> interrupted, stating that she had not been given a chance
> to explain herself. "All right," said her mother, why were
> you late?" "I had to help another girl. She was in trou-
> ble," explained the daughter.
> "What did you do?"
> "Oh, I sat and helped her cry."

Emotional nonresponsiveness in the therapist can stalemate
a treatment; some clients do need our help to cry when they
too are emotional underresponders. Lack of emotional display and response logically prevents cognitive–emotive integration, a key feature in effective therapy (cf. Littrell, 1998).
As Alice Miller (1990) wrote, "it is not possible for someone
really to clarify their situation and dissolve their fears until
they can feel them rather than discuss them" (p. 184).

More immediately dangerous to the therapy, however, is

emotional nonresponse in the presence of appropriate or exaggerated affect. This pairing tends to be (at best) anger producing and possibly humiliating to the client, exacerbating his or her feeling of aloneness. Webster (1991) presented an abused client's description of therapy of this type with an "uninvolved" therapist:

> During session five I experienced an enormous feeling of grief and aloneness. I became overwhelmed with these feelings and began to sob uncontrollably. It was as if I had fallen into the abyss and was going deeper and deeper. She just sat there writing, then she said "Time is up. If you need some time to get yourself together you can sit in my front room." Nothing more was said.
>
> The session was over. I sat for a moment in disbelief, confused, disoriented, feeling out of control. Somehow I got myself out of the building and to my car. I felt abandoned, abused. I never went back (p. 141).

Several participants in the Trauma Countertransference Study told similar stories. David, a Vietnam veteran was among them:

David: I found myself shaking. Really shaking.

Interviewer: As you told your Vietnam stories.

David: As I told one story.

Interviewer: Do you want to tell it first?

David: [Retells story: deleted at participant request]

Interviewer: It makes me shake just to listen to that. What did your therapist do with it?

David: (tearfully) Nothing. If I heard "uh-huh" one more time I was going to deck him.

Interviewer: Uh . . . oops

David: (laughs) Habit, huh?

Interviewer: (laughs) So you didn't deck him. What did you do?

David: I sat there quivering like a jackass, well, like a rabbit . . . like a child, really. It was . . . what's a bigger word than embarrassed . . . mortifying. How's that? Mortifying. Does your tape recorder work? Write that down.

So I wrote it down, believing then, as I do now, that this client was highlighting a very real and underresearched danger in the "objective" or "neutral" response to trauma. Nonresponse can transform appropriate emotion to mortification in a patient already predisposed to view his or her distress as weakness. This predisposition, as Crittendon (1997) noted, is found disproportionately in those raised by punitive caregivers.

The issue of countertransference disclosure is multifaceted and complex, embedded as it is in broader theoretical frameworks regarding the mechanisms for therapeutic change. An alternative use of the material above for those who choose nondisclosure as a thoughtful strategy would be to consider the dangers above as "side effects" of the clinician's therapeutic choice. Many of these effects might well be minimized if the client is helped to understand that they can be normal reactions to the structure of therapy rather than pathological states in and of themselves.

Dangers of Countertransference Suppression for the Therapist's Psychic Health

In supervising hundreds of doctoral students, I have watched many clinicians go through an initial experience of attempting to suppress their countertransference feelings. This effort might be made for theoretical reasons or for defensive ones. In either case, the sense of distance does come quickly for most therapists, some of whom then feel more sanguine about their "neutrality." Even in the short term, however, uninvolved therapists tend to report boredom and "burnout." This style also can put the therapist at risk for dissociative symptoms, in which the feelings that are suppressed during daily clinical hours are acted out in extratherapeutic settings (cf. Stamm, 1995).

Suppression of affect in the name of neutrality also could be a disguised version of posttraumatic stress disorder, the symptoms of which appear at clinically significant levels in at least 40% of those therapists who work with substantial numbers of traumatized clients (Kassam-Adams, 1995). Finally, there is a growing literature suggesting the health dangers in suppressing emotional response to trauma (Esterling, Antoni, Fletcher, Margulies, & Schneiderman, 1994; Pennebaker, Kiecolt-Glaser, & Glaser, 1988; Pennebaker & O'Heeron, 1984), suggesting that the therapist should choose between or combine (a) countertransference disclosure to the patient and (b) emotional disclosure to a support system regarding the indirect experience of the patient's trauma.

Advantages to Countertransference Disclosure

In addition to avoidance of the dangers of countertransference suppression, disclosure has several distinct advantages within the treatment of traumatized clients. The list below draws heavily on the work of Ferenczi (1931, 1933/1949), Little (1951, 1957), Gorkin (1987), Tansey and Burke (1989), and Maroda (1991).

Reinforcing the Patient's Reality Testing Function and Modeling the Universality of Transference

Traumatized patients often have lived daily with the experience of having physical and emotional reality denied and distorted ("Your behavior deserved this punishment." "Mommy's not drunk." "It was not harassment." "Tell Daddy you love him."). This experience leaves the patient in doubt about many of the emotional truths within various relationships (cf. Davies & Frawley, 1994). The therapist who is unwilling to own countertransference feelings is less able to help the client learn to have faith in his or her own emotional perception—when it is accurate—or to differentiate projected from actual emotional experiences.

Consider this brief exchange between one of my colleagues and his patient, upon which I was asked to comment.

Ms. C: You look angry.

Therapist: We have to look at that, don't you think? I'm not angry at all. I think if you search for negatives in me all the time, you are likely to find some.

Ms. C: But you just look angry. Your brow is furrowed. You don't smile. (She begins to cry.)

Therapist: But why would I be angry at you? What do you think you have done that would make me angry? What is so bad and anger-provoking about you?

Now let's say we believe the therapist, Dr. A. He was not angry, or at least he was not conscious of being angry. What message does he send with his comment to the client? For me, his claim of objectivity—he was right about his lack of angry display and his client was wrong (and therefore it is transference and not countertransference)—implies the following:

- □ He, the therapist cannot be wrong about what he is feeling.
- □ The emotional display that he shows to others must match the internal state that he believes to be present.
- □ Therefore, if he is experienced in another way, the perceiver is misconstruing the situation.

In contrast, Dr. A will be trying to convince Ms. C that she can be quite wrong about her own affective state. He believes that she is unaware of her own anger at her mother, a difficult and at times abusive woman. He also believes that this suppressed and unexperienced anger is felt by others in Ms. C's workplace as disdain for them, and that it might explain why she has difficulty making friends in this setting. She does not agree.

My point here is that although Dr. A and Ms. C are at odds about the source of Ms. C's problems, they agree about the process of self-perception. Dr. A believes that he can know that Ms. C's perception of him is wrong, and Ms. C believes that she can know that Dr. A is off track in his interpretation. I disagree, believing that such perfect self-knowledge is an ideal, not a state actually achieved by anyone. The therapist's willingness to self-examine, to treat all countertransference reactions, indeed all therapy-related behaviors, as potentially multidetermined, would serve a necessary role-modeling function for the client. It would suggest that it is not sickness or pathology to fail to know completely oneself or one's influence on others and that other people are useful tools for the acquisition of self-knowledge.

In this case, it would imply that Dr. A should tell his client that, although he is not aware of any angry feelings, he respects her ability to observe, he considers her perceptions worthy of discussion and analysis, and he is curious as to what specific evidence leads her to her perception of anger in him. He can explain that her observations might be useful to him in understanding his effect on her, just as he hopes that his observations will help her. Interestingly, Dr. A tells me that anger is one of his more pervasive emotional states. He is often told that he appears angry when (to his knowledge) he is not.

Countertransference disclosure, then, whether or not it parallels the transference accusation or question, models willingness to critically analyze internal experience. It takes considerable courage for the client to try on the idea that his or her perceptions of the therapist (and of the self) might not be trustworthy—bravery some clients never marshal. Many analysts refer to this capacity as the ability to maintain an "as-if quality" to the transference, that is, understanding that one might experience one's therapist as if he were your father, while simultaneously knowing that he is not in fact your father. The as-if quality is purportedly particularly difficult for traumatized clients to develop (cf. Levine, 1982, 1990).

Dr. A's willingness to self-examine in his client's presence signaled to her that reality testing about the appropriateness of emotions is work best accomplished in an interpersonal setting. By not privileging his own emotional perception as truth, he allowed the client to consider adopting the same strategy. The difficult sessions that followed taught both Ms. C and Dr. A something about their effect on others and reportedly deepened their therapeutic alliance.

Establishment of the Therapist's Honesty and Genuineness

In any type of therapy, countertransference disclosure at times is advanced as a necessary tool for demonstrating the honesty of the therapist (cf. L. Epstein, 1979; Gorkin, 1987; Little, 1951, 1957; Maroda, 1991). Within trauma therapy, such honesty, linked as it is with trustworthiness, is even more critical, particularly for clients whose traumas were dealt out at the hands of attachment or authority figures. Writing of his work with Vietnam veterans, Jonathan Shay (1994) concluded:

> To be trustworthy, a listener must be ready to experience some of the terror, grief and rage that the victim did. This is one meaning, after all, of the word compassion. Once the vet sees that the listener authentically experiences these emotions, even though with less intensity than in combat, the vet often loses the desire to shout in the listener's face, "You weren't there, so shut the fuck up" (p. 189).

The client's experience of the therapist's honesty, when honesty is often difficult, also builds the capacity for the therapist to point out (in a believable way) that what is experienced as hostility, rejection, and anger toward the patient could be frustration and exasperation on his or her behalf. Perceived withdrawal and disdain could be the therapist's efforts to manage compassionately induced fear or pain. For complex reasons (see chapter 6), adult survivors of chronic trauma also often continue to live in environments that are deceptive, and honesty is a rare and welcome event. At times, belief in the power of honesty is the only viable hope that both members of the dyad possess.

As an example, I wish to return to my first session as an intern with the client mentioned in chapter 1, Mr. B, who had recently lost his job:

> When I met Mr. B in the lobby and showed him back to one of the graduate student offices, he followed without expression. Upon arriving, however, it became clear that he thought me to be the receptionist showing him to the "real doctor." When I told him that I was his therapist, he laughed derisively, picked up the briefcase he had dropped on the floor, and turned to leave with the line "I may be broke but I'm not stupid." He spoke angrily. "I have to start my whole life over again. What could you know about that?" At the door he paused, shaking his head, and asked "How old are you, anyway?"
>
> I knew the correct therapeutic answer to this question. It had been in a role play I had attended the week before, and the recommended response was "I see that my age may concern you. Would you like to talk about that?" I didn't think I could pull it off. Instead I sat down on the desk, picked up a book and began thumbing it through. Stopping near the back of the book, where an index might be, I spoke aloud as if to myself, "Patient asks how old you are. If he means you look like a kid and probably can't help, see p. 18. If you are a kid, stay out of your mother's books." I looked up at him and smiled, still thumbing through the text. He laughed, putting his briefcase back down, but still standing. Leaning against the doorjamb, he asked what I thought it said on p. 18. I told him that I hadn't read it yet, but thought it probably talked about the value of emotional and intellectual commitment to a person and a problem. We probably bantered back and forth for 10 minutes or so, during which time I disclosed my anxiety in working with him, and my intention to do so effectively. I told him that he had begun honestly, and that it was possible that both of us would get over our anxiety, although it would help me a lot if he sat back down. He did so, and we began to work.

In preparing this text, I wrote to Mr. B and asked him to review this passage and others for fairness and to give me permission to discuss it. I also asked whether he had anything to add, looking back over many years from the position of a new and passionately loved job to this most difficult time of his life. "Yes, I do remember that meeting," he wrote.

> I'm surprised you call both of us frightened, because I was trying to go for contempt and domination at the time. I was frightened though, and embarrassed that they put me with an intern, which seemed to confirm that I was a loser. If you want me to add to your presentation, I would say that I knew you were frightened of me right away, but I thought at first that it was because you felt cowed by me. When you talked about being nervous, and joked with me about it, it seemed as if you were frightened because you felt an obligation to me. It became a positive thing. Another thing was that I felt humiliated by my own fear of breakdown at the time, and honest expression of fear without embarrassment was the therapy I needed. My own memory of what you said was "I think you're scared, Mr. B, and I know I am." You made some analogy of finding our way out of a forest. A little odd given our age difference, but I felt the "we" of "us" right away.

Psychotherapists within the field generally agree that honesty is important, although we forgive (and even compliment) the therapists' sins of omission more than sins of commission. We rarely acknowledge, however, that honesty is very difficult and that this is more true, not less true, in intimate relationships. DePaulo and Bell's (1996) empirical study of the frequency of everyday lies is aptly titled "Lies Are Told to Those Who Care."

Establishing and Cementing the Therapist's Involvement With the Client

The therapist's involvement with the client and the client's perception of this involvement are obviously separable dimensions, but both seem critical to successful therapy. In my own studies of dissatisfied and satisfied trauma clients, dissatisfied clients almost universally stated that their therapists appeared distant, uninvolved, or cold (Dalenberg, 1995; Dalenberg & Cuevas, 1997). Their behavioral evidence of this lack of involvement almost always involved their inability to identify therapist feelings or to believe that they influenced the therapist enough to produce empathic involvement.

The best known studies of client improvement also show that a primary predictor of negative outcome in psychotherapy is the patient's claim that the therapist is cold, bored, and fails to understand (cf. Strupp, Wallach, & Wogan, 1964). The finding crosses theoretical boundaries and appears to be powerful in behavioral treatment (Sloane, Staples, Cristol, Yorkston, & Whipple, 1975) as well as in psychoanalytic therapy (Colson, Lewis, & Horowitz, 1985). Beck and his colleagues (e.g., Beck, 1989; Beck & Emery, 1985), along with other cognitive theorists (Friedberg & Fidaleo, 1992; Merali & Lynch, 1997) highlighted the relationship under the label of *collaborative empiricism*, the requirement that the therapist work in partnership with the client rather than attempting to impose the therapist's will or definition of health on the client.

The theoretical framework presented here would support countertransference disclosure both of genuine involvement and the discomfort of felt noninvolvement, which might be worked through if it is discussed. To the extent that we believe that true involvement affects client perceptions of our involvement, it follows that our engagement with them will serve several treatment-related functions.

- □ Positive countertransference facilitates positive transference, the foundation for the acceptance of therapist interventions within either cognitive or analytic theory.
- □ The therapist's involvement, particularly in long-term therapy, is a sign to the client of the client's inherent likability. "It is natural for people to feel friendly and caring toward each other when they spend time together, especially when they are talking so intimately

with each other," writes psychiatrist Peter Breggin. "Not to acknowledge this is to perpetuate the client's original feelings of unlovability, alienation and worthlessness" (Breggin, 1991, p. 380).

□ Involvement will increase the therapist's capacity for empathic understanding of the client's feelings, so that countertransference will yield information about the patient rather than unrelated or tangentially related data.

Mr. S, a well-to-do man who had seen 14 therapists in eight cities before his treatment with me, states now that the continual negotiation of the degree of our emotional involvement *was* the therapy to him, as opposed to a prerequisite to therapy. He was an angry individual with a variety of symptoms that took center stage in serial fashion, so that I often felt that he was frustrating any possibility for me to help him examine any specific problem in depth. The following is an excerpt from a session approximately six months into our work:

Mr. S: You don't like me very much, do you?

Therapist: Where did that come from? Oh, I'm sorry. You make me crazy, but, yes, I like you. Where does that come from—that I don't like you?

Mr. S: You're frowning. You frown a lot when you're with me, and I don't take you to be a natural frowner.

Therapist: Well, I think I might be concentrating. When do I do it?

Mr. S: I make you crazy?

Therapist: I feel like I am always chasing you, trying to get you to sit down and stay involved in something. I want to rest with the pleasure of liking you, and I'm always one sentence behind. Like now. ... You're on crazy-making now, and I'm still on why am I frowning.

Mr. S: The pleasure of liking me, huh? That's a new one.

Mr. S grew up as the son of a career criminal and saw his father engage in many illegal and violent acts. He felt that his father was always on the verge of getting caught, and he listened secretly more than once to police interviews that took place at his home. His father was never jailed, but he died in a suspicious accident when Mr. S was a young adult.

In response to reading the excerpt above, Mr. S wrote:

> You were the first person I ever fully, completely, genuinely liked in that oh-I-have-to-tell-her-that way. I find your choice of [excerpts] interesting. I did come to believe that you took pleasure in puzzling out my personal mysteries. That's what I eventually thought about between sessions. Carrying memories to someone else and having that person treat them with some emotion is really an extraordinary experience to have for the first time as an adult.

Certainly, involvement is a dangerous as well as a life-giving function for those who have been traumatized by attachment figures. To me, this underlines further the need to manage involvement well within trauma therapy. Given the acknowledged importance of the working alliance within all forms of therapy, it is interesting that so little has been written about methods for building such a foundation.

Providing a Source of Information About the Patient

The idea that countertransference might be an important source of information about the patient's inner life is perhaps the most accepted of the positive arguments for countertransference disclosure. "If the analyst is well identified with the patient and if he has fewer repressions than the patient," Racker (1968, p. 17) argued in his important theoretical text, "then the thoughts and feelings which emerge in him will be, precisely, those which did not emerge in the patient, i.e., the repressed and the unconscious." The argument is traced to a well-known statement by Sigmund Freud describing the analyst's response to the patient's unconscious:

> To put it in a formula: he [the therapist] must turn his own unconscious like a receptive organ towards the

transmitting unconscious of the patient. He must adjust himself to the patient as a telephone receiver is adjusted to the transmitting microphone. Just as the receiver converts back into soundwaves the electric oscillations in the telephone line which were set up by sound waves, so the doctor's unconscious is able, from the derivatives of the unconscious which are communicated to him, to reconstruct that unconscious, which has determined the patient's free associations. (S. Freud, 1912/1958, p. 115–116)

Initially, this argument may not appear to bear directly on countertransference disclosure, because countertransference could be experienced with the therapist engaging in "silent use." If the newly gained information is to be shared with the client, however, the therapist is still disclosing countertransference, albeit indirectly. To the sensitive and involved patient, the phrase "Could it be that your employer is angry at you for doing X?" is quite similar to "I find it plausible that your employer is angry at you for doing X," which in turn can be heard as "I am [or would be in your employer's place] angry at you for doing X." One could even argue, in a moral sense, that the client is owed the information that the therapist's interpretations, advice, judgments, or pointed questions about the patient's inner experience or effect on others stems from the therapist's (perhaps idiosyncratic) countertransference rather than from a more general theoretical–scientific base. If told, the patient might be able to make use of his or her own knowledge of the therapist (e.g., that the therapist is or is not easily moved to anger) to weigh the likely validity of the proposed information. As argued earlier, the inherent subjectivity of both transference and countertransference is part of the definition of the terms. Further, the acknowledgment of this subjectivity is at the heart of the educational subtext of therapy.

The idea of the countertransference as information has sound empirical backing within biologically based theories of human interaction, including attachment theory. The similarity in human expression of emotion across race, age, and culture (cf. Ekman, 1973) and the ability of infants to show appropriate reactions to their parents' emotional expressions (Klinnert, 1984; Tronick, Als, Adamson, Wise, & Brazelton, 1978; Stern, 1985) suggest that involuntary facial expression of emotion is the product of evolution. Certainly there is species survival value in programming the animal to quickly "catch" fear or disgust from another proximate animal who was first to see the danger or taste the tainted food.

Racker (1968) identified this type of countertransference— resonating with the client's felt emotion—as "concordant." The therapist might also experience complementary countertransference—feeling placed in the role of abuser to the client's victim (cf. M. Davies & Frawley, 1994; Pearlman & Saakvitne, 1995). These interactions also could have biological subtexts, as client and therapist play out dominance– submission themes or sexual seduction and conquest.

To the extent that countertransference is based on these basic emotional communications, which will at times (but not always) be the case, it might not be mediated consciously. The therapist simply finds herself or himself feeling worried, upset, angry, or threatened. Typically, the lack of known referents for the emotion (I have no reason to be angry), the anomalous nature of the feeling (I do not usually feel or act this way), or both, are clues to the patient-generated source of the countertransference.

Another rich descriptive source for this use of countertransference, although I have theoretical problems with the term, is in the literature on "projective identification." Melanie Klein (1946) described *projective identification* as a process whereby the infant splits the emotional self to separate the "good internal objects" from the "bad internal objects." The infant then fantasizes expelling or projecting the split-off objects (typically the bad objects) into another person (usually the mother). In the last step, the infant identifies with the recipient of the projections—hence projective identification. The concept was expanded in the work of Bion (1955, 1959), Malin and Grotstein (1966), Kernberg (1975), Langs (1976), and Sandler (1976).

The conceptual danger in the concept of projective identification is the degree to which it is presented within some case studies as a real rather than a fantasy projection of the emotions of one individual into another. "You have been pushing into my insides your fear that you will murder me," Bion (1955, p. 224), for example, states to his schizoid patient (after Bion became aware of his own fear). Similarly, although Sandler's version of the therapist is less passive in the projective-identification exchange, the concept was again described as "an attempt [by the patient] to impose an interaction . . . between himself and the analyst" (Sandler, 1976, p. 44). Gabbard and Wilkinson (1994) describing the concept within the context of work with patients with borderline personality disorder, label it as a "highly coercive force," that "disables the therapist's ability to reflect on meanings and assign them to one's subjective state. . . ." [Such therapists are] locked into a 'dance' with the patient that is inevitable and obligatory. . . . [T]hey cannot think their own thoughts because they have been transformed into a repudiated part of the patient" (p. 74).

The feeling of inevitability of emotional states is a key element within trauma therapy, and one of the major obstacles to recovery. Although countertransference, even as it is drawn out by the patient's projective identification, can feel "obligatory," the argument that it is so disowns the therapist's responsibility for his or her own thoughts, feelings, and behaviors, inviting the client to do the same. Again, the therapist's public struggle to climb out of the disturbing interaction in which he or she has fallen with the patient, whether or not the therapist believes he or she has been pushed into the abyss, could be the much-needed sign for the patient that the pattern of the interaction is not inevitable.

An example of the projections of a patient with borderline personality disorder is instructive here (Gabbard & Wilkinson, 1994, p. 92):

> As Ms. U went on and on about how Bill was secretly attracted to her, Dr. F became rather bored and realized that he had not been listening to what she was saying. When he realized that his attention had become distracted, he blinked and refocused on the patient's words.

Ms. U: (shouting) I'm boring you! You really don't care!

Dr. F: You've suddenly shifted gears.

Ms. U: You blinked!
The patient delivered her observation in the form of an accusation, as if Dr. F's blinking was the most heinous of acts.

Ms. U: (now more seriously and angrily) This therapy isn't working! You don't care. This is obviously not a good match. You don't give me insights. You don't talk about my envy? I can't develop a relationship with you. It's no use to keep at this!
Dr. F groaned inwardly. The complaints he was hearing were part of a familiar litany about how he should change to meet the patient's needs. He felt completely controlled by the patient, so that he did not even have the freedom to blink or shift his attention away from Ms. U without being blasted for it.

Dr. F: A few minutes ago you wanted me to hold you. I haven't changed. Something inside you has changed.

Ms. U: No, it hasn't.

Gabbard and Wilkinson's main purposes in presenting this case were (a) to demonstrate the extreme reactivity of the borderline patient and (b) to suggest that the therapist must learn to contain the patient's projections rather than defending himself against perceived attack. Both are valid and important points. My own assessment is that the therapist and client here share a common failing: Both deny their separate roles in the interaction. For example, the therapist did indeed change, as he acknowledged earlier to his professional audience, if not to his patient. He became bored and momentarily diverted his attention. It is true that the interaction with Ms. U implied that "he did not even have the freedom to blink or shift his attention away from Ms. U without being blasted for it." But it is also true that he did not give Ms. U the freedom to notice that shift in attention without being forced to deal with a challenge to her reality testing.

In my view, if one goal is to help the client become more

clear about her own contributions to intimate interactions, the therapist's obscuring his or her own role is unlikely to serve this end. Disclosure also aids the traumatized client in allocating responsibility and blame—an issue of enormous concern for many victims of life-changing circumstances.

Breaking Through an Impasse or Mending a Countertransference-Based Enactment

Of the published reasons for countertransference disclosure, there is perhaps most agreement on the occasional necessity for disclosure to bring the therapy back on track after a countertransference enactment. Several published accounts reviewed in later chapters present a psychotherapist who is frustrated by a patient's dogged attachment to a particular symptom or way of relating. One can almost hear the therapist's sighs of exasperation in the descriptions of intervention after failed intervention. The patient's behavior is often labeled *repetition compulsion,* setting the stage for a patient-based explanation of the retraumatization that follows. Finally, the narrator reaches the point in the therapeutic story in which (a) the therapist disclosed a powerful countertransference feeling, typically blurted out without a good deal of thought, or (b) the therapist acts out—forgetting the client's appointment, overcharging, or losing track of the client's account. The entire vignette is often chosen to illustrate the positive effects of countertransference disclosure by an astonished therapist.

Not surprisingly, I would advocate a more consciously reasoned and accepting approach to the disclosure process. I believe that these enactments and thoughtless or rude disclosures tend to occur with therapists who attempt to withhold any lower-level expression of their negative feelings. Supervision of students and discussions with colleagues has led me to conclude that many who are uncomfortable with countertransference disclosure have had the experience of disclosing material with an intensity that frightened their patients. A good rule of thumb, discussed in detail by Maroda (1991), is that countertransference disclosure generally should take place on occasions of patient choice. If the therapist feels a strong urge to disclose, the source of that urgency deserves examination before it leads to an enactment. Countertransference explosion is not countertransference disclosure, and it will not have the same effect.

The most important countertransference disclosure that can be made after an enactment is expression of sincere remorse. Therapists are often deeply ashamed of their spontaneous and thoughtless hostile remarks or actions and, being human, respond defensively to the patient's wounded cries. How many of these reactions seem familiar?

- □ Ok, so I was not tactful. I did have a point, though, and my patient is overreacting. This is more her pathology than my bad character.
- □ After months of tolerating my patient's attacks, I think I have earned the right to respond at least once. It is not as though I do this all the time.
- □ My patient is searching for a reason to suffer. She has been waiting to catch me in this. In fact, she probably pushed me into it so she could be in the victim role and make me feel guilty.
- □ It is important that my patient knows that this is the reaction he invokes in people. Obsessing on my error does little good. Let's learn from it.

Posttraumatic growth is a true phenomenon, and certainly one hopes to move the situation in this direction if one errs in a major way with a patient. I would submit, however, that most of us need training in designing and implementing a sincere and effective apology (see chapter 9).

Increased Toleration of the Affect of Others

Countertransference disclosure is one tool for moving a client toward more capable approaches to the emotion of others. Particularly for those whose trauma occurred through human malfeasance, affect tolerance is likely to be a major difficulty in therapy. Chapter 1 states that several types of interactive strategies designed to minimize the experience of the therapist's anger, disapproval, or disgust are characteristic of clients in the midst of traumatic transference. Changes in these strategies, disabling strategies that are designed to avoid confrontation with true emotion could depend on the client learning in fact, rather than in fantasy, that low doses of negative affect from an attachment figure can be tolerated.

Caveat: Dangers of Countertransference Disclosure

I have argued implicitly above that the more traditionally understood dangers associated with countertransference disclosure are not highly applicable to the trauma population. The preservation of neutrality, for instance, is less commonly valued in general in modern writing, but can be an active obstruction to the psychotherapy of survivors of trauma. As in Greenson's (1967) example of the young analyst who showed no emotion when told of the serious illness of his patient's child, neutrality to trauma in many cases could be synonymous with a lack of compassion. Two other common reasons for nondisclosure, the facilitation of negative transference and the encouragement of transference in general, seem less applicable to populations known for their propensity toward uncontrollable transference explosions, at times destroying therapy in the process. Bringing the negative transference to full force in most trauma populations, I would argue, is a very bad idea. Nonetheless, caveats for the recommendation to disclose countertransference are important.

The trauma therapist considering disclosure for therapeutic reasons should consider at least three facets of the intervention, which could be used to generate a more sophisticated plan for disclosure that is matched to a particular client–therapist pair.

1. Is the reason for disclosure appropriate, in that it is information relevant to the client's need to know rather than the therapist's need to discharge affect, to protect his or her own ego, or to advance his or her own needs?
2. Are the method and timing of disclosure appropriate, offered in the manner most likely to be perceived as

information rather than as an assault, mindful of the client's ability to hear?

3. Is the type or content of countertransference disclosure appropriate, responsive to client needs, and unlikely to overwhelm the client?

The choice of timing of therapist countertransference disclosure as presented in published literature often belies the claim that the disclosure was in the client's best interest. Occasionally, authors admit they "couldn't take it anymore" or that the form of the disclosure embarrassed or shamed the author. Such disclosures typically are in response to a client's sexual or hostile transference, and they can have predictably devastating consequences. From the comfort of distance, for instance, I do wonder how Hilton's supervisor (Hedges, Hilton, Hilton, & Candill, 1997, p. 206) thought it would be helpful for any adult male client to hear his therapist say (in response to his sexual transference) that she would never have been interested in him because he was not "man enough" for her. The client subsequently terminated therapy.

Countertransference disclosure is a tool, and like most tools, it makes a handy club. It is most commonly unwise to make any nonemergency intervention, including countertransference disclosure, when intense emotion could be blurring the capacity for cognitive evaluation. Such disclosures can be (a) poorly disguised hostility, often immediately recognized by the patient; (b) an effort to distract self or client from painful material; or (c) an effort to reclaim the therapist's ravaged self-image.

On the last point, I believe that the lengths to which many authors go in their case histories to detail the unfairness of their clients' verbal assaults illustrates the therapists' immense discomfort with being placed in the role of attacker. This is particularly true when the therapists are working so hard to restrain themselves from actually acting out this very role. In some instances, countertransference disclosure might be forced on the client to stop such a perceived assault on the therapist's self-image, simply due to the therapist's increasingly strong wish to be known as the person that she believes that she is. Sadly, this is often the same internal struggle that clients wage as they protect themselves against perceived therapeutic attacks. The disclosure of therapist achievements as a defense against attacks ("No, given my advanced education, I am not bothered by your anger") also is risky, although it could be a defense against more destructive, hostile countertransference disclosure.

The method of countertransference disclosure should emphasize that the therapist's feeling state is not the client's responsibility. There are times when it might be useful to say "I think I phrased that comment poorly because I was feeling a little confused (anxious, frustrated)," but there are fewer justifications for comments of the type "You are making me feel X" or "You are trying to get me to do Y." I agree with Searles (1986) that it is unlikely that we will help the traumatized patient become well "if we unwittingly use him as a receptacle for our own most deeply unwanted personality components and . . . require him to bear the burden of all the severe psychopathology in the whole relationship." (p. 22)

Summary

I have argued here that the frequency, method and form of countertransference disclosure are important dimensions of clinical work in trauma therapy. The following points were made:

- □ The provision of safety in trauma therapy is intimately connected to the management of countertransference and to countertransference disclosure patterns of the therapist.
- □ Nondisplay of countertransference is display, and therefore must be evaluated in regard to risk–benefit ratios for the client (just as display and disclosure would be so evaluated).
- □ The nondisclosing therapist must be aware that countertransference nondisclosure is not entirely possible. Thus the therapist must develop tools to mitigate the possible damage of unintentional countertransference

display. The hypervigilance of the trauma client and his
or her sensitivity to unpredictable emotions in attachment figures makes this task particularly important.

☐ Countertransference disclosure can serve many positive
purposes: reinforcing clients' reality-testing function,
modeling the universality of transference, establishing
and cementing involvement with the client, establishing
the therapist's honesty and genuineness, providing a
source of information about clients' psyches and their
effect on other people, breaking through impasses, and
mending damage from countertransference-based enactments. As stated in a Hebrew epigram, words that
come from the heart are more likely to enter the heart.

☐ Countertransference disclosure does also carry atten-
dant dangers. Therapists would be aptly warned to be
careful that they are pointing with the sword of truth,
rather than stabbing the patient with it.

3

Speaking Trauma:
The Inadequacy of
Language in Trauma Treatment

He'd say in a quiet, reassuring voice "I know what you lived through. I know one doesn't return from there without scars that bleed at the lightest touch. That's why I never raise the subject with you. I want to help you forget." (Delbo, 1995, p. 266)

We can begin a description of the life of trauma therapy with the obvious—or at least with what should be obvious. Trauma is hard to speak and hard to hear. Traumas tend to be sudden, negative, and uncontrollable events (Carlson, 1997) that are by common clinical definition difficult to assimilate into existing systems. Anna Freud wrote that the word *trauma* is overused and should be reserved for events that are "shattering, devastating, causing internal disruption by putting ego functioning and ego mediation out of action" (A. Freud, 1969, p. 242). The *Diagnostic and Statistical Manual of Mental Disorders* (American Psychiatric Association, 1994, p. 424) provided the following definition:

Direct personal experience of an event that involves actual or threatened death or serious injury, or other threat to one's physical integrity; or witnessing an event that involves death, injury, or a threat to the physical integrity of another person; or learning about unexpected or violent death, serious harm, or threat of death or injury ex-

perienced by a family member or other close associate
(Criterion A1). The person's response to the event must
involve intense fear, helplessness, or horror (or in children, the response must involve disorganized or agitated
behavior) (Criterion A2).

This is, of course, a nonexhaustive list of potential stress-
ors, focusing on those events that commonly lead to the intense emotion that is thought to mediate later symptoms. Notice, however, that learning about the trauma of a close
associate could qualify as a trauma for the listener if the req-
uisite emotional response occurs. Therapists who treat
trauma clients, who thus might fall into that close-associate
category, have high rates of posttraumatic stress disorder
(PTSD) symptoms (Kassam-Adams, 1995). Therefore, it would
be understandable, and in fact psychically healthy, for therapists to resist a closeness that would leave them vulnerable.
There is good reason, then, not to hear trauma. Perhaps it
should not be surprising that clinicians tend not to ask about
trauma background (Briere & Zaidi, 1989) or that as many as
one-third of incest victims go through therapy without sharing information about that experience with their therapists
(Dalenberg, 1994).
   As a thought experiment, imagine that in the next room is
a client with whom you will work. Suppose that this is his
story, actually taken from the book *Fragments: Memories of a
Wartime Childhood* by Binjamin Wilkomirski (1996, pp. 60–61).
He is describing seeing several little boys outside a barracks
where he was housed:

> They were forbidden to come back into the barracks.
> They were meant to be a warning to the rest of us. Hud-
> dled over, crying constantly, they knelt in the filth. I
> stared horrified at their trousers, which were all spotted
> with red.
>   The older children explained:
>   On the way to the latrines they hadn't been able to
> hold their water anymore. Two of the block wardens had
> caught them as they were peeing against the wall behind
> one of the barracks. As a punishment, they'd taken little

sticks and pushed them up into the boys' penises as far as they'd go. Then the block wardens had hit their penises, making the sticks break off. The wardens had laughed a lot and had a good time.

"Now all they'd do is pee blood," said one of them.

When evening came they were still whimpering. Then people came and took them away.

Workshop participants tell me that they experience a number of emotions as they contemplate seeing this client. The most common reactions reported in free responses are anger at the perpetrator, vicarious fear, horror, shame at what happened to this individual, sadness, the wish to protect or rescue the children, and disgust and nausea. Most of the psychologists in the workshops affirm that they wish both to help and to turn away. In either case, *they don't know what to say.*

The Inadequacy of Language in Describing Trauma

At times, in clinical training, I offer students a chance to respond to "Written in Pencil in the Sealed Railway-Car," a poem by Don Pagis written in the voice of a woman in a cattle car, riding to Auschwitz (Pagis, 1995, p. 588):

> Here in this carload
> I am eve
> with abel my son
> if you see my other son
> cain son of man
> tell him that I

When I ask my students why the woman stopped writing, they most commonly give what I call "obstacle explanations" for her failure to continue. The pencil fell or was wrenched from her hands. She was killed, or taken from the boxcar. She was overcome with emotion. Only rarely do they mention an important alternative: She stopped speaking because of the inadequacy of language to convey her meaning. She stopped speaking not because she was afraid to share the words, but because there were no words.

I recall listening to a mother at a local vacation park chastising a park employee. Standing outside a petting pool, her daughter had been splashed by a dolphin, surprising both mother and daughter. The mother was "horrified" that her daughter was wet, "terrified" that her 8-year-old daughter would fall, "aghast" that the park would allow such a thing to happen. We should not be surprised, perhaps, that when confronted by an event that really is deserving of such words, patient and therapist alike can lapse into silent search for adequate descriptors.

An interesting example of the point I am trying to make here came to my attention during the interview process for the Trauma Countertransference Study. Lisa, a multiple-trauma victim who had recently been raped, described for me her termination with her therapist after about a dozen sessions. With Lisa's permission, I spoke to her therapist for an extended period. Here are their initial descriptions of their final session:

> *Lisa:* She just would not listen. She kept shifting the subject. I would be trying to figure out how to tell her something and she would cut me off. It hurt so much.
>
> *Interviewer:* How would she cut you off?
>
> *Lisa:* She would not let me speak. She would ask me about something else. I think she must have thought I was to blame for the rape. [Begins to cry.]
>
> *Interviewer:* Did she say anything like that, that you were to blame?
>
> *Lisa:* She didn't say much at all, really, except for the questions. She was so . . . silent. That's part of why I think she was ashamed of me.

Next, her therapist speaks:

> *Dr. B:* She just couldn't talk about it. I tried to make it easier for her, you know, did all the usual things.

Interviewer: What . . . what usual things?

Dr. B: I tried to support her defenses while they were still needed. I respected her silence. I could tell the whole thing was too much for her. I actually feel very badly about it. I don't usually have clients leave this way.

Interviewer: I understand. How did you respect her silence?

Dr. B: I knew that she was not able to talk yet, and I understood that. It was a really terrible rape, from what I could tell about it. I knew she was ashamed. I know I didn't deal with it well.

Interviewer: What do you think you should have done?

Dr. B: Interpreted her resistance, probably.

Interviewer: OK, well, I'm not saying that I think you should have done that, but why didn't you do that?

Dr. B: I felt sort of . . . incompetent . . . from being faced with that much pain. It threw me off.

Embedded in these excerpts are therapist and client interpretations of each other's silence. Dr. B believes that Lisa's silence is her shame and resistance, and feels incompetent to fight it. Lisa believes that Dr. B's silence is disrespect, and she feels shame in response. My own feeling, in speaking with each of them, was one of profound loneliness, which each of them seemed to share.

I do not discount the possible role of shame and resistance in Lisa's silence and the wish to distance (even through disrespect) in Dr. B's silence. Both possibilities are explored in later chapters. I would argue, however, that the fragmented, silence-riddled language of the trauma victim is in part a limitation of speech, not of the speaker. In his introduction to his eyewitness account of the Holocaust, Romaine Anteime states that "it seemed impossible for us to bridge the gap that we discovered between the language available to us and the experience which was still continuing in our bodies" (Lang, 1988, p. 42). Elie Weisel believes that the high rate of suicide among those who write about the Holocaust results from their profound disappointment that their work "is not what they want it to be. ... " "Where language fails, what can be its substitute?" (Weisel, 1993, p. 161).

Facing the Inadequacy of Language

It is unusual in my clinical life to find single lines or paragraphs that change my approach to a countertransference or general clinical problem. I confess that my more reliable insights regarding my clients tend to be the lumbering kind, moving slowly and awkwardly into the room before settling down comfortably between us. In reading the Holocaust literature, however, one phrase from Lawrence Langer struck me immediately, as he described the testimony of Edith P, a survivor of Auschwitz:

> She pauses, looks down, and for a moment seems to lose her power of speech. Everything conspires to remind her of her inadequacy to face this issue. But then she proceeds, as if in pursuit of a controlled inaccuracy, not as a calculated breach of truth, but as a concession to what words cannot do, an assent to the partial collapse of verbal power (Langer, 1991, p. 105)

Controlled inaccuracy captures something quite important in the potential solution to the countertransference–transference dilemma created by the inadequacy of trauma language. The concept of *concession* is also important here, suggesting as it does that there is a need for therapist and client to give up the belief that perfect articulation is possible, and instead to struggle together to reach a good-enough disclosure. One Trauma Countertransference Study participant put it this way:

> *Brian:* I guess the most helpful thing my doctor did ... well, this is going to sound strange, but he tried to guess what it must have felt like to me as a kid. And when he was groping around for the words he just hit on a couple

that worked. And until that happened, I couldn't grip
them in my mind, you know? They kept slipping away.
His descriptions weren't exactly right, but they were like
sandpaper. My own truth stuck to his words well enough
for me to trap it and talk about it.

Because I see this point as an important one, I have chosen
a more extended clinical example of controlled inaccuracy.
The anecdote is given from my client's point of view, and it
is her unedited free account of her therapy. I remember several details differently, but I interrupt the narrative here only
to clarify. The narrator is a young adult, describing an experience that occurred in our sessions when she was 9 years
old:

> I remember my father used to hold me by the elbow, with
> my hand flopping in the air strangely. About our meet-
> ing, I remember he would always hand me over with
> that line "Here's my bit of nothing." He said that all the
> time—it got to me. I don't remember why or when it
> started. So he stands in your lobby, pinching my elbow
> and you come out and he jerks my elbow over for you
> to take it. And you took my hand instead and twirled
> me around and said "Hello, little ballerina. What's your
> name?" I must have had my leotard on from ballet class
> or something. I don't remember that part. [I don't recall
> what she was wearing either, but she was moving up
> onto her toes and down again as she stood by her father,
> her arm dangling in the air. The two of them created
> quite a memorable picture.] You never did that again and
> I was waiting for it. But you always offered your hand
> and I always took it.
>
> General things I remember are the way you would
> watch me when I was doing things. I watch my daughter
> like that. And I remember a few of your toys, like the
> blocks. I recall that you were a pretty good storyteller,
> and that you'd put parts of my life in the story, which
> was fun.
>
> That day that you call our turning point is very mem-
> orable to me. I remember that I was crying over the "bit
> of nothing" comment. You figured out what the problem

was immediately. [This is a kind exaggeration of my clinical intuition. She was under the table, pounding herself on the leg, repeating "bit of nothing" over and over. The source of her distress was maddeningly evident to me.] So you told me we were going somewhere and you took me over to the computer center. I'd never been there. Then you showed me spectacular things that it could do —there was a program that talked back to you when you typed and a kind of picture-drawing program. And you were selling me. "Look at this. Look at that." I was intrigued despite myself. Then you made me close my eyes and you popped some chip out of the back of the computer and you had me open my eyes to see that it didn't work. [I think I found the chip in the lab.] Then you called the computer tech over and had this conversation with him that used the word "bit." I remember that part well. You kept talking to him about what this "bit of nothing" could do. You were holding that tiny thing in your hand. You were talking to him about how many memories it could hold and what it could learn. I knew the computer tech could tell he was teaching me something, and he picked up your jargon. He said "this little bit of nothing can do anything, depending on where it is placed." [I repeated this line to her often.]

When he left, you turned to me and you said that my father's nickname was well-chosen because I was small but "immensely talented" and you called me "little bit" and touched my hair.

I know you want me to be honest. I hope you won't be disappointed at this part. I remember looking at you and *choosing* to let you take over his word. I knew we were lying to ourselves, kind of. You weren't just changing the word for me. I was part of it. We were making a true lie together. I knew he didn't mean "Bit" that way, your way. But it was like we were robbing him of his power to use that word against me. It suddenly belonged to you and me and we could do what we wanted with it.

I have tried to explain this moment to my husband [a psychology graduate student], and he says that I discovered my own power. That's partly right, probably, but I would say it was that I discovered the power of words.

Just because he meant a word one way, doesn't mean I have to hear it that way. I developed a whole dictionary for my father. When he said selfish, he meant that I wanted to do it my way sometimes, and when he said I was arrogant, he meant that I was self-confident. Do you remember when you were trying to explain to me why I felt the way I did about my father, and you said that he was erasing me? That's what I visualize now. Erasing his definition and writing in my own. And here's the really weird part. Now he's kind of come around to my meanings and he's proud of me for a lot of the things that he used to hate. I forgive him now.

There are several examples of controlled inaccuracy in the case study above. The redefinition of "bit" and the concept of erasure were two of a dozen metaphors I used to meet my own need for words to describe and thus to "grip" the emotional abuse of E's father. I was trying, with E, to affect my own countertransference frustration and E's corresponding despair by substituting metaphor for literal description. Personalizing this despair through individually designed metaphor can rescue the suffering from the anonymity of the clichés that leap to our minds at such moments.

As is demonstrated throughout this text, one solution to many countertransference–transference dilemmas is to attempt to transform the patient's pain ("your despair") into a joint problem worthy of the attention of two bright and concerned people ("our despair"). Such a reformulation typically changes the nature of the problem, to make "our despair" more accurate as a description, which in turn facilitates the collaborative relationship championed by cognitive and analytic theorists alike (cf. Beck & Emery, 1985; Meissner, 1996). Even though E recognized that her father did not share the meaning she and I had concocted for her nickname, she expressed great comfort in moving the dilemma from hers to ours. Dr. B and Lisa also found comfort in learning that their self-blame and misinterpretation of silence were shared problems, and decided to resume their therapeutic work.

Duty to the Trauma

Both therapist and client in the extreme trauma case often feel an uneasy obligation, something I have called a "duty to the trauma." This too helps maintain a preference for silence, as both believe that they are unworthy of telling or discussing the trauma story. Again, the inadequacy of language is one culprit: Therapist and client struggle to find the "right words" and are convinced that they have come up short. "The issue is not merely the unshareability of the experience but also the witness's exasperated sense (not uniformly borne out, as we have seen, by the effects of his or her testimony) of a failure in communication" (Langer, 1991, p. 61). Here, my point is the vague sense in both members of the therapeutic dyad (but, I have found, particularly in the therapist) that there is something morally wrong with speaking inaccurately or inarticulately about trauma. Oral description of the trauma becomes not only a clinical goal that is unmet, but also a duty that is unfulfilled.

Therapists fear they minimize the trauma by using "normal" language, and indeed at times this is the case. Dolan (1991), for instance, speaks of *language muting*, the adoption of an abstract and indirect vocabulary by both participants in discussing tragedy. This possibility is discussed in more detail later. At present, however, I would argue that there also is a danger that the therapist's or client's fear of potential minimization might drive them into silence. "That was not it, not quite it," one of the Holocaust Remembrance Study participants repeated over and over throughout his narrative. "Damn it, I should shut up. I can't do this right. It was more, more than that. You should talk to my son" (Dalenberg & Epstein, 1999).

Moving portrayals of the tension between the necessity to describe and the felt incapacity to do so are found most frequently in the literature of war trauma—particularly within the Holocaust literature. Elie Weisel (1995), a brilliant teacher and scholar in this arena, still claims that to understand well enough to describe accurately would be to "blaspheme—the frightened smile of that child torn away from his mother and transformed into a flaming torch. Nor have I been able, nor will I ever be able," he continues, "to grasp the shadow which, at that moment, invaded the mother's eyes" (p. 142). Claude Lanzmann, commenting in Caruth (1995, p. 155) on his acclaimed film *Shoah*, states that

> there is an absolute obscenity in the very project of understanding. Not to understand was my iron law during all the 11 years of the production of *Shoah*. I had clung to this refusal of understanding as the only possible ethical and at the same time the only possible operative attitude.

Insincere or hypocritical speech from outsiders does have a strong and negative effect on survivors, and many therapists are uncomfortably aware of this fact. They know that easy claims of understanding are disrespectful, and they distrust their own press to know more. Their awareness of a sense of "privileged voyeurism" (Dolan, 1991) shames them, and they fear representation in Weisel's (1995, p. 140) parody of the listener below:

> Well, now, what was it really like? How did you feel in Minsk and in Kiev and in Kolomea, when the earth, opening up before your eyes, swallowed up your sons and your prayers? What did you think when you saw blood—your own blood—gushing from the bowels of the earth, rising up to the sun? Tell us, speak up, we want to know, to suffer with you, we have a few tears in reserve, they pain us, we want to get rid of them.

Weisel, himself a prolific author, stated that he sometimes is reduced to regretting the passage of the days when Holocaust speech was considered taboo, "reserved for the initiates, who spoke of it only with hesitation and fear, always lowering their eyes, and always trembling with humility, knowing themselves unworthy and recognizing the limits of their language, spoken and unspoken" (1995, p. 140). A Holocaust Remembrance Study participant told me that her rabbi had quoted a Holocaust scholar as stating that "no words should be spoken about the Holocaust that cannot be uttered in front of burning children."

There, of course, is the center of our anguish. There are no words, these authors imply, that can be uttered in front of burning children—no words that should be spoken as we vicariously reexperience (in our work) the rape of a woman, the torture of a prisoner, the beating of a child. Any speech is blasphemy. So as we sit with our patients as they relive these experiences, we should be silent. "All the words of the philosophers and psychologists are not worth the silent tears of that child and his mother," Weisel (1995, p. 143) stated, and he is right. I would simply add that, in trying to be worthy, to pay homage to the magnitude of the trauma, one can betray the traumatized. By identifying the issues of the inadequacy of language and the duty to the trauma, and by offering to share the anguish and moral uncertainty of discussing these issues, the clinician can transform and overcome both transference and countertransference shame.

A Priori Countertransference or Event Countertransference

In reviewing the literature, it appears that the greatest difficulty that clinicians face in refusing to hear (or in imposing a prior view on the client) comes when the therapist feels strong a priori countertransference (Tauber, 1998) or event countertransference (Danieli, 1981). These terms are applied to countertransference that is triggered less by the client than by the client's trauma. The issue is most commonly discussed in the literature on rape or war.

I sometimes ask my first-year students to fill out a questionnaire about their perceptions of difficult patients. I ask them to fill in an answer within the statement: "If a patient came in and told me _____, I would wonder if I could work with [him or her]." Most students either fill in a perpetrator group or claim to be able to work with anyone. I worry about the latter. If they are required to consider only potential tragedies, they most commonly choose incest, child abuse in general, or the loss of a child.

For a priori countertransference, one advantage is that the clinician can confront the issue without the presence of a true victim. Advances in computer simulation have opened some possibilities, and we have experimented in our laboratory with interactive computer programs that simulate bulimic, depressed, or battered women. In this type of clinical training, the "client" might confront the "therapist" with a realistic story like the one given in Exhibit 3.1, which is adapted from one of our simulations (Baskin-Creel, 1994). The "therapist" selects the content upon which he or she chooses to comment by typing the sentence number and then typing in the intervention or response. The therapist then categorizes his or her response (which is repeated as a memory cue at the top of the screen) using a structured category system. The branching program then generates a believable follow-up, given the therapist's response.

For instance, one participant in the above research paradigm might choose sentence 9, the description of battering,

---

Exhibit 3.1

Patient Simulation in Interactive Computer Training Studies

I'm 27 years old and have been married for 5 years. (1)
We have one great kid, a boy, 4 years old. (2)
I don't work outside the home. (3)
My dad says I'm lucky to find a sucker to take care of a worthless female like me. (4)
And I guess I am lucky. (5)
When I first met my husband I would have described him as the most exciting man I'd ever met. He has an exciting career. (6)
But even before I moved in with him, he was abusive to me. (7)
I feel confused because he can be so sweet and romantic. (8)
But there's been physical abuse all along—hitting, slapping, pushing. Once he broke my arm. (9)
He felt real bad about that. (10)
It might have been my fault. (11)

and ask for further detail. Another might choose sentence 7, the woman's first statement that she was abused, and offer empathy. A third clinician might choose the same sentence, and offer an interpretation (perhaps connecting the woman's choice of husbands to her father's treatment of her). The patient simulation paradigm is useful as a research tool, but also can be useful for clinical training. As the "therapist" interacts with multiple "clients," a profile is developed. The clinician-in-training potentially learns that he or she moves toward or away from the event itself, avoids feelings or concentrates on them, interprets more or less than do others confronting similar material (or than do experts), and so on. The computer can track the content the clinician chooses to address and the characteristic intervention as it is tied to that content.

Thus far, we have found that clinicians (graduate students) do seem to have well-established styles (Baskin-Creel, 1994). The feedback given by these programs can be quite private, and it is possible that privacy will allow clinicians to engage in self-evaluation in a useful way. Alternatively, the feedback could be used by a supervisor or provide substance for a group discussion.

Another useful technique for self-evaluation of event countertransference is to engage in discussion or consideration of case histories. To be most valuable to the clinician, however, the collections should be those that offer the clients' stories with as little interpretation as possible—raw stories that evoke the emotions clinicians fear.

Therapist as Obstacle to the Patient's Disclosure

Both held captive by the trauma and avoidant of it, the client often arrives at the therapist's door at a point in time when avoidance has momentarily become impossible. Unfortunately, that same dialectic as it applies to the therapist (also being confronted with a potentially traumatic event) might result in the therapist serving as an obstacle to client disclosure.

Therapist Resistance to Traumatic Information

There is no substitute, I believe, for the honest disclosure of the difficulty of confronting trauma within trauma therapy. If the trauma is extreme or otherwise touches the therapist deeply, such disclosure is even more important for several reasons. First, the unconscious operation of avoidance of traumatic material operates to block therapist understanding. Failure to acknowledge this likelihood leads both therapist and client to blame the client for the inevitable breaches in rapport. This example, for instance, comes from Lawrence Langer's (1991) Holocaust testimonies (p. 117):

> *Moses S:* All right. A few weeks later, the English people came in and bombed the concentration camp [Mauthausen]. And I said "Yankel, get up, it's no good lying here, you'll be a piece of gornisht [nothing at all]." So we got up, and we found a hand from the bombing . . .
>
> *Interviewer:* A hand grenade?
>
> *Moses S:* No, a hand. [The interviewer still does not respond, presumably still not understanding. Another voice, presumably a family member, interjects "A human hand."]
>
> *Moses S:* A human hand.
>
> *Interviewer:* Oh, a human hand.

When I asked participants in the Trauma Countertransference Study whether their therapists said it was difficult to listen to their traumatic material, 70 of the 84 survivors (83%) stated that their therapists denied any difficulty. On the other hand, the clients themselves overwhelmingly agreed that their trauma *was* difficult to hear, and more than 60% felt a desire to protect their therapists. In discussing how the clients knew their therapists were distressed, I seldom heard that the therapists disclosed this feeling. Instead, survivor clients stated that their therapists avoided, misheard, and minimized. As in the example above, the survivor often had to repeat the material that was most difficult to disclose, attempting to overcome the therapist's resistance to hearing it. Below is an example from the Trauma Countertransference Study, a woman who had been in therapy as a teenager after a particularly brutal rape:

> *Kathy:* This was the worst part, I mean I am still just furious at this.
>
> *Interviewer:* I can tell. Go ahead. Blast me with it. I'm sorry already.
>
> *Kathy:* Well, there was this part of the rape, this part, it was . . . there was this part of the rape. . . . He. . . . There was. . . . He [Deleted at patient request: a brutal and humiliating act against her.]
>
> *Interviewer:* Aah. Ooh. So furious seems like an understatement. [I am incorrectly assuming her fury is with her assailant, when it is with her therapist.]
>
> *Kathy:* No that's not it. I mean I kept telling him [the therapist]. I told him three times. *Three* times. And he said that I didn't tell him. He kept saying that I hadn't quite said it. And I did say it. I practically had to shout it. It was him. It was him. It was him, it was him, it was him. [It was her therapist who didn't hear.]

As a group, the survivors found their therapists' denials of emotional distress annoying, humiliating, and devaluing. Understandably, they felt that if their therapists were emotionally connected, as the therapists typically had said that they were, and if the trauma indeed was serious, as both participants typically conceded that it was, then some therapist distress would be expected. Countertransferential denial of distress thus often indirectly signaled either a lack of concern about the client or a minimization of the trauma (already likely to be concerns of the survivor). Moreover, if the distress resided totally in the client, then the disagreements about who was "resisting," who was "repressing," and who was "avoiding" would generally be resolved in "favor" of the survivor: That is, it was the client who did not disclose clearly.

A serendipitous finding in the Child Disclosure Study also bears on this point (Dalenberg, 1996b). In that study, recorded disclosures of children of sexual abuse, physical abuse, or both were rated by professionals and nonprofessionals along several dimensions. To develop an accurate transcript, each recorded interview was transcribed by one rater, and the accuracy of the first rater was checked by two more. We expected to find, and we did find, that the interviewers of severely traumatized children were more likely to misapprehend and to misstate the facts with the children. We also found that the mistakes in the transcription by those simply listening and typing the accounts were biased toward (a) deletion of traumatic material and (b) distortion of material toward the mundane. For instance, when a child said in one interview that his father "bites" him regularly, the interviewer and the first transcriptionist heard "fights." The child did not correct the interviewer's misstatement.

Advances in the study of trauma and meaning also have underlined the potential for therapist resistance to the threat to worldview presented by a client's past (Harvey, Orbuch, & Fink, 1990; Janoff-Bulman, 1992). People who have survived a life threat have commented on their sudden awareness of their own mortality (see Chapter 4) and on the "shattering" of their assumptions (Janoff-Bulman, 1992). Trauma clients force therapists to enter and accept worlds that have been held at an intellectual distance through theory and novelistic case studies. The pretrauma world—where the sick become well, effort is rewarded, and talent and good intent are generally recognized and predict success—is a decidedly more pleasant place to live than are those more realistic worlds inhabited by traumatized clients.

For me, these findings suggest close attention to a client's accusation that it is the *therapist* who misunderstands, avoids, or distorts meaning. "Yes," we should acknowledge, "trauma leads to distortion and avoidance. It is likely that we are both doing that." Both members of the therapeutic alliance need to work to stay out of the client's way in the disclosure of trauma.

Therapist Fear of Triggering Personal Traumatic Reactions

In a series of empirical investigations and theoretical papers, Wilson and Lindy (1994) have contributed greatly to the study of transference and countertransference in PTSD. In their conceptualization, empathic withdrawal (avoidance) is more characteristic of those who have been spared personal catastrophe, because "their worldview preserves the ideas that life is decent and just" (Wilson & Lindy, 1994, pp. 40–41). Empathic repression, a state in which the therapist both withdraws and denies the significance of the withdrawal, and empathic enmeshment (overinvolvement) are said to be more characteristic of previously traumatized therapists.

A few of the therapist participants in the Trauma Counter-transference Study were quite candid about their wish to avoid triggers of memories of their own traumatic past. Two of the seven therapists stated that they would avoid clients with histories that mirrored their own if they could do so, although neither asked clients at intake whether these traumas had occurred. I see no problem myself in avoidance of some client populations, but I do suggest that relevant investigation of such factors might be done at intake.

As noted in chapter 1, it is also clear that posttraumatic reactions are common in therapists who are constantly exposed to trauma. Avoidance thus can be healthy, in that it occurs in the service of psychic health. General arousal and pain in listening to the distress of another also is common. In fact, Pennebaker and his colleagues have shown that, although skin conductance levels dropped in survivors as they recounted their traumatic memories, their listeners became more aroused, and their skin conductance levels increased (Pennebaker, Barger, & Tiebout, 1989; Shortt & Pennebaker, 1992).

Therapist avoidance also can pose difficulty when therapists confront traumatic events that they fear will happen in the future to themselves or others. In my own case, I was confronted a few years ago by one client whom I hurt badly by minimizing (speaking casually about) her sister's recent diagnosis of cancer. Ms. Y, who was being treated for symptoms related to sexual abuse, remembers it this way:

> I do remember that, and I think it will always hurt some. My sister had been on the phone to me for most of the day, crying and sobbing and all that. She never stopped thinking about it, and I was in that state too at the moment. I had not stopped thinking about it for a minute. I even dreamed about it. So your treating it as unimportant, putting it in a string of all the bad things that had happened to me that week, really was upsetting.

As the reader might guess from the placement of this anecdote, I too had a relative who had recently been diagnosed with the same type of cancer. I did not wish to hear Ms. Y's list of the dire consequences that might follow in my relative's future, particularly the low base rate and devastating consequences I had not yet contemplated. At the time, I believed Ms. Y was dwelling on unlikely negative consequences—"catastrophizing"—and that this was psychically damaging to her. Whether or not this was true, my finding temporary refuge in cognitive theory did not justify dodging the related emotions, which I also did.

The above would be a more impressive clinical example if it ended the way that many such anecdotes do within the countertransference literature. There, the therapist catches himself or herself, corrects the problem, and prevents the client from suffering at the therapist's hands. I, on the other hand, blithely continued the session, and I do not know if I would have caught the mistake myself had my client not left a rather clear message regarding my malfeasance on my answering machine that evening. I told her that I agreed that I was avoiding, and I took responsibility for the cruelty of the incident. Yes, Ms. Y did eventually allow me to make the alliance rupture useful to us by examining her reaction to my failings, but no, it probably was not an ultimately therapy-advancing mistake. I would echo here the statement of a senator accused of one ethical violation and railing against the sins of another, that the defense of virtue cannot be left to the virtuous.

Therapist Fear of Client Emotion, Primitive Impulses, and Deterioration

Therapists and clients alike also refer to therapists' perceptions of the fragility of survivors and clients' parallel fear that clinicians "can't take it." Transcript analysis of the Trauma Countertransference Study interviews illustrated the fine line that therapists must walk, respecting the magnitude of the trauma while not implying that they are incapable of hearing it. It is my impression from the data that both client and therapist in trauma therapy often use the protection of the other as an excuse for or defense against their own resistance to immersion in the emotions related to the traumatic event. Kathy, for example, the patient discussed earlier who believed that her therapist, Dr. D, could not hear the most brutal aspects of her rape, also allowed me to speak to her therapist. The two of them appeared to provide an example of this dynamic, as each accused the other of avoidance. Each also believed that the other would be harmed by full knowledge of the patient's trauma and emotional truths:

> *Interviewer:* It sounds like the two of you kept moving toward and away from this piece of it.
>
> *Kathy:* I don't know if I did. He [Dr. D] did though. It's just that . . . he had a hard enough time with the rape itself. I mean, I did too, and I could see that he did. This part disgusted him. If he knew everything about it, I think it would have backfired on both of us. The whole relationship would have unraveled . . . well, it did anyway.
>
> *Interviewer:* Why would it have unraveled?
>
> *Kathy:* Because he wouldn't have been able to sit with me

anymore, I think. It . . . I think it would have made him sick.

And Dr. D:

> *Interviewer:* It seems like both of you were trying to stay away from it
>
> *Dr. D:* I'm not sure I was. She was, certainly. Actually, I take that back. I did try to slow her down. I didn't want her to tell me something that would have made her feel embarrassed to be with me.

Dr. D and I then sidled off into a clinical discussion of the possibility of therapy without embarrassment. Dr. D believes that the therapist should seek to build the relationship to the point that such disclosures no longer embarrass the patient, and only then to encourage them. I believe that such a scenario is unlikely, if not impossible, and that exposure of the potentially embarrassing beliefs is necessary to detoxify and disempower them. My own approach is more similar to that of Pearlman and Saakvitne (1995), who described the parent–therapist standing *within* the patient experience—interpreting, normalizing, explaining. The therapist's understanding of his or her own countertransferential response to embarrassment and shame (see chapter 5) is one important element of this strategy.

Along the same line, therapists fear client emotion because of its power, primitive nature, and the likelihood that it will be aimed directly at them. Again, I believe that for many patients, this dynamic is unavoidable within good psychotherapy. I have some doubts that Winnicott (1974) was correct when he argued that client fear of breakdown in therapy is a projection into future time of fear experienced in the infantile past, but I have frequently seen the terror, helplessness, rage, dread, and sense of loss of control that he described. I have been frightened by it, as my patients are frightened.

One countertransference reaction frequently reported by patients, related to minimization as discussed in the previous section, is the presentation of invulnerability by the therapist paired with encouragement toward rapid disclosure. From the patient perspective, the therapist seems to be proving something at the expense of the treatment. Patient L, for instance, told me that she disclosed the death of her son, the death of her husband, and a brutal attack by a guard in the first session with a therapist who seemed to her to be ripping the details from her throat. Living with lethal authorities in the camps had left her unable, or at least unwilling, to slow the pace of the questioning. Instead, she never went back. As her second therapist, I met with her for the first time 20 years after her first course of therapy had ended.

I mention this example here in a chapter on obstacles to disclosure because I believe that dramatic emotion on the part of the client can serve as a shield behind which both therapist and client can hide from a deeper, more threatening appraisal of the meaning of the events. Emotional display can persuade both individuals that a "good session" is occurring (cf. Biaggio, 1987), despite the lack of evidence that catharsis itself is curative (Littrell, 1998).

Therapist Fear of Involvement in Litigation

An additional source of therapist fear of involvement centers on subgroups of victims within the child abuse survivor group. These clients, who are perceived as particularly dangerous, include children who have alleged abuse that the perpetrators deny, children who have alleged abuse within a custody dispute, adults who have alleged abuse based on recovered memory, adults who suspect that they have a repressed memory, dissociative adults, and adults who have alleged ritual abuse. As can be seen in Table 3.1 therapists in training workshops have become less positive about the treatment of each of these groups, particularly the groups of clients with repressed memory and dissociative adults. The data in Table 3.1 was taken from a questionnaire given to those who entered my licensure workshops for psychologists in 1987, 1992, and 1997. Participation rate was over 90% of those who attended each workshop.

Table 3.1

Willingness to Treat in Samples of Newly Licensed Psychologists

Diagnosis	1987	1992	1997	F[2.85]
Major depression	M = 7.77	M = 7.83	M = 7.41	.36
Anxiety disorder	M = 7.54	M = 7.53	M = 7.72	.06
Psychosis	M = 3.2	M = 3.33	M = 3.41	.05
Abuse by therapist	M = 7.58	M = 8.37	M = 7.59	1.15
Perpetrator of abuse	M = 7.42	M = 7.13	M = 7.53	.27
Child sexual abuse	M = 7.34	M = 6.57	M = 6.13	1.47
Recent recovered memory	M = 6.85	M = 5.93	M = 4.16	8.72***
MPD/DID	M = 5.62	M = 4.73	M = 3.50	6.24**
Ritual abuse		M = 7.00	M = 4.84	10.13**
Suspected repressed memory		M = 5.83	M = 4.19	4.69*
Child custody case (accused denies)	M = 6.77	M = 6.07	M = 4.31	6.20**

Responses to question: "On a 1 (*definitely would refer*) to a 10 (*definitely would accept*) scale, how likely would you be to accept referrals with the following diagnoses (assume a full-fee client)?" Note: $n = 88$, $*p < .05$, $**p < .01$, $***p < .001$

Denying the risk myself here certainly defeats my purpose. The American Psychological Association thought it worthwhile to publish a text (Knapp & Vandecreek, 1997) entirely devoted to legal risk management in treating persons with memories of abuse. A 750-page compendium, *Memory, Trauma Treatment, and the Law*, by D. Brown, Scheflin, and Hammond (1998), is an outstanding volume, unparalleled in its integration of legal and psychological material on this subject. It should be read by every trauma therapist. Similarly, Pope and Brown's (1996) text on clinical issues in recovered memory is a must. Readers are particularly referred to the informed-consent guidelines included. Finally, no well-read trauma therapist is unaware of the concerted efforts by advocacy groups to target those who treat members of these groups. Such groups encourage lawsuits, support picketing, and engage in shameful name-calling. (See Pope [1996] and Lindsay & Briere [1997] for discussion and a call for more reasoned behavior.)

The fear of such risk is described in a painful segment of the analysis of a woman who may or may not have been a victim of incest, as presented by analyst Sue Grand (1995). The clients' stepfather, as represented in her continuous-memory accounts, was an alcoholic and "pathological liar" who had been arrested and jailed for embezzlement when the patient was very young. He also was open in his sharing of pornographic material with her, and he engaged in behavior that was clearly sexually inappropriate. In the second year of the analysis, the client recounted a dream that involved the receipt of an envelope containing pornographic pictures and literature about incest. The segment has been edited to focus on the points of greatest interest here:

> "In the pornographic pictures [the patient said], there is a girl who looks like me, around age 11 or 12. There is writing next to the picture of the girl but I am not sure what it says. I was terrified." At this point, my patient begins sobbing and says, with fear and tentative conviction, "Did my father do this to me, take these pictures?"
>
> On this particular day, I have read yet another media exposé on the false-memory controversy. I realize that this outspoken, serious, and assertive woman would confront her stepfather if thoroughly convinced that [he] had incested her; this litigious volatile man would lie and very possibly sue me for "implanting" an incest memory. Her stepfather suddenly appears to me powerful, vindictive, and relentless in his retaliation; I am helpless, vulnerable, small. . . . Even as she weeps, she does not yet know, but she has lost me. . . . Suddenly I feel I must demonstrate to the patient that these images may be more symbolic than literal, expressive of other issues and anxieties. . . . Even as she weeps, I question her differently, drawing her away from the image of actual incest. She attempts to follow me where I am going, desperate for us to stay together, willing to be confused, deflected. . . .

In subsequent sessions, she does not mention either incest or the moment of analytic rupture I have described. Her symptoms increase. ... Her inability to know becomes the focus of her analysis (Grand, 1995, pp. 247–251).

Turning first to the reality base of the therapist's fears, it is clear that third-party lawsuits are still being filed against therapists, and that some are being won. Calming countertransference fear here can be aided by reviewing such texts as those of Pope and Brown (1996) and D. Brown et al. (1998) and by the substance of recent third-party decisions, such as *Hungerford v. Jones* (1998) and *Ramona v. Ramona* (1994). Both decisions appeared to turn on the perception that the therapist orchestrated the confrontation or public accusation of the parent. The Hungerford decision, for instance, reads in part:

Accordingly, in response to the district court's questions, we hold that a therapist owes an accused parent a duty of care in the diagnosis and treatment of an adult patient for sexual abuse where the therapist or the patient, acting on the encouragement, recommendation, or instruction of the therapist, takes public action concerning the accusation.

Although it might seem as though I am working against my own wish to decrease the clinician's existing fear, I must mention that the act of obstructing action by the client also can lead to legal liability, because it can place the client at risk for injury and can prevent recovery of damages if the statute of limitations is passed.

The best defense against the real possibility of a successful legal attack, then, is to follow the risk management guidelines recommended in the texts cited above. Most importantly, these involve appropriate informed consent, good documentation, monitoring one's countertransferential wish for the client to take public action (or more commonly, not to take it), and using consultation. Pope and Brown (1996) presented an excellent discussion of notes and record-keeping. Informed consent and informed refusal are thoroughly discussed by Pope and Vasquez (1991/1998, p. 74), who noted:

> Nothing blocks a patient's access to help with such cruel efficiency as a bungled attempt at informed consent . . . . The doors to our offices and clinics are open wide. The resources are all in place. But not even the most persistent patients can make their way past our intimidating forms (which clerks may shove at patients when they first arrive), our set speeches full of noninformative information, and our nervous attempts to meet externally imposed legalistic requirements. A first step in remedying the situation is to recognize that informed consent is not a static ritual but a useful process.

At best, informed consent is a useful process. At worst, it is our first countertransference enactment, crystallizing our own fear of the client in a way that implies that we are now (or can become) uneasy adversaries. The Trauma Research Institute Informed Consent form, which is available from the author, was developed to provide consent that aids the process of therapy for traumatized clients.

Summary: Addressing the Therapist's Avoidance of Trauma Material

Many participants in the Trauma Countertransference Study stated that their therapists addressed joint avoidance of the trauma material. A few (9 of the 84 participants) stated that it was never avoided. When asked how they and their therapists helped the dyad move past the therapist's avoidance, the following participants gave these responses:

> *John:* I think the most effective thing was that he always admitted it when I would point it out. He seemed to think it was so normal that I got to thinking it was normal, so it was easier for him to point it out in me. At first, I found the whole avoidance–repression thing

pretty insulting until it started getting clear that we all did it.

Sandra: She would catch herself sometimes and say "Oh, now I'm doing it. This is so hard." It was so helpful that she said it was hard.

Ann: She would be all, you know, "Damn it, I shouldn't be acting this way." I could tell she was fighting. She fought for me.

Richard: Because it didn't stay avoided. The next time he would talk about it again, and I could see he had been thinking about it.

Kate: [A therapist participant]: Because he let me know it was hard for him. It goes against many ideas that I've been taught, but one of the most valuable things he said was that if it had happened to him, he didn't know if he would be handling it as well as I have.

To mitigate the negative effects of the avoidance and ob-struction of client disclosure and to minimize the instances of such events that occur in psychotherapy, I would thus em-phasize the following:

- □ It is not only clinically useful but also morally respon-sible for the therapist to take responsibility for his or her own avoidance and obstruction of disclosure.
- □ Avoidance of traumatic material should be presented as a normal response, one to be expected in both therapy participants and fought against when appropriate.
- □ As a model for the client, therapists are well-advised to search out and identify for the client instances in the therapist's own behavior of selective memory, defensive forgetting or avoidance, or distraction of the client from traumatic material.
- □ To the extent possible, it is therapeutically useful to present each instance of avoidance as a cooperative act between therapist and client. It is virtually always true that both participants allow the client, the therapist, or both, to avoid and to participate in the events that lead to avoidance. The trauma therapy is unlikely to succeed

unless both participants are willing not only to accept but also to actively search for their own roles in unpleasant or disappointing interactions.

□   Finally, the discomfort of the therapist in listening to trauma might not be an active (or even unconscious) wish to avoid, but rather a manifestation of the fear of causing further client distress. In our chapter of the *Handbook of the Psychology of Interviewing* (Dalenberg & Epstein, 1999), we recommended disclosure to the client of the reality that listening to trauma is painful and difficult adding that this does not mean an account is not worth hearing or that receiving the disclosure is not an affirmative choice for the therapist. In a sense, we argued,

> the helper is hoping for the outcome described in a Midrash story, in which we are told that when God gave Adam the gift of fire, He directed him to take two stones, called in the legend Darkness and the Shadow of Death, and to rub them together. The meaning of the legend [described in Wolpe, 1992, p. 120] is said to be that with the proper environment, one can take even darkness and death and turn them to light (Dalenberg & Epstein, 1999, p. 45).

4

Do You Believe Me? Countertransference Responses to Client Doubt and Reality-Testing Disturbance

> Chronic doubts about what did and did not happen, along with a persistent inability to trust one's perceptions of reality, are perhaps the most permanent and ultimately damaging long-term effects of childhood sexual abuse (Davies & Frawley, 1994, p. 109).

It is said that Abraham Lincoln once greeted Harriet Beecher Stowe, author of *Uncle Tom's Cabin,* as "the little woman who wrote the book that started this great war." Poet Paul Laurence Dunbar (1913/1993) upon reading Stowe's story of the slaves stated that "the whole world wept/At wrongs and cruelties it had not known" (p. 119). The disclosure of important traumatic truths can have the same effect on a more personal level—a change in worldview can be brought on when a seemingly obvious but destructive truth is stated aloud.

But changes in worldview are resisted, understandably, because so much cognitive work is necessary to readjust to a transformation in meaning. This transition period, a time in which the survivor attempts to find a cognitive "place" for the trauma in continuing thought (often after years of avoidance), challenges reality-testing for the victim. Trauma has an "alien feel" to it in the period during which it is most generative of symptoms; that is, at least for a time, one can both know that it is true and not believe that it has happened.

Traumatized patients, one might say, "carry an impossible history within them, or they become themselves the symptom of a history that they cannot entirely possess" (Caruth, 1995, p. 5).

The false memory–recovered memory controversy has had one of its most profound negative effects in the distraction of clinical psychologists from a more complex view of doubt and truth within trauma therapy. The examination of these complicated issues is the focus of this chapter. The extended discussion between Julia, a participant in the Trauma Countertransference Study, and myself gives a starting point for a more thorough reevaluation. Julia is a therapist who herself has a history of multiple trauma, including (a) a car accident that killed one sibling, injured her, and injured another relative, (b) extreme physical abuse, (c) witnessing of her mother's battering, and (d) a recovered memory of sexual abuse by her father.

> *Interviewer:* So if you had to say one thing your therapist did that made it harder for you in therapy rather than easier, what would you say it was?
>
> *Julia:* I'd say he did help me, but I'd say that it was that doubt was so unsafe.
>
> *Interviewer:* What do you mean?
>
> *Julia:* I really doubted my memories a lot of the time, and it was really unsafe to mention that, because he would leap on it and say that it did not matter if it was true or not, etc., etc.
>
> *Interviewer:* OK, so help me out here. I would like to learn something from you. How was that not supportive? You say you doubt, he says it's OK that you doubt. . . .
>
> *Julia:* I . . . No. It just wasn't helpful. It's as if—I tried this on him once—it's as if you say to your mom, "Mom, I am afraid I'm ugly," and you want her to say, "You're not ugly." And instead she says, "Looks don't matter, honey."
>
> *Interviewer:* First of all, that's wonderful, a wonderful

analogy. Let me stick with that. See, I get the point emotionally, but what if your mother's blind? What if she doesn't know if you're ugly?

Julia: Oh, very good. He didn't say that.

Interviewer: What did he say?

Julia: More about looks not mattering, truth not mattering.

Interviewer: Ah, and what should he have said and still be honest, ethical, clinically effective, and all that?

Julia: I don't know. "I believe you," is what I wanted, but I suppose that's not always possible. So can I ask you? What do you think the blind mother should say?

Interviewer: Well, I don't know how far we can push this. I would say she should find out if there is anything practical that her daughter can do to feel better. But in the moment, if she was my daughter, I suppose I'd tell her that I knew she was beautiful.

Julia: I think that's like "I believe you."

Interviewer: Is it?

The analogy that developed between Julia and myself does share some features with the dilemma of "believing" the victim of trauma. The push for the response "I believe you" comes from at least four sources—the search for the therapist's compassion, the search for a tie to reality, the search for narrative reality, and the search for validation of the past.

The Search for the Therapist's Compassion

In the literature on false memory the most commonly alleged source for the client's desire for belief validation is the wish to be a victim (cf. Loftus & Ketcham, 1994; Ofshe & Watters, 1994). I believe that this motive is not as common as nonclinical sources suggest. It is true that some individuals seek victim status (discussed below), but it is more common that

"Do you believe me?" is more akin to "Will you join me here?" or "Are you with me?" than it is to "Is my past abuse history historically accurate?" In a content analysis of the 17 trauma patients in the Trauma Countertransference Study who claimed to have had an experience of disbelief with a therapist, the reaction of the patient to therapist disbelief typically was not memory centered ("Maybe it isn't true"). Instead, it was relationship centered ("He won't be able to help me." "Her compassion would be fake." "I was going to be alone with it."). Therapists also can experience their disbelief as disloyalty for this reason; disbelief is likely to alienate therapist and patient.

It thus is important to concede that the client or therapist who fears that clinician disbelief will distance therapist from client is right to be concerned. If a therapist does not believe a client—and particularly if the therapist believes that the client is purposely exaggerating or malingering—compassion is likely to dissipate. In the Child Disclosure Study sample, for instance, in which interviewers typically were extremely compassionate in their responses, noticeable changes occurred in the child–interviewer interaction when unbelievable material entered the discussion (Dalenberg, 1996b). Interviewers who heard fantastic material from children alleging child abuse were statistically less likely to offer comfort ("That must have been hard"), to ask for more information about how the child thought or felt ("What did you think/feel when he did that?"), or to compliment the child ("You are being very brave") than they were when more "believable" stories were told. Interviewers often try not to "reinforce" fantasy (for clinical reasons and to avoid lawsuits). It is unfortunate, however, that the response to a lack of compassion is often *increased* exaggeration or malingered responding, as the client seeks to reinstate the therapist's good feeling toward him or her.

For reasons we do not completely understand, emotional support and comfort appear to increase the accuracy of memory. Gail Goodman and her colleagues (Goodman, Quas, Batterman-Faunce, Riddlesberger, & Kuhn, 1994), for instance, examined the accuracy of children's memories of a painful medical procedure. The children were likely to re-count fewer inaccurate details if their mothers had sympa-thetically talked to them or hugged them during the proce-dure. In earlier work, Goodman and colleagues also found that noncontingent rewards and smiles led to more accurate memory performance in young children than did more "neu-tral" interviewing (Goodman, Bottoms, Schwartz-Kenney, & Rudy, 1991). It is not clear whether these advantages for chil-dren who have supportive mothers are a function (a) of more opportunities for the children to talk, (b) of less discomfort in thinking about the trauma in the presence of a supportive mother, or (c) of fewer memory-interfering emotions in the presence of a supportive mother—any of which might pro-vide more opportunity for consolidation of memory. None-theless, it is interesting to speculate about the role of emo-tional support in providing an atmosphere of safety for emerging memories.

If felt compassion does allow for safe emergence—or safe ownership—of difficult memories, the question, "Do you be-lieve me?" could logically emerge when the client perceives a distancing or lack of compassion in the therapist. When the question arises, the therapist might first examine his or her own recent countertransference feelings. Is the therapist of-fering a degree of support and sympathy that is in keeping with belief (whether or not the therapist actually believes the client)? If not, perhaps it is this compassion that is sought, rather than the therapist's solving of the mysteries of the pa-tient's past. Julia made this point:

> *Julia:* I wanted him on my side to hold my hand in a way while I tried to believe this thing. But he wanted to be neutral.
>
> *Interviewer:* Being a therapist, you know that we are sup-posed to be neutral, so I understand the problem that you are pointing out. But the answer is hard to find. It's hard to be neutral and compassionate in this instance.
>
> *Julia:* Neutral isn't how it feels, you know. I realize that ["neutral"] might be the right word. But "neutral" sort of sounds like it can't be harmful.

Interviewer: So you're saying, correct me here, you're saying that a therapist doubting you doesn't feel like objectivity.

Julia: Doubt is disbelief. Doubt is . . . disconnection.

The therapist's wish to remain close and available, as he or she senses this fear of disconnection in the client, then can become merged with a wish to believe. With rare exceptions, most therapists that I have interviewed or supervised do not appear to wish to find trauma in an individual's past when the issue of "did it happen or did it not" arises. Instead, they feel the anguish of the patient's confusion and loneliness and wish to meet this anguish with an appropriate salve. "Yes, I believe you," seems to be an answer to that problem, one that might appeal to client and therapist alike.

When Julia said that doubt is disconnection and that it is not "neutral," I believe that she was making an important statement about psychologists' glib promises not to take a stand on memory veracity. I do not believe that a therapist can easily "suspend judgment" after being confronted with a trauma story. It is more likely that he or she will waiver between belief and disbelief rather than remain in some state of suspension. This wavering also is experienced by the typical trauma victim, and it can be understood by most victims within therapy. Doubt in the therapist, like doubt in the victim, is part of trauma therapy.

I am arguing here that the question of belief might arise from the client as a response to countertransferential withdrawal of the therapist confronted with disturbing material (cf. Savitz, 1990). The therapist's corresponding wish to believe might be a wish to support the client rather than to validate the belief. In such circumstances, it is thus worth exploring with the client whether there has been an unnoticed betrayal on the part of the therapist that has led to this quest for belief as a symbol of caring. If betrayal is acknowledged and overcome, it is possible for the therapeutic dyad to tolerate the uncertainty together that is an inevitable part of trauma therapy. Encouraging an atmosphere in which both doubt and certainty can be entertained does not, in my opinion, mandate that the therapist remain "neutral" to the truth, but rather that the therapist try not to substitute his or her own answer for the client's conclusion.

The Search for a Tie to Reality

> What happened—really happened.
> What happened—really happened.
> What happened—really happened.
> I believe with perfect faith
> That I will have the strength to believe that
> What happened—really happened. (Carmi, 1977, p. 102)

The question of belief also can arise when the client or therapist feels the terror of loss of reality testing. Here, the client is indeed asking the therapist to affirm a truth, to state that the trauma occurred. However, again the client might not be seeking—as an end point—the therapist's view of the truth of the trauma. Rather, "Do you believe me?" here could mean "Tell me I am not crazy" or "Tell me that I know truth from fiction." Herman (1992) wrote that a sense of unreality in the therapist might be the first sign in the relationship that the client has an unspoken trauma history. Nonetheless, as Courtois (1999, p. 303) argued in her indispensible text on memory of sexual abuse, "in the absence of memory, neither transference or countertransference, no matter how compelling, should be interpreted as always indicative of past abuse."

Chronic doubts in the reliability of their own perceptions appear to be the fate of many who experience chronic trauma. (See Shay [1994] for a discussion of this symptom as exhibited by war trauma victims and Davies and Frawley [1994] for a discussion of the same symptom in incest victims.) Countertransference withdrawal or avoidance, or over-reliance on a "blank-screen" approach, can further undermine a client's sense of reality. Almost 70 years ago, Ferenczi argued that a therapist's "cool" and "unemotional" attitude is inappropriate when "events are of a kind that must evoke, in anyone present, emotions of revulsion, anxiety, terror, vengeance, grief, and the urge to render immediate help. . . . The patient prefers to doubt his own judgment rather than believe in our coldness" (Ferenczi, 1932, pp. 24–25).

The therapist who empathizes (consciously or unconsciously) with this aspect of the wish to believe might seek to concretize the trauma prematurely to gain some hold on reality. This is particularly true when bizarre or implausible elements enter the trauma account—which is likely for a variety of reasons (Dalenberg, 1996b; Everson, 1997). The study of the frequency and meaning of these disclosures was one focus of the Child Disclosure Study series. In this research, a "gold standard" sample (n = 142) was located—abuse accounts supported by evidence from medical exams and police reports. Supportive medical evidence, a perpetrator confession, and (in 80% of the cases) some physical or eyewitness evidence was available for all children in the gold standard sample. In the comparison sample, a questionable account group, none of the children's accounts were supported by medical evidence, eyewitness or physical evidence, or a perpetrator confession.

Children's disclosures of sexual abuse also were rated as severe and nonsevere. "Severe abuse" was defined as abuse containing force or oral-genital contact, repeated abuse, or abuse by a family member with frequent access to the child. Abuse labeled "nonsevere" involved single, nonviolent incidents of molestation by perpetrators who were not likely to be attachment figures in the child's life. Fantastic elements (those judged unbelievable or highly implausible by raters independent of the evidence) were more than four times more likely to occur in children known to have experienced severe trauma (the gold standard severe group) than in those known to have experienced milder incidents of punishment or molestation or those in the questionable account sample (Dalenberg, 1996b). Thus, "unbelievable" accounts of abuse are likely to be characteristic of the most serious and dangerous cases, leading to the frightening conclusion that the most serious cases might be most difficult to prosecute. Similar descriptions of lapses in reasoning in adult traumatized populations are given in the literature on attachment (Main, Van Ijzendoorn, & Hesse, 1993, as cited in Shaver & Clark, 1994) in portrayals of "D-like" adults (who typically have abuse or trauma backgrounds). D-like individuals are described as showing "lapses in the monitoring of reasoning" when responding to questions regarding potentially traumatic events. This description is said to apply particularly when participants were asked to discuss abuse or the deaths of important others. Bizarre elements or lapses in reasoning not only distance the therapist (in an observable way in our Child Disclosure Study research), but also leave the therapist feeling disoriented, confused, and uncomfortable.

The fantastic and bizarre elements of trauma accounts in children can result from a child's misunderstanding, confusion between nightmares and reality, or traumatic hallucinations (cf. Dalenberg, Hyland, & Cuevas, in press; Everson, 1997). These distortions, however, are not limited to children. Adults can show short-term reality distortion after trauma— an effect that research in our laboratory has shown dissipates more slowly for patients who also were traumatized in childhood (Strauss, 1996). These elements add to the therapist's sense of disorientation, because they often appear within an otherwise credible trauma story.

Dissociation, a key trauma symptom about which so much has been written (cf. Putnam, 1997; Spiegel, 1994), also contributes to the client's and the therapist's sense of unreality and need for confirmation. The therapist's dissociation to the client's trauma or the patient's dissociation to the memory of trauma create fundamental feelings of fragmentation in the self. The need for reality testing for such clients (or in such states) becomes quite concrete. Reaching for reality might include reaching for a statement from the therapist about the past.

A patient of mine, a victim of severe childhood trauma, lost two close relatives in bizarre accidental circumstances within a period of four months. For many weeks after the second event, our meetings began as does the sample below:

Mr. D: You're here.

Therapist: I'm here.

Mr. D: You aren't sick. You aren't dead.

Therapist: Not sick, not dead. I feel fine.

Mr. D: The office looks the same.

Therapist: The office is essentially the same.

Again, if the therapist senses that the request for belief by the client or the wish to offer belief in himself or herself is driven by need for a more stable reality, this hypothesis might be shared with the client. Such a possibility should be considered particularly for the therapist if he or she is being confronted by bizarre or implausible elements.

The Search for Narrative Truth

A third transferential motive for belief that could be shared by client and therapist is the wish to find a coherent narrative for one's life. Much has been written about the disruptive effect of trauma on meaning in samples of sexual assault victims (Harvey, Orbach, & Fink, 1990), cancer survivors (Barkwell, 1991), victims of incest (Silver, Boon, & Stones, 1983), and individuals who have experienced a recent, important loss (Harvey et al., 1992). Those with debilitating psychic or physical symptoms who are unsure of the cause for these problems are arguably even more likely to be in search of a reasonable life story that might offer guidance and closure.

One of my clients, Ms. I, is a brilliant woman who works in the helping professions. Despite a childhood with a physically abusive and emotionally confusing mother and memories of violations by two sexually abusive relatives, a difficult first marriage, and many years of single motherhood before her second marriage, she has been a remarkably inspiring and effective mother to her children and a successful professional. She has very few memories of her childhood, however, and she struggles with profound depression and anger that she does not fully understand. At times, in periods of greatest stress, she will ask me if I believe that some specific trauma, related to but perhaps more severe than the events she recalls, could be in her past. I believe that it is her wish for narrative understanding (and therefore, she believes, control) that drives her search for the past.

One source for a recurrent request of this type—that is, a request to find and believe in a narrative foundation for symptoms—is the shared societal underestimation of the effects of neglect and parental coldness. "After all," some of my clients at times state, "it's not as if I was raped, ritually abused, or hospitalized from the beatings." Both therapist and client must come to respect the human need for deep and reliable connection and for the idea that a betrayal of that connection is "enough" to produce a traumatic transference or a generally symptomatic client. It is important for case studies and empirical work to counter the prolific arguments that "gentle tender fondling by an older and bigger person with a context of a caring and loving interaction" is not abusive or potentially traumatic (Wakefield & Underwager, 1994, p. 59).

Among the most difficult therapies I ever conducted was my work with a woman who had walked in on her father as he was being given oral sex by a young woman. My client was about 12 at the time; the young woman was a slightly older teenager whom my client knew. It was a one-time event, and it did not appear to be violent, although my client's father chased her when she fled the room to order her silence. This event, however, was a true "betrayal trauma" (Freyd, 1996) and was the central traumagenic episode that had to be integrated within therapy.

The Search for a Validation of the Past

Certainly, in some cases the therapist's or client's wish to know is exactly what it seems to be. The truth of the trauma allegation can have practical implications, as for example in a forensic evaluation, in a custody or criminal allegation, or for those clients considering the type of relationship they wish to have with the alleged perpetrator of the crimes. The therapist also can increase the client's need to know by feeling or showing an obsession with trauma detail, leading the client to believe that such knowledge is crucial to a "cure." Even if recovery of certainty in one's own past is curative in some cases (and it might be so), it is not clear that premature closure from the therapist will facilitate this self-knowledge.

It could be in the cases in which "Do you believe me?" *does* mean "Is my trauma real?" that premature cognitive commitment (Pope & Brown, 1996) is most dangerous. I believe that it is fair to state that most trauma therapists distinguish between taking on the role of arbiter of truth, advocating for one among many answers to the client's questions about his or her own past, and trying to enhance the client's capacity to find his or her own truths. As I have stated

> the therapists' advocacy role is not for an end point, that the memory must be true or must be false, but for a process that includes reasonable reality monitoring skills, openness to consideration of alternative explanations of one's own experience, and willingness to tolerate ambiguity in circumstances in which unknowns will continue to exist (Dalenberg & Carlson, in press).

Briere (1996) appears to have made a similar point: The therapist in such incidences should

> endorse the reality of the client's pain, as well as the general plausibility of his or her explanation for such distress (if, in fact, it is plausible), while giving [him or her] sustained permission and support to avoid a prematurely definitive conclusion regarding what exactly happened. (p. 76)

Davies and Frawley (1994), speaking of therapy with incest victims, stated that therapist communication of beliefs about the specific likely nature and likely validity of the trauma might have various negative effects. The client might accept the therapist's reality as his or her own and construct matching memories in an effort to please. Alternatively,

> as is more often the case, the patient becomes uncomfortable exploring her own trauma-related image and memories, because the therapist's certainty about their meaning forecloses on her own psychic elaboration of these thoughts. Here the therapist treads dangerously close to the parent who superimposed his view of reality onto that of the child during the original abuse. In either of these scenarios, something is being forcefully inserted into the experience of the child. (Davies & Frawley, 1994, p. 110)

Three distinct minority groups of theorists have argued for other ideal countertransferential positions toward the request for belief. Pope and Brown (1996) described the position of the False Memory Syndrome Foundation (FMSF), as highlighted in its publications and by some of its board members, as requiring that the therapist take responsibility for answering the validity question (rather than leaving primary responsibility to the client). Writing in the *FMS Foundation Newsletter*, board member Paul McHugh stated that, "To treat for repressed memories without any effort at external validation is malpractice pure and simple" (McHugh, 1993b, p. 1). Because there is no evidence that memories presented by the client as formerly repressed are less reliable than those presented as continuous, and because convincing evidence exists that they are equally reliable (Dalenberg, 1996a; Williams, 1995), it is unclear how this moral position could be applied solely to repressed memories by the scientifically informed practitioner.

In either case, the FMSF position seems to require that the therapist assume falsity in the client accusation of traumatic injury unless offered proof of trauma validity. It also mandates investigation of the truth of traumatic memory with or without client permission. McHugh (1993a) recommended that the therapist freely share information about the patient with the accused perpetrator of rape or assault to show "good faith." Most important, here, the FMSF stand seems in general to be that the therapist must take a position on the memory in order to treat and that this position should be generated through extratherapeutic investigation. How can a therapist do trauma therapy, these scholars ask, when it is not clear that any trauma occurred?

A second group of theorists, largely writing within the grassroots literature, highlights belief as a duty to the victimized and powerless client from the therapist as a representative of the majority. "You must believe that your client was abused," Bass and Davis (1988) wrote. "Your client needs you to stay steady in the belief that she was abused. Joining a client in doubt would be like joining a suicidal client in her belief that suicide is the best way out" (p. 347). The lay literature on rape, war trauma, and battering has similarly pushed the therapist to believe in and for the client, as an effort to sustain and support the individual whose efforts to disclose have traditionally been silenced. This group of theorists also claims that therapists should take a stand on truth in order to treat but argues that the trauma account should be believed unless there is obvious evidence against it. Extratherapeutic investigation is not recommended.

The third proposed countertransferential stance at first appears to be the most neutral. Here, theorists argue that the investigation of the validity of trauma is not in their job description, and the therapist should remain uninvolved in the validity issue. Cognitive therapists taking this position argue for symptom abatement through empirically proven methods; analytic theorists argue that they are engaged in analysis of the patient's psyche, not the patient's life. Such theorists state that the truth of the allegation becomes a nonissue—virtually irrelevant to the treatment process.

To address this last position first, I do not believe that veridicality of trauma is a nonissue, because the client's concerns about veridicality of trauma are so personally wrenching. It is arguably a major goal of long-term therapy to enhance the client's ability to perceive reality more objectively and to live with reality more comfortably. The therapeutic relationship itself, Sigmund Freud once said, "is based on a love of truth—that is, a recognition of reality" (1937/ 1964, p. 248).

The argument that the therapist can operate clinically while suspended between belief and disbelief presents what to me is a misunderstanding of the nature of doubt and truth. As an analogy, perhaps the reader can recall the perceptual illusions presented in introductory psychology texts, in which a focus on the foreground produces the visual impression of one image (for instance, a vase), while a focus on the background convinces the viewer that another image is being displayed (for instance, two faces in profile). One does not, even if one is aware of both possibilities, remain suspended between the two images. Instead, the perceptual experience flips back and forth, capturing the viewer in one way and then another. Similarly, belief and disbelief capture the client and the therapist *at different times*, sometimes concurrently and sometimes singly, as they struggle with the difficulty of the material. The therapist does not stand halfway between alternatives; instead, he or she, at times leading and at times following the client, takes excursions into the realms of belief and disbelief.

Captured in different moments by the unreality of a trauma description and by its compelling truth, the countertransference responses of the therapist will mirror the patient's anguished attempts to make peace with the past. The messages that the therapist would wish to send are compassion with the agony of not knowing and honest confession of the press to doubt and to believe as countertransferential responses to trauma. "I can't know what happened to you," although true, should be a painful admission, not a prideful declaration of "neutrality." Belief in the trauma is usefully presented to the trauma patient as a living rather than a static thing. Clear discussion of this view of doubt allows the patient a cushion to the blows dealt by occasional sensing of the therapist's disbelief. Furthermore, participants often presented therapists' doubt within the Trauma Countertransference Study as examples of betrayal—proof that the therapists had lied about prior statements or that their prior compassionate responses that implied belief were deceptive. Countertransference disclosure in this arena could address this painful issue.

The FMSF position presented earlier (unlikely, by the way, to be characteristic of the entirety of this diverse group) and the position of those advocating constant belief as support within the lay literature also cut both client and therapist away from aspects of the therapeutic experience. One group forbids belief in the absence of extratherapeutic evidence; the other forbids disbelief. Both rigid countertransferential positions, even if they are realistically maintained, are likely to produce damaging rigidity in the corresponding transference. Courtois (1999) discussed both extremes, noting the destructive effects on therapy of cynicism, suppression, and paranoia (leading to avoidance of the memories) and over-involvement and attraction to trauma (leading to overemphasis on this facet of the therapy).

Unbelievable Accounts of Trauma: The Countertransference Press to Disbelieve

In a defensive letter to an editor about a work of fiction that I had written, I once responded to his criticism that an aspect of my story was unbelievable by telling him that I was incorporating an event that had actually happened to an individual whom I had known. Helpfully, he pointed out that many things were too strange to be believed, but fewer were too strange to have happened (a comment he attributed to Thomas Hardy). I think of this when I listen to accounts of trauma that I find unbelievable.

The countertransference press to disbelieve is strong and could stem from many of the same factors reviewed earlier in this chapter and in chapter 3—the defense of the therapist against vicarious trauma, a compassionate and empathic response to client doubt, and incorporation of the societal contempt for victims. Armsworth (1989) and Dale, Allen, and Measor (1996) found that therapist disbelief was a major factor in trauma victims' negative appraisals of the helpfulness of their therapy. I suspect that some of what the clients experienced as disbelief was actually poorly communicated empathic doubt (see below) or the temporary withdrawal from trauma that might be expected occasionally in intense therapeutic work. I agree, however, that flat rejection by therapists of client accounts of trauma (attributing them to fantasy or to conscious lying) is common and has become more so over the past decade. I now regularly have at least one workshop participant in my training for licensure (mandated by California) who states in the initial questionnaire that 75–90% of trauma accounts heard in therapy are false. Several authors have argued that exaggerated doubt in the victim's story is more common among therapists and evaluators than is zealous overinvolvement (Armstrong, 1994; Bernardez, 1994).

As therapists try to place barriers around their nontraumatic approach to human encounters—to preserve a benevolent worldview—their disbelief in trauma is a major method of self-defense. As Janoff-Bulman (1992) wrote, most of us live in an unrealistically safe world, full of protective illusions. We believe that, although accidents are common, they will not happen to us or to those we love. We can simultaneously believe that no friend or relative will ever commit suicide, injure another while driving drunk, assault a loved one, or suffer serious injury through negligence and yet believe that such events are not rare in the world we inhabit. We can dispassionately agree that we are mortal without having a real emotional connection to the idea that we could die.

Trauma "shatters assumptions" (Janoff-Bulman, 1992) about this benevolent world. The personal or impersonal force that so carefully protects those within our empathic bubble from the inevitable pain of life can disappear when pricked by the patient's sharp-edged story, and this is a distinctly unpleasant sensation. Going back to one example from chapter 3, if I must hear from my patient about her sister's cancer (that so parallels my own family concern), then I consciously prefer to believe that she is exaggerating the rate of health deterioration, the likelihood of recurrence, and other horrors of the disease. I do not like the world she asks me to share with her. It is hard to be afraid with her so that she (and I) can learn to contain that fear.

To the extent that the therapist feels endangered by the account of trauma—perhaps through parallels in his or her own past or present—it is more likely that the countertransference response will be more extreme. This can lead to overinvolvement and overemphasis on the trauma (Wilson & Lindy's [1994] Type II countertransference reaction) or to the unconscious avoidance of the material, mediated through disbelief and minimization (Wilson & Lindy's [1994] Type I countertransference reaction). When the therapist has this sense of disbelief, the source of the reaction deserves careful, conscious examination.

Disbelief as a Compassionate Response: Empathic Doubt

The more pleasant assumptions associated with the nontraumatic views will be defended by client and therapist alike, and neither wishes to rob the other of the peace of disbelief. Were it not for the resiliency of truth and its tendency to rise from the ashes no matter how often it is destroyed, one might agree with Ralph Waldo Emerson that God offers to every mind its choice of truth and repose. It is extremely compelling in the moment to choose repose.

The client who is considering the truth value of a traumatic element (rather than asking about belief because he or she doubts the therapist's connection) may well hope to be proven wrong. As an example, I recall listening to a tape of an interaction between Mr. S, a black business executive and his superiors. Mr. S had recorded their exchange surreptitiously. The way that Mr. S was treated was so appalling to me, so blatantly and obviously racist, that I felt shame at being present. He did not look at me as I listened and showed little feeling, although I frequently looked across at him. At the end of the tape, Mr. S's supervisor told him that Mr. S's references to racism (in a previous meeting) were unacceptable, belligerent, insulting, and typical of his race, and

the supervisor hoped that Mr. S could negotiate more pro-
ductively in the future. If he could do so, he would eventually move into an important and well-paid position, one that
Mr. S wanted very much.

Mr. S, head still down, said that he supposed that I agreed
with his supervisor, but that his rage was so out of control
by the end of the meeting that he had to leave in silence to
preempt a violent reaction. We had spoken a great deal about
his rage, which we had traced to his violent and chaotic past.
Our own relationship had been rocky. When he asked me if
I believed that his supervisor was correct, however, I was at
the moment so caught up in my own anger on his behalf that
I had a difficult time believing my intuitive sense that the
question was real. At that exact moment, he wanted me to
tell him that his rage was of intrapsychic origin, that his supervisor was well-intentioned and fair in his assessments,
and that the signs of racism he saw in his environment were
illusory. He wanted my doubt, in part to hold back his own
helpless anger at the truth. It was a difficult time for me, as
I tried to support his efforts to view his supervisor in as
positive a manner as possible to preserve their relationship
and yet to empathize with his anger and find ways to contain
it.

Mr. S and I climbed in and out of intrapsychic explanations
of his rage (and disbelief in his racial explanations for his
failure to get along well at work) and interpersonal explanations (with accompanying belief in the same racial explanations). Our success in finding a way through doubt without losing connection rested on clear communication
between us that his objective anger at his employers did not
truly preclude other intrapsychic causes and that the same
was true for my countertransferential anger. Here is one such
discussion:

Mr. S: I wanted to rip him apart, kick his pompous ass.

Therapist: He's a lot like your father, you know. He was
being an ass, I agree, but he was also reminding you of
your father.

Mr. S: Bastards are the same all over.

Therapist: Seems to me like they come in stupifying variety. And this one is like your father.

Mr. S: A fat white pig is a fat white pig. No offense, Missy D [a nickname he often used when he was aware of my whiteness].

Therapist: None taken, unless you want me to take offense. This fat white pig is like your father.

Mr. S: All right. You're right. I'm going to give you this one. But I want to talk about his . . .

Therapist: His pigitude?

Mr. S: His pigasity.

Therapist: Cool. So talk.

Mr. S: [Laughs] He's a lot like my father. And he's a lying fat ass.

Such discussions underline the point made earlier: that is, that doubt and belief (like transference-based and reality-based reactions) can be living entities within the therapy relationship, surfacing and moving into the background as needed during various periods. Still, it is important to emphasize that disbelief in trauma, although it can be compassionate and empathic, also can be a way for therapist and client to avoid confronting the powerful. As Herman (1992, p. 267) wrote,

> It is very tempting to take the side of the perpetrator. All the perpetrator asks is that the bystander do nothing. He appeals to the universal desire to see, hear and speak no evil. . . . The victim demands action, engagement, and remembering. . . . The more powerful the perpetrator, the greater is his prerogative to name and define reality, and the more completely his arguments prevail.

Disbelief as a Response to Client Prevarication

Judith Herman (1992), an important founding theorist in trauma therapy, listed truthfulness as one of the requisites of treatment. Those traumatized individuals who have been raised "in an atmosphere of deception and secrecy," wrote R. Epstein (1994), "need to be informed that treatment cannot be effective without a commitment to honesty" (p. 121). He went on to state that therapy can be easily destroyed if the client consciously deceives the therapist.

A countertransference response of distance and disbelief to a trauma story or to a general account from a trauma client can be the result of the therapist's picking up signs that the emotions are not in fact genuine or that the factual information is not accurate. I am not saying that the client with the consciously false story of trauma is encountered frequently, but I do find that use of social deception is a symptom of living with trauma. It follows from other descriptors of traumatic transference (its life-or-death quality and intensity, the threat associated with potential abandonment by the therapist or with the therapist's anger) that clients will lie to prevent negative feeling from surfacing in the therapist. It is for this reason that I do not emphasize to my patients, as R. Epstein (1994) suggests, that lying will undermine the possibility of success in the therapy, but instead suggest that it is difficult to speak traumatic truths aloud. With clients from physically abusive homes or with histories of concentration camp or prison experiences, I discuss the immediacy of the wish to protect oneself that leads to a social lie to which one might feel committed. However, I should mention that 71 of the 84 participants in the Trauma Countertransference Study said that they told an "important lie" in therapy at least once. Fifty of the 71 never corrected it.

At times, I have shared with clients the story of a woman (repeated with her permission) who "borrowed" the car of a neighbor when he was at work. The car was a showpiece that was seldom if ever driven, and the woman thought that she could take it out for a drive without her neighbor's knowledge, because she knew his schedule. As she drove into his driveway and was stepping out of the car, she was confronted with her enraged friend, who said angrily "You stole my car!" Keys in hand, one foot still in the car, the woman said "No, I didn't."

The discussion here bears on the general issue of traumatic morality (chapter 5) and on the efforts of the therapist to remain nonjudgmental in the face of seemingly unnecessary deception by the client. "I can't be your therapist if you lie to me" is one recommended response, although not my own. Instead, I try to say, "Lying is not a great interpersonal strategy, but it's a hard habit to break when you are so afraid of someone's anger. It's just a symptom, like any other, and I'll help you with it. You need to try to catch yourself though, and let me know, so we can look at when you feel pushed to lie."

A "retractor" whom I met on a false memory list on the Internet, Ms. X, once had an extended discussion with me about her therapy, her suit against her therapist for false-memory implantation, and her symptoms throughout her hospitalizations and thereafter. The woman describes being bullied by her therapist to accept a diagnosis of multiple personality and ritual abuse. It is interesting, however, that she admitted to me that she did not begin stating her agreement with her therapist because she had a "false memory" that resulted from hypnosis and suggestive questioning, although both hypnosis and suggestion had been used. Instead, she reported wanting to please him, and she lied consciously to become more favored in his eyes. (Parenthetically, his apparent technique of pairing closeness and attention solely with disclosure remains a clinical mistake, whether or not a false memory of abuse resulted.)

The retractor above, to the extent she is now accurately describing her doctor (noting that she is now part of another system that pushes for accusations of a different type), had very poor therapy. It is important for me to provide examples, however, that do not provide an easy out for the reader (and writer) to distance from the possibility that we too at times create a countertransference environment that favors the lie. One mechanism for creation of this environment, I believe, is to equate the lie with immorality, trapping the patient into defensive protection rather than admission of the lies that are told. However, two other more developmental mechanisms for patient lies within basically competent therapy come to mind—lies in response to therapist lack of compassion and lies in response to therapist privileging of trauma material.

Dishonesty in Response to Therapist Withdrawal of Compassion

First, particularly with children, exaggeration or conscious lying can result from the clinician's "compassion fatigue" (Figley, 1995). The therapist's deep compassion and caring response to first hearing the trauma account often feels so life-giving that the client wishes to re-create it repeatedly. Unfortunately, therapists sometimes are unaware or otherwise incapable of meeting this need. The subsequent responses of the clinician to the same material are less compassionate, even taking on a "Let's get on with it" quality by patient report. The desperate client might manufacture trauma to reach toward that prior connection.

I have listened to more than one client story of therapy beginning to flounder over this dynamic. The new trauma material might not be believable, and the needed compassion is not given. Furthermore, the therapist's disbelief is shaming to the client, and the client's lies appear manipulative to the therapist. The way out of this dilemma is for the therapist to recognize his or her role in the interaction and to take responsibility for it. Typically, this allows the client to face his or her own responsibility without shame. Jean, a participant in the Trauma Countertransference Study, describes such an interaction:

> *Interviewer:* Did you ever lie to him?
>
> *Jean:* Did I . . . you mean a big lie?

Interviewer: A big lie. Well, an important lie.

Jean: Yeah. This is really bad. I swear the other stuff I told you is true.

Interviewer: OK.

Jean: I told him that I was raped.

Interviewer: And you weren't.

Jean: I wasn't. This is the story, see. I was just desperate, desperate for him to act like he liked me. And he was acting all cold and everything, and I thought if I was raped it would . . . he would care. So I tell him, you know, and he was really really nice, and it made me cry, which made him believe me, I think. So then he starts asking me about the police, and I tell him I didn't go to the police, and he's "Why not?" and I get more and more caught up and confused and it just . . . just . . .

Interviewer: Came apart, huh?

Jean: Yeah. But boy, it was almost a good thing. I mean I just started crying and begging him to understand, and he really did. He said he felt bad about being distant and sending me . . . driving me to that.

Clients also have come into therapy with me carrying lies that they had told for similar reasons to friends, relatives, employers, Alcoholics Anonymous, Narcotics Anonymous, or incest groups. Even when I have good reason to believe from the beginning that this is the case, I have found that a compassionate response to other aspects of the client's life is most useful in allowing or encouraging eventual honest disclosure.

Dishonesty in Response to Therapist Privileging of Trauma Material

In the retractor story above, the client clearly believed that therapist approval depended on specific content in disclosure. This might not be consciously true for the therapist, although he or she may think that a specific type of trauma material must be discussed with greater depth. Alternatively, for some therapists, a rare type of trauma might be compelling for the clinician, who will engage in the privileged voyeurism of the consulting room. Several patients in the Holocaust survivor samples (Dalenberg & Epstein, 1999) believed that their therapists were guilty of this countertransference-based mistake.

An example in my own practice involved a woman who heard me speak on Holocaust history to a community gathering. The room was a small one, and a surprising number of people arrived to hear my talk. Extra chairs were brought in, and the crowd sat shoulder to shoulder as I paced a small stage in front of them. About 10 minutes into the talk, a baby began to cry loudly. Her mother was trapped, and the baby was disrupting the seminar. As I continued to speak, I reached to the mother, and she handed her daughter to me. I paced with the baby, who calmed down quickly with the movement and space, and I gave my speech about lost Jewish children as the baby played with the Star of David necklace that I was wearing.

Three potential clients called in the weeks following the seminar. Each came in knowing my love for Jewish literature and my interest in the Holocaust. One trauma survivor, Ms. V, seemed in particular to share that love. She would tie in her present-day dilemmas to rabbinical stories or Midrash tales, asking me to do the same. She frequently read Talmudic texts in the waiting room, at times making appropriate references from her reading to her everyday struggle. During the period in which she felt my absence between sessions most acutely, she took to wearing a Star of David, explicitly discussing her felt connection to me through Judaism. I would see her briefly at times at my temple, but she stayed discreetly apart from any group with whom I was interacting. She responded enthusiastically to any analogies that I would make that used Judaic content, and I thoroughly looked forward to the exercise of tying together two worlds that I so enjoyed. Her therapy flowed easily, and marked improvements in her life brought us to termination earlier than I had predicted. A week before our planned last session, however, she dropped the bombshell that added three months to the end of our work. She was not Jewish. The daughter of a cold and abusive mother and a drunken and absent father, she wanted a connection with that person that she saw holding the baby in the seminar. Not trusting her ability to form one on her own, she created one and then felt trapped by it.

Ms. V and I did not substitute religious discussion for therapy, and there was nothing inherently inappropriate about the content of our sessions. In thinking back on my time with her, however, I believe that I privileged those sessions that allowed me to stretch my psychic muscles in a new way. The intensity of my pleasure in her unique offerings was so intoxicating that I do not wonder that she was pulled into playing her role with more and more complexity and finesse. Such fascination with one feature of the individual's personality, one way of interacting, one talent, or one story, can spur the client to feed that fascination at the expense of other useful foci, even if it involves a lie. As in the example above, traumatized clients might believe that truth is expendable if it could get in the way of the relationship.

Therapy in the Context of Disbelief

When the patient is offering an account of trauma that is either fully disbelieved or in doubt, it is not clear to me that it is ethical for the therapist to continue treatment without disclosing and discussing disbelief as a problem. My experience with those who have fabricated and maintained histories of child abuse is limited; most patients (of those I discovered) either confessed the fabrication spontaneously or began to minimize the history (in favor of other real issues) over time. However, I have had the experience of treating three men who presented with symptoms of trauma after a claimed alien abduction. Two of these men dropped their claims during therapy, but one did not. It is his story that I will discuss briefly here.

Mr. R came to therapy with debilitating anxiety that bordered on agoraphobia, nightmares, panic attacks, and flashbacks of abduction. Basic cognitive techniques helped, but not as much as I typically expect. When I stopped to examine my countertransference reactions—as I do when I find that I am not being helpful to a client in my own or the client's view—I found myself so overwhelmed with the magnitude of my countertransference that my first reaction was a wish to refer. I did not want it known that I treated this man. The very act of accepting him as a client seemed to pronounce me gullible and antiscientific. Although his emotions appeared genuine, the content of the sessions made me feel as if I was dishonoring my profession. Moreover, I wondered whether I could help him, given the distance that was created by my disbelief. (I distinguish this, by the way, from doubt. Doubt was something that we could share; my own state was one of firm disbelief.)

Two months into therapy I began to talk to him about it. I told him that I was concerned because I believed theoretically that my being fully with him as he confronted his trauma was an important part of the therapy process and that my disbelief was getting in my way. On the other hand, I knew of no one to whom to refer him who met the twin criteria of (a) real openness to the possibility that he had been abducted and (b) expertise in the empirical foundations of trauma therapy (particularly cognitive therapy, given his anxiety symptoms). He asked what plausible explanations I had for what happened to him, and I discussed a few. He pointed out that I had no more evidence for my explanation than he had for his. I could not cite proof that a compelling belief or memory of alien abduction could emerge as a result of the combination of drugs, sleep paralysis, and hypnogogic hallucination that I proposed. Mr. R stayed in therapy during this period, he said, because he thought that I was struggling to find a way for us to talk on the same plane; he saw that it mattered to me that we were not emotionally communicating.

Mr. R's symptoms did not resolve until I found a way to join him in the cycle of belief and doubt during his cognitive sessions, fully empathizing with his terror. I found that I was able to do this without knowing the "perpetrator" of the terrifying events, thinking instead (to myself) of various real events that could be symbolically represented by the abduction memory (belief) and intrapsychic causes that might generate this experience (doubt). Moving past the countertransference block created by my disbelief allowed therapy to proceed.

I find the same approach to be most effective in work with ritual abuse and clients with dissociative identity disorder who offered unlikely or impossible accounts of violent assault, rape, or cannibalism. The countertransference distance created by disbelief is an impediment to therapy. Instead, I have found that decreased anxiety and dissociation is produced through allowing the cycle of belief and doubt in the essence of the traumatic injury to occur, while simultaneously educating the client to the possibility of nightmare confabulation and other sources of distorted or misremembered trauma.

As a final brief example, I recently conducted a consultation on a dissociative identity case in which the client told her therapist that her parents sexually abused her and put her to bed with a hot curling iron (set on high and still plugged into the wall) between her legs and forbade her to remove it during the night. Genital examination conducted after a rape in adulthood showed no scarring. That same week, I listened to a 7-year-old girl who had been raped by a relative (who had confessed). In the days following the rape, she stated that she felt something hot inside of her (a sensation that disappeared after inflammation decreased) and feared that the perpetrator had left a hot object behind. She spoke about her dreams about the hot object and about the rape itself. I wonder if the two individuals had the same experience and if the adult might have been remembering vivid dreams about the aftermath of childhood rape. The expression of simple disbelief would be an acting out of the countertransference rather than the provision of a fair and therapeutic response.

Summary

A number of conclusions about validation of and challenges to belief flow from the arguments above. Belief and doubt will cycle in the therapist and client for complex sets of reasons related to the transference–countertransference matrix. The negotiation and acceptance of these cyclical changes is an important feature of trauma therapy, as the participants work on emotionally arousing and provocative material. It is crucial during this negotiation, however, that the clinician respect the bravery of the client as he or she breaks silence and asks to be believed.

Part of this respect is an increased understanding of the degree to which therapist behaviors can signal belief (e.g., compassion as belief, withdrawal as doubt), and the related transference–countertransference tangle that might be produced by these connections. Both therapist and client could temporarily fuse belief and care, doubt and withdrawal, or doubt and protection from evil.

The prolific historian and psychologist Erna Olafson once brought to my attention a quotation from Shakespeare's *Measure for Measure*. In the scene, Angelo, an official in the duke's court, tells Isabella that he intends to kill her imprisoned brother unless she yields herself to him. When she answers that she would "tell the world aloud what man thou art," Angelo replies scornfully,

> Who will believe thee, Isabel? My unsoil'd name, th'austereness of my life, my vouch against you, and my place i' th' state, will so your accusation overweight that you shall stifle in your own report and smell of calumny . . . Say what you can: my false o'erweighs your true. (act II, scene IV)

Today, we read that, although less than 10% of trauma reports are likely to be false, more than 80% of media attention is devoted to allegedly false accusations (Beckett, 1996). We learn that, in states with mandated sentencing of sexual offenders of children, a large number of confessed rapists still receive probation (Cheit & Goldschmidt, 1997), in part because it is so difficult to try a case on the word of a child. Clinicians are told in risk management workshops that, although many or even most recovered memories are probably true, for reasons of self-protection, therapists should refer or express disbelief in any client with such an experience. One gets the distinct impression that "false o'erweighs true" in many of these cases. It is important that therapists continue to champion a more complex view of this phenomenon.

5

It's Not Your Fault:
Countertransference Struggles
With Blame and Shame

It was not your fault.
Then whose fault was it?
I shall find out. And I shall tell. I swear to you, little sister.
I shall.

Elie Weisel (1978, p. 180)

The survivor is silent, and we encourage him or her to speak. We tell survivors that once the trauma is spoken, it will seem less dangerous, less shameful, more a part of the everyday imperfect world. It's not your fault, we tell them. You were young. You were not as strong. You didn't know it would happen. And then we hear the story, and the life of the therapy becomes one notch more complicated.

When I discussed shame and blame with participants in the Trauma Countertransference Study, I heard some stories of therapy that surprised me. The 84 clients who participated in the in-depth interviews responded to solicitations that asked for feedback to psychotherapists. Such introductions arguably elicited clients who had enough respect for the process of therapy through their own experience to spend their time in this way. Their criticisms were for the most part thoughtful rather than vengeful, and the psychiatrists, psychologists, and social workers described (again, for the most part) were lovingly reproached for their failings. I was surprised, therefore, to note how many participants (40 of 84) believed that their therapists were ashamed of them.

That finding itself is not dissonant with other research in the area. Armsworth's (1989) sample of 113 incest victims reporting on their therapies also found a high incidence of clients reporting therapist shock or disgust at the disclosures. The literature on blaming the victim is quite old (see Lerner [1980] for a review) and also seems in keeping with the victim report. I have yet to find a therapist sample, however, no matter how the question is phrased, that self-reports high levels of shame or disgust. The exception is shame reported by therapists regarding their *own* unacceptable feelings, for example, of sexual attraction to clients (Pope, Keith-Spiegel, & Tabachnick, 1986). So what is the client seeing?

One possibility is that clients are projecting their own feelings. The propensity of trauma victims toward self-blame and feelings of shame is well known, supported in the theoretical and the empirical literature. Trauma populations reporting self-blame have been diverse, including incest victims (Hunter, Goodwin, & Wilson, 1992), spine injury patients (Schulz & Decker, 1985), parents of infants with perinatal complications (Tennen, Affleck, & Gerschman, 1986), and burn patients (Kiecolt-Glaser & Williams, 1987). In some cases, patient shame and self-blame are attributed falsely to the therapist. In other cases, however, shame in the therapist is accurately perceived.

Shame and the Trauma Therapist

Tracking down potential sources of the therapist's shame (or the client's perception of that shame) has been a fascinating process. The most obvious sources, such as the nearly universal tendency to blame victims for their misfortune, are addressed first below. However, my own clients, together with the participants in the Trauma Countertransference Study, have led me to consider other possible sources for the problem of therapist shame.

Blaming and Judging the Victim

While therapists can be rather glib in their statements to patients about self-blame ("The battered woman/incest victim/
rape victim is never to blame for the action of the perpetrator"), they do admit to struggling with understanding
trauma behavior. Sometimes the failure to ask an obvious
question is shaming to the client, who has the same question
preying on his or her mind. One participant in the Trauma
Countertransference Study, a rape victim, spoke about such
a dilemma:

> *Karen:* [Description of rape deleted.] And then he told me
> to stay there, on the bed, and I did. That's the part my
> doctor couldn't understand.
>
> *Interviewer:* So he told you to stay, and he had a
> knife . . .
>
> *Karen:* He left. He told me to stay on the bed, and he left
> and went to his car to get cigarettes, and he told me to
> stay on the bed, and I did.
>
> *Interviewer:* Oh. So your therapist didn't understand why
> you didn't do something while he was out of the house.
>
> *Karen:* Yes.
>
> *Interviewer:* Oh. Did she ask you why?
>
> *Karen:* No, she just said "You didn't leave?" "Was there
> a phone nearby?" Yes. "You didn't call anybody?" No.
> "You didn't lock the door?" No. "What's wrong with
> you?"
>
> *Interviewer:* She said "What's wrong with you?"
>
> *Karen:* She didn't say it. She just . . . my answers were
> just hanging in the air. I should have protected myself,
> and I didn't. She was too nice to say it. She felt . . . se-
> cretly she felt ashamed of me.

Even to the well-trained therapist who understands traumatic reaction, some behaviors associated with trauma seem

"abnormal" or "illogical." Both members of the therapeutic dyad can evaluate trauma-related behavior in this way, and might fear closer examination of the event. The client fears discovery of a major character flaw or a setup for an accusation that seems plausible and yet hurtful ("You deserved this." "You wanted this."). The therapist fears being misunderstood, wishing to appear compassionate and to avoid causing further pain. The exaggerated obedience and the abnormally normal behavior (behaving normally in abnormal circumstances) of many victims during trauma (see Terr [1990a]) are particularly strong triggers for such ruptures in the alliance. For those who are uncomfortable with countertransference disclosure, education alone might be useful to explain the discomfort that therapist and patient share. Carlos's therapist apparently tried both of these approaches:

Interviewer: Was there ever a time that you felt your therapist was ashamed of you?

Carlos: No. Once. Once.

Interviewer: Can you talk about that?

Carlos: Well, the assault . . . I'm a pretty big guy.

Interviewer: I noticed.

Carlos: I didn't turn around, you see. I could have taken him out, the one that had me. He hit me in the back, and I fake fell, so . . . and I was trying to seem unconscious or close to it.

Interviewer: I get it. Smart.

Carlos: But I could have taken him out. And [Name deleted, Carlos's friend] he was much smaller than me, and I was lying there while they beat him nearly to death. I didn't run, I didn't fight, I just fake slept. And I could have done . . . done a lot of things.

Interviewer: So how was your therapist? Did he say anything about that?

Carlos: He . . . when I told him the story, that's when, in answer to your question, he was ashamed of . . . us.

Interviewer: What an interesting way to put it, "ashamed of us."

Carlos: Well, Dr. P, do you know him? He's a big guy, too. And he was saying that in this kind of situation you just do what you have to do to live. It's sort of instinctive. And then later, when you look at it from outside, you doubt your own manhood. [Dr. P] was noticing that he didn't think to ask me how [my friend] was, and [Dr. P] was ashamed of himself for a minute. We were both ashamed of ourselves for a minute.

Interviewer: So was that [disclosure of the therapist's shame] a helpful thing for him to say?

Carlos: Helpful. Very helpful.

The application of nontrauma morality to the trauma setting is also an instigator for shame for both therapist and client regarding the client's actions. Dr. P and his client felt shame over what they each believed were his own unethical or immoral thought processes. Carlos felt that he should have risked his life and health for his weaker friend, and Dr. P (according to Carlos) believed that he should have modeled such concern. These dilemmas were ubiquitous in our Holocaust survivor sample and might explain the prevalence of shame–guilt reactions in Danieli's (1981) groundbreaking study of therapists treating these individuals. Danieli identified 45·of the 61 participating therapists in her study as showing countertransference themes related to shame.

In reading the general Holocaust literature, I have found the concept of "choiceless choice" (Langer, 1991) valuable in thinking through these difficult dilemmas. Langer referred to situations that provide the victim with the superficial features that would define "choice" together with alternatives that are incompatible with humanity. An example was memorialized in William Styron's Holocaust novel *Sophie's Choice* (Styron, 1979), in which a young mother was asked to choose which of her two children should live and which should die. The story of stealing bread from the mouth of a dying fellow prisoner also is often told. Hearing these stories myself, at times from my own clients, I am struck by how often my clients and I will lapse into silence, one of us insisting to the other that we "shouldn't judge." And yet we do judge, and there is shame in knowing that we do so. Both client and therapist must learn that refraining from judgment is continuing work.

The empirical literature on blaming the victim does support a "just-world hypothesis" (Lerner, 1980). Knowing that an innocent person is to be punished or that he or she must bear great suffering leads to a search for the reason for this suffering; if no negligence, malintent, or unsavory associations can be found, the observer of suffering appears often to distort the character of the sufferer. Thereby we preserve the world in which "bad things happen to bad people" (Kushner, 1983). This mechanism could explain the frequency with which participants in the Trauma Countertransference Study and those in the Armsworth (1989) therapy evaluation study stated that their therapists believed that the client deserved or shared the blame for the trauma.

It is clear that the process above might become cyclical in a context such as psychotherapy. Because the therapist may well feel shame over his or her perceived contribution to the client's pain—particularly when explicitly blamed for being cold or withholding—defensive blaming of the victim serves a personal function (protecting the benign view of the self) as well as a general one (protecting the benign view of the world). As the client reacts negatively to the therapist's blaming behaviors, shame in the therapist can increase, perpetuating the cycle.

Shame Over Unacceptable Feelings

The focus on containing and eliminating countertransference and the continuing advice to avoid sharing countertransference feelings are other sources of shame in trauma therapy. Suicidal behaviors and gestures, self-mutilation, hostility, anger, aggression, repetition compulsion, and self-endangerment all commonly appear in traumatic transference, often entangled with a primitive terror that verges on psychosis. (See Hedges, Hilton, Hilton, & Caudill [1997] for a discussion of organizing transference.) Such extreme transference manifestations produce by definition extreme countertransference reactions in therapists. One simply cannot face this degree of pain in someone with whom one is involved and not feel changed.

A special problem for the therapists most likely to feel shame at the power of their feelings is the potential of reactivity of patients to this shame. It is extremely important to note that therapist evaluations (e.g., Danieli, 1981; Pope et al., 1986) frequently note shame over unacceptable strong feeling. Therapist studies infrequently mention self-perceived tendencies to blame the victim, whereas client studies (e.g., Armsworth, 1989; Dale, Allen, & Measor, 1996; the Trauma Countertransference Study sample here) do find this problem in the therapist. These findings support the tentative conclusion that, in any given case, client and therapist can misinterpret the relative proportions of the causes of shame. The client, already prone to self-blame and shame, takes the nonverbal signs of shame in the therapist as confirmatory of his or her own self-degradation ("He is ashamed of me so I should be ashamed of myself.") and might not consider other sources. Similarly, the therapist might believe that his or her affect-related shame is invisible to the client and see reactive shame in the patient as generated solely by the traumatic event.

Unique countertransference reactions can transform into shame when therapists find that their specific feelings toward their clients are inappropriate. Sexual countertransference is experienced this way by a significant number of therapists (Pope et al., 1986) and has been most thoroughly discussed. However, my experience of supervising student trauma therapists has led me to believe that shame over other strong feelings (anger or hatred, for instance) also is common. In fact, one of the more difficult supervisory problems I have encountered in this field has been to help trauma therapists tolerate their own shame without acting out punitively toward the client (Hahn, 1995a, 1995b). A useful sign of such a problem for our continual self-analysis is the sense that the client is "making" the therapist feel something. Such a statement or conceptualization (which might remind the reader of some versions of the projective identification concept) implies the disowning of the affect in the therapist, which in turn implies the therapist's shame over the existence of the feeling. It is important in such instances not to ask or expect the client to take on the responsibility for the therapist's unique responses to trauma.

Another source of shame that I have not seen discussed in the trauma literature is the therapist's envy of the patient's intensely felt and vivid past. Erik and his therapist, for instance, apparently went through such an experience.

> *Interviewer:* Was there ever a time that you felt your therapist was ashamed of you?
>
> *Erik:* That actually . . . that's actually an interesting story, because I was wrong about that. We were wrong about that. It was an interesting story.
>
> *Interviewer:* Would you mind telling me?
>
> *Erik:* It was important. From my end, I was thinking she was ashamed of my being such a basket case over my son's death, because, you know, I was ashamed. But really it turned out that she was uncomfortable. I was seeing her uncomfortableness, her discomfort.
>
> *Interviewer:* Do you know what she was uncomfortable about?
>
> *Erik:* Yeah. She ended up talking about it because I was threatening to leave therapy because I had had it with her cold . . . it looked like disgust. But it wasn't. She was ashamed of herself, you see. This is pretty personal.
>
> *Interviewer:* Would you rather not say?
>
> *Erik:* I mean, it makes her sound like a bitch, which I don't mean to do, really.
>
> *Interviewer:* I see. Well, I mean I don't see, but it's OK if you don't want to talk about it.
>
> *Erik:* It just turned out that she had a very easy life, rich parents, big doctor, nice family, no hassles, and here I

come with my whole series of disasters. And it turned out that she felt as if she had not been tested the way I had. She'd never been in a fight. She felt like she couldn't talk to me.

Interviewer: You mean like she had no right to talk to you about your losses because her life had been so easy?

Erik: Oh, more than that. That she wanted to have that past, to brag that she had conquered something. And what she had to say there was so nothing, so puny . . .

Interviewer: Did you feel that way?

Erik: Oh, a little. Mostly she did. It even rubbed off a little positively on me, after I got the hang of it. I felt courageous.

Another example comes from [Paul] Shaffer's play *Equus* (1977), discussed by Scaturo and McPeak (1998) as an example of a therapist overidentifying with a client and losing perspective. In the play, a psychiatrist, Dr. Dysart, treats an adolescent who has blinded six horses with a spike. This discussion taks place between Dr. Dysart and his friend Hester Saloman, the magistrate who referred the patient (*Equus*, act 2, scene 4):

Dysart: [Earnestly.] Look . . . to go through life and call it yours—your life—you first have to get your own pain. Pain that is unique to you. You can't just dip into the common bin and say "That's enough!" . . . He's done that. All right, he's sick. He's full of misery and fear. He was dangerous, and could be again, though I doubt it. But that boy has known a passion more ferocious than I have felt in any second of my life. And let me tell you something: I envy it.

Hesther: You can't

Dysart: [vehemently]: Don't you see? That's the Accusation! That's what his stare has been saying to me all this time. "At least I galloped! When did you!" . . . [Simply] I'm jealous, Hester. Jealous of Alan Strang.

Hesther: That's absurd.

Erik's therapist was able to move through her own shame, and not exacerbate her patient's shame, by reframing the client's life-in-trauma as an act of courage. As such, her client's survival was worthy of the therapist's admiration.

Feeling Shame Due to the Restrictions, Limitations, and Boundaries of Therapy

One form that shame over unacceptable feelings may take is "bystander's guilt" (Danieli, 1981). Here the focus of the shame can settle on the restrictions imposed by the therapeutic setting. Several trauma therapists have noted their struggle with their wish to "prove" to clients that their commitment is real. I know of few senior theorists in the field who have not had moments in which they longed to step out of role and reclaim their compassion as a gift rather than as a paid service. Ablow (1992, p. 35) wrote:

> I rent my soul ... I still feel embarrassed when my patients mention clinic fees. No matter how much I care for a patient, the fact that dollars are the life blood of the relationships seems to color my concern as impure—a hint of the prostitute feigning romance.

To the extent that the therapist has a more stable personal and financial life than the patient, which is often the case in trauma therapy, shame associated with the slow movement that can characterize the therapy is potentially increased. Long-term psychotherapy is extremely expensive, possibly the most significant financial investment in the client's life. Many patients make great sacrifices to continue their psychotherapy, including postponing career decisions and improvements in practical life circumstances. I almost always feel a twinge of guilt when my patients give me a fiscal accounting of our relationship ("Do you know how much money I have spent on you in the last year?").

That phrase, "money I have spent on you," is the key to both the therapist and the client working through this shame–blame dilemma. Trauma patients are notorious for their difficulties with maintaining the "as if" nature of therapy that allows processing of traumatic and nontraumatic material (Levine, 1982, 1990). Given this limitation, client and therapist at times feel that the client is paying solely for the experience of connection without moving toward internalization of this capacity for attachment.

Shame is exacerbated in both therapist and client by the reduction of the therapy experience to some narrow subset of allowable interactions. The client might be shamed by the knowledge that he or she is a "difficult patient" who cannot tolerate the full range of typical therapist expression. Participants in the Trauma Countertransference Study typically stated that they expected a lot from their therapists, and at times they felt humiliated by what they saw as their therapists' grudging acceptance of the job. Low-fee patients often emphasized that they were "unfair" to their therapists and exploitative of their therapists' emotional generosity.

Pay also was a focus among therapists with whom I spoke. Most clinicians reported vacillating between their sense of being exploited and their guilt at playing the role of exploiter. A large minority of the participants (33 of 84) accused their therapists at least once of being not worth the expense, because the clients' traumatic issues were not quickly or satisfactorily resolved.

Therapists who find the above statements familiar as they consider a specific patient might ask themselves whether the shame might indicate a stalemate within therapy that deserves attention. Does the therapist have a clear conceptualization of the patient? Alternatively, is the patient leaving all or most of the responsibility for therapeutic change in the hands of the clinician? The following excerpt from session 31 of Mr. H's psychotherapy illustrates such a discussion of my struggle to redistribute therapeutic responsibility with Mr. H, a patient who had a history of multiple loss and trauma.

> *Mr. H:* I think nothing is happening to me, and I'm paying you a lot of money to make nothing happen.
>
> *Therapist:* I think you're right. I feel really frustrated about that. Am I doing anything specific that is getting

in your way, or do you just find something missing in general?

Mr. H: You don't know any more about what I should do about [my relationship with my wife] than I do.

Therapist: I don't. You're right. Help me.

Mr. H: I can't help you. If I could help you I would do it myself.

Therapist: Well, but you're asking me to do it myself, too. I'm not copping out here. I know I haven't helped you enough, and I really want to. It's just that this is totally about us, not about me. I am not going to just figure it out by thinking about it. I will keep trying different ways of working on this until we find something that works. You just have to keep up your energy too.

The client's anger and projection of blame on the therapist is particularly to be expected in clients who are shame-prone themselves (Hoglund & Nicholas, 1995; Tangney, Wagner, Hill-Barlow, Marschall, & Gramzow, 1996). Such clients will almost inevitably react with shame to the process of therapy, because the setting has many of the features most associated with shame-eliciting situations. I strongly believe that therapists do not adequately share responsibility with clients for the creation and maintenance of this shame-inducing situation, and they therefore make it more difficult for themselves and their clients. I offer this chapter as a critique both of my own nontherapeutic behavior and of what I see as frequent issues for others.

For instance, we ask the client to disclose the most personal and potentially shocking details of his or her life. Speaking these truths aloud, for reasons discussed above, is likely to cause initial shame. This much tends to be acknowledged by both therapist and client. However, clients often expect that the shame will dissipate quickly when their speech is not punished by the therapist. They are thus ashamed of their shame—a secondary emotional response that is common in trauma therapy (see chapters 6 and 7).

Furthermore, the dependency that can develop in trauma

therapy often is felt to be toxic to the client. Shame over dependency was the most common shame-related theme in my own research. Clients felt unprepared by their therapists for the degree of their dependency (particularly the men, who also sometimes think that therapeutic dependency is a feminine trait; Osherson & Krugman, 1990). Many therapeutic dyads fell victim to a "blame boomerang," in which a client comes to feel blamed by a therapist for behavior that initially was acceptable. When therapist and client underestimate the stress on the therapist of the client's dependency, the subsequent aggressive reaction from the therapist (when his or her tolerance limit has been passed) is likely to shame the client even more.

The lack of reciprocity in the therapeutic setting is another shame-eliciting feature: Clients have little direct access to information that their emotional interaction is valued by their therapists. After all, the client must pay to be near the clinician and, by the rules of therapy, must always be the one who seeks further contact. Client and therapist can either forget or fail to recognize that the boundaries and restrictions of therapy forbid many of the ordinary exchanges that would allow one individual to assure the other of his or her personal meaning. For instance, for reasons related to therapeutic process, therapists often do not call clients to assure them that they remain in the therapist's mind, do not ordinarily give gifts even to those clients who offer gifts to them, do not request that clients come in when clients make no such requests, and so on. Moreover, some processes of therapy, such as interpretation, are recognized as inherently shaming (Alonso & Rutan, 1988).

A remarkable 70% of the participants in the Trauma Countertransference Study stated that they had tried at some time to discuss with their therapists the issues of shame at the need for proof of care and their frustration at the absence of this proof. About half of the participants thought that their therapists handled this well, although virtually all believed that the interaction was stressful for the therapist. Those who found that countertransference reactions were a hindrance to their resolution of the dilemma claimed that their therapists were angered by their requests. Erin, a Trauma Countertransference Study participant, offers an example:

> *Interviewer:* Was there ever a time that you felt ashamed of something in therapy?
>
> *Erin:* Sure.
>
> *Interviewer:* Could you tell me what your therapist did in response to your shame, and if that was helpful?
>
> *Erin:* I was ashamed of my feeling so needy, clingy. It's hard to describe her response. On the one hand, she said it was normal. But when I would tell her that I couldn't believe that she cared, and I called her machine a lot, she would say that I should know she cared [about me] from her emotions and she would get frustrated. But who can know from that? What is she going to do? Like, does she expect me to believe that she wouldn't be nice to me whether or not she felt anything? She was my doctor.

Kate, one of the psychologist participants who allowed me to speak to her therapist, also reported this phenomenon. Using an analogy of a restaurant, she argued that the patron does not make attributions about a waiter's behavior from the fact that the waiter asks for an order but would make one if the waiter refused an order or disparaged the patron's taste. Kate argued that compassionate behavior on the part of the therapist, which genuinely comes out of caring (in her own work), is the expected background behavior for the therapist (like the waiter asking for an order). Its presence is not noted, and it does not suggest caring or any other personal motivation to a subset of clients. Negative behaviors, on the other hand, such as therapist ill-humor, do provoke explanation. This is actually a well-known phenomenon in social psychology and likely to be widespread (as it is widespread in empirical research in nontherapy settings). Despite Kate's awareness of this research, her own history and pathology (her labels) led her to be unable to "see" the therapist's compassion as anything but a likely outgrowth of the setting during much of her therapy.

Both Kate and her therapist saw a turning point as occurring when the therapist moved away from his anger and frustration at not being "seen" and shared his pain that he could not reach his client. Client and therapist then discussed in some depth what the therapist might do to show his caring that would not violate his role. Although the partial solutions that they found were healing on one level and unsatisfying on another, both members of the dyad report that the discussion helped divert the therapist and the client from blaming client pathology for the existence of the problem. Instead, they began to jointly recognize and acknowledge the limitations of therapy and the effect of these limitations on the patient's ability to "see" care. This allowed Kate to come to the conclusion that true compassion might be present even though it is not always visible; she too had difficulty coming up with acceptable "proofs" of the therapist's connection that did not violate the therapy contract. For his part, Dr. G (with whom I also spoke) realized that he found the client's shame difficult to tolerate, particularly because Dr. G. was targeted as the cause of it, with no obvious "out," and came to understand that he then often became angry (at himself). Furthermore, because shame is feminizing, fragmenting, and a sign of vulnerability, and because anger is organizing and empowering, the slide from shame to anger is a smooth one. In Dr. G's case, his anger was then interpreted by the client as anger at her attachment, and this increased her shame.

Turning to the social psychological literature that Kate provocatively raised as relevant, I also believe that the issue of characterological versus situational attribution is of interest. In coming to any causal analysis, such as of the client's behavior in traumatic settings or in therapy, the causal analyst could choose dispositional causes (references to character) or situational ones (references to setting and context). The tendency to overweight dispositional causes is so great that it is called the fundamental attribution error within the vast literature on causal reasoning (Miller, Ashton, & Mishal, 1990). The same empirical literature reports that people are likely to see the cause for another's behavior as dispositional and to give inadequate weight to situational features in these cases—although situational causes are used to explain one's own actions (Jones & Nisbett, 1987; Malle & Knobe, 1997). Thus, I see you as behaving badly toward me because you are ill-mannered, hostile, and a poor communicator. I, on the other hand, behaved badly toward you because I am busy today, because I slept poorly last night, and because you caught me before my morning coffee.

The therapy setting conspires to give dispositional explanations for client behavior (paranoia, poor boundaries, shame-proneness), which are more likely to be shame-inducing, and situational ones for the therapist (the difficulty of the patient, the limitations created by necessary boundaries). Our professional bible, the *Diagnostic and Statistical Manual of Mental Disorders* (American Psychiatric Association, 1994), is a compendium of client dispositions. It is worth considering that our training might lead us to behaviors that increase the likelihood of shame, as we underestimate the role of the strange world of the therapy room and overestimate the role of client pathology in such dilemmas as (a) the inability of the client to notice compassion in the therapist, (b) the frustration of the client regarding therapy boundaries, and (c) struggles that at times emerge between client and therapist over what types of information the client should learn about the therapist's personal life.

The unique goals of psychotherapy also often shame the therapist, because no one person could be equal to the task of wrestling with the full variety of life dilemmas that clients bring to therapy. The wrenching moral and practical decisions that the client places in the therapy space include unanswerable human questions that have puzzled and frustrated ethical scholars for centuries. What human therapist could treat a full range of trauma clients and not at times see himself or herself as incapable of offering solace? I agree with Wachtel (1982, p. xiii);

> Practicing psychotherapy is a difficult—if also rewarding—way to earn a living. It is no profession for the individual who likes certainty, predictability, or a fairly constant sense that one knows what one is doing. There are few professions in which feeling stupid or stymied is

as likely to be a part of one's ordinary professional day, even for those at the pinnacle of the field.

The therapist protects himself or herself from drowning in shame by keeping close watch over the tendency of both members of the dyad in trauma therapy to idealize the therapist and see him or her as a potential rescuer (Davies & Frawley, 1994). To the extent that the therapist honestly admits that trauma provides all individuals with mind-fragmenting dilemmas and that the therapeutic hour is not a meeting between one person affected by trauma and another who would have been unaffected, shame in both individuals is minimized. On the other hand, the magnitude and complexity of the material does not excuse lack of expertise in the therapist. Shame also will be affected by an increase in knowledge and time spent in serious thought about issues such as those discussed throughout this text.

Perhaps the most controversial statement I make on this topic is that therapists are likely to respond more helpfully to client shame regarding the structure of therapy if they have experienced excellent psychotherapy themselves. I cannot give empirical support for this statement—it is based on my own experience and on the experiences of those whom I supervise. And this is not a "physician, heal thyself" statement, although I do believe that many therapists place a stigma on the perceived need for mental health treatment and therefore avoid it. Rather, it is a statement that the power of transference is difficult to describe and remarkable to experience fully. Although, admittedly, the typical clinician will not experience a transference intensity that is comparable to traumatic transference at its height, he or she will more often feel the frustration and narcissistic injury of the poor interpretation, the anxiety-provoking sense of being less powerful and vulnerable to someone whom you do not know well, and the wish for a more reciprocal and complete relationship with a valued therapist. Such an experience appears to lead a therapist to be more aware of the effect of the setting of psychotherapy and at the same time to believe more strongly in the possibility of profound change or important self-evaluative experiences within this setting. The former outcome can yield an attitude in the therapist that is less shaming to the client, whereas the latter affects the therapist's own internally generated shame.

The Shame of the Just

The last point to be raised here has been discussed only tangentially in the literature I have reviewed. The most relevant description that I have seen came from Primo Levi, who in 1947 wrote a description of the Russian soldiers who first entered the concentration camps. It was restated in an essay in his book, *The Drowned and the Saved* (1986, pp. 73–74):

> They did not greet us, nor smile: they seemed oppressed, not only by pity but also by a confused restraint which sealed their mouths, and kept their eyes fastened on the funereal scene. It was the same shame which we knew so well, which submerged us after the selections, and every time we had to witness or undergo an outrage; the shame that the Germans never knew, the shame which the just man experiences when confronted by a crime committed by another, and he feels remorse because of its existence, because of its having been irrevocably introduced into the world of existing things, and because his will has proven nonexistent or feeble and was incapable of putting up a good defense.

Later in the same essay, speaking of his own shame, Levi wrote (p. 86):

> It was useless to close one's eyes or turn one's back to it because it was all around, in every direction, all the way to the horizon. It was not possible for us nor did we want to become islands; the just among us, neither more nor less numerous than in any other human group, felt remorse, shame, and pain for the misdeeds that others and not they had committed, and in which they felt involved, because they sensed that what happened around them and in their presence, and in them, was irrevocable.

Like many survivors, Levi openly questioned the competence of those in the mental health profession who "pounced on our tangles with professional avidity" (p. 84). Most specifically, he questioned this knowledge base because it was "built up and tested 'outside'" (pp. 84–85). Here is where I disagree, although some might reasonably take me to task for doing so. True, psychologists and psychoanalysts have used theory and intellectualization to distance themselves from trauma. But there also are moments in any well-conducted trauma treatment in which the therapist is by no means "outside." Listening to the survivor's tale of rape, battering, child abuse, sexual abuse by a therapist, and other trauma by human agency, the therapist often feels that shame that Levi references. It is the shame of the just, shame that any decent human being feels when forced to know how cruel human behavior can be, shame associated with the wish to push away any connection between ourselves and those who would commit such acts, including connection mediated through the victim.

Levi speaks of the shame felt in witnessing a traumatic (and evil) action "because of its having been irrevocably introduced into the world of existing things" (p. 73), implying a resistance in the witness–therapist to the change in worldview that would be necessary to accommodate this event. He adds that the shame of the survivor relates to his perception that "his will has proven nonexistent or feeble and was incapable of putting up a good defense" (p. 73). It is possible that the latter type of shame, blaming the victim–survivor for "feeble will," is not shared by the therapist. However, the survivor's intuitive sense of shame in the therapist could lead him or her to misinterpret the therapist's nonverbal signals of shame, confusing accusatory shame (rejection of an interpersonal tie to a client because of the client's unjust actions or pathological reactions) with the shame of the just (rejection of the act perpetrated against the client). One can refuse to be part of the client's accusatory shame (a variation of Briere's [1996] nonparticipation principle [p. 99] regarding sexual transference), while still sharing and working through with the client the shame of the just. This approach provides a reinterpretation of upsetting therapist behavior and emotional reaction, transforming rejection into empathic connection.

The Relationship Between Self-Blame and Other-Blame

One common response to confrontation with extreme and resistant self-blame in a client is oppositional other-blame. Here the therapist, trying to protect or rescue a client who seems unable to protect his or her psychic (or physical) self, begins to urge the client to blame others for the trauma. The initial stages of such encouragement, although they may be born more of therapist anger than therapeutic planning, can be positive for the alliance. The client responds positively to the therapist's just allocation of blame for the traumatic event to the individual who was its author. "You were not to blame for the rape/the battering/the abusive act," we argue. "You could have done nothing to affect it."

Of course, blame and responsibility are many-sided concepts. In attempting to disown responsibility for an event caused by a malevolent other, a reasonable therapeutic effort, both therapist and client slide easily into disowning responsibility for the psychological aftermath of these events. The question "Am I to blame?" can be translated in many ways, some of which were described in a review article:

> To what extent am I to blame for my own and/or another's pain? To what extent am I responsible for the continuance of this pain? What facets of the incidents were subject to my influence? Did I make the right practical and logical decisions? Where was my mistake? Where was my moral transgression? What does an answer, any answer, to these questions mean about me as a daughter/son and as a person? If I am not responsible for the injury, can I still assume responsibility for its cure? (Dalenberg & Jacobs, 1994, p. 42)

Similarly, the statement by the client that he or she is to blame for his or her trauma can reflect many meanings. Perhaps it is a statement that he or she made choices within the situation and that these choices influenced the outcome of the trauma. Perhaps he or she believes that the probability that the trauma would occur was influenced by his or her behavioral decisions. More subtly, the client might be acknowledging voluntary aspects of his or her relationship with the perpetrator—perhaps that affection was valued or attention enjoyed. Or, as argued earlier, he or she might believe that the trauma-related behavior deserves our moral approbation, particularly if the victim shared a forbidden act.

Therapists often join clients in fighting self-blame with other-blame, believing the two to be opposites. Empirically, the correlation between the two is negligible. Therapists and clients might conspire to protect the abuser, particularly if the abuse stems from a system or from the client's parents (Miller, 1990). In clients with child abuse histories, self-blame and other-blame are often related in a series of quasi-logical steps that Briere (1992) labeled the *abuse dichotomy* (See Exhibit 5.1). Here, the client reasons that, because blame must be allocated when injury occurs and because injury caused by parents is deserved punishment, the client must be "bad" and must deserve to be ashamed.

The therapist's tendencies to join or lead the client away from self-blame and toward other-blame have costs, particularly if the meaning of blame and responsibility are not fully explored. Self-blame, particularly behavioral self-blame (blaming one's actions for subsequent consequences), potentially has a positive psychic function. Believing in a role for the self in important events could allow a continued belief in a just world (Lerner, 1980), could encourage a sense of control or safety (Janoff-Bulman, 1979, 1982; McCann & Pearlman, 1990), and could confer meaning on a previously meaningless event (Taylor, Lichtman, & Wood, 1984). Similarly, other-blame has been associated with poor outcomes in a diverse set of samples (Janoff-Bulman & Wortman, 1977; Schulz & Decker, 1985; Tennen et al., 1986).

Although the question is not settled, most empirical re-

Exhibit 5.1

The Abuse Dichotomy

1. I am being hurt, emotionally or physically, by a parent or other trusted adult.
2. Based on how I think about the world thus far, this injury can only be due to one of two things: Either I am bad or my parent is (the abuse dichotomy).
3. I have been taught by other adults, either at home or in school, that parents are always right, and always do things for your own good. (Any other alternative is very frightening.) When they occasionally hurt you, it is for your own good, because you have been bad. This is called punishment.
4. Therefore, it must be my fault that I am being hurt, just as my parent says. This must be punishment. I must deserve this.
5. Therefore, I am as bad as whatever is done to me (the punishment must fit the crime: Anything else suggests parental badness, which I have rejected). I am bad because I have been hurt. I have been hurt because I am bad.
6. I am hurt quite often, and/or quite deeply, therefore I must be very bad.

From *Child Abuse Trauma* (p. 28), by J. Briere, 1992, Newbury Park, CA: Sage. Copyright 1992 by Sage. Reprinted with permission of Sage Publications, Inc.

search (including our own: Dalenberg & Jacobs [1994]) makes a case for the differential operation and outcome of behavioral and characterological self- and other-blame. Thus we argue that many therapists tend to press countertransferentially toward other-blame, staying within the characterological column of Table 5.1 (moving down). Both client and therapist might be better served, however, if they fought to move from dispositional to situational (moving from right to left within Table 5.1). If the client develops a dispositional style of allocating blame which, I have argued earlier, could be a bias of the therapeutic literature, the situation will feel less modifiable than if behavioral attributions of cause are made.

Other-blame is also a seductive concept for victims

Table 5.1

Theoretical Model: Effects of Self- and Other-Blame for Trauma

	Dispositional	Situational
Self-blame	Prototypical statement: "I was a difficult child." Associated symptoms: Depression* Self-destructiveness	Prototypical statement: "I was careless that day." Associated symptoms: Excessive self-examination or behavior change
Other-blame	Prototypical statement: "My parent was mean." Associated symptoms: Pervasive anger* Externality* Depression*	Prototypical statement: "My parent was under great stress that day." Associated symptoms: Anxiety

Note. *Relationships tested and confirmed. From "Attributional Analyses of Child Sexual Abuse Episodes: Empirical and Clinical Issues," by C. Dalenberg and D. Jacobs, 1994, *Journal of Child Sexual Abuse, 3,* p. 44. Copyright 1994 by The Haworth Press. Reprinted with permission from the Haworth Press.

who long for absolution. In a surprising number of cases in both the Trauma Countertransference Study and an earlier study of transcripts of intern-conducted trauma therapy, a pattern of interaction developed that I call the *blame boomerang*. As summarized in Exhibit 5.2, this transference–countertransference interaction follows a fairly predictable pattern.

Initially, the client presents with pervasive self-blame. Both therapist and client feel despair and shame at this outcome of the trauma, and the anger of the therapist is expressed in other-blame. To be understanding, the therapist reminds the client that his or her hypervigilance, overreactivity, and avoidance behaviors are traumatic symptoms. These too were "caused" by the other. Often, the therapist's under-

Exhibit 5.2

The Blame Boomerang

1. The client presents with severe self-blame.
2. The therapist counters with other-blame.
3. The client, feeling supported by this stance, escalates other-blame in his or her external life.
4. The crisis:
   a. An extreme or self-endangering episode of other-blame.
   b. Other-blame turns toward the therapist.
5. The therapist has a strong countertransference response, typically anger or fear.
6. The therapist "confronts" the client about his or her failure to take responsibility.
7. The client feels betrayed.

standing also represents a haven for the client, especially if the client is a survivor of chronic trauma who has alienated and exhausted his or her own support systems. The therapist becomes the "life raft" in a sea of unsympathetic faces.

The idealization that occurs so predictably in this phase is hard for the therapist to resist. Having sat through verbal assaults from prior clients, the therapist might greet his or her idealizing client with relief and a sense of excitement. "If only my husband understood me the way you do," the client says gratefully. "Why won't my friends give me more time, more space, more understanding?" The therapist commiserates and basks a bit in the light of superior empathy and knowledge. Often it does seem to the clinician that the trauma client's support system has moved on too quickly and failed to give the victim the chance to display his or her rage and despair.

The destabilizing effect of early stages of therapy (and perhaps the recovery of memories) can have a negative effect on the victim's symptoms (Hedges et al., 1997), placing further stress on colleagues and personal supporters. The victim also could be increasing his or her disparaging comments about these supporters, asking them to behave more like the therapist. Both the negative comparisons and the seemingly harmful effect of therapy understandably lead some among the client's friends and relatives to question the therapist's skills and motives. Hearing this feedback, the therapist sees the support system as undermining therapy and is likely to respond defensively. The dyad easily moves into a more intense and reciprocally supporting relationship. Therapist and client assure each other that those in the client's life who question either person are not empathic, not knowledgeable about trauma effects, not aware, and not kind.

As the client continues to escalate other-blame, it is not unusual for a blame-allocation crisis to occur. The crisis for Sharon, a participant in the Trauma Countertransference Study, was feedback from her supervisor, who made what the therapist saw as reasonable demands for change in the workplace. Sharon exploded in anger, left work in a rage, and called for an emergency appointment with her therapist. The crisis for Marsha was an unexpected need for the therapist to cancel a session due to the death of one of his parents. Marsha accused her therapist of being like the rest of her support system, always deserting her at the moment of crisis. Gabe was caught by his wife when he was fondling their young babysitter. When he pleaded vulnerability to flirtation due to trauma-related self-esteem problems, his wife shouted obscenities at him and left their home.

All three clients went to their therapists expecting support, with Marsha also expecting an apology for the therapist's lack of compassion. According to the clients, all three therapists then took a strong confrontational stance. It is likely that the therapists treating Sharon and Gabe were worried about the consequences of the client's impulsive actions. Marsha's therapist, with whom I spoke, stated that he was angry with Marsha for her preoccupation with herself in the face of the therapist's loss. He felt he had "earned" better treatment from her, having rearranged his schedule many times for her convenience.

All three of these clients stayed in therapy. Two believed that the incidents recounted had harmed their relationship but were outweighed by other positive features of the treatment. The third, Sharon, presented this incident in the "turning point" section of the Trauma Countertransference Study, highlighting that both therapist and client came to understand their joint contribution to the client's reaction. Although all three patients initially felt betrayed, Sharon said that she no longer was upset about the episode.

The pattern illustrates the danger of the therapist's failure to balance self- and other-blame. Again, the cruelties with which fate (or a more personal villain) treats clients can leave trauma therapists understandably reluctant to add to clients' burdens. Interpretations, which naturally highlight the clients' own contributions to their difficulties, seem to distance client and therapist. Further, as Briere (1992) pointed out, because interpretations are by definition not yet part of the client's self-understanding, they often appear false and disconfirming—if not assaultive. This is no doubt one reason Winnicott (1968/1989) specifically cautioned against using interpretation in the midst of a client attack on the therapist. Therefore, as we think through our existing therapy relationships, we might consider whether countertransferential fear or anger leads us to confront excessively or to blame the client too strongly for a series of events. Alternatively, our countertransferential wish to protect and show compassion can lead to overreliance on other-blame. Breaking both therapist and client out of the abuse dichotomy ("either he is evil or I am evil"; Briere, 1996) is a fundamental goal for trauma therapy.

Negotiating the Shame–Blame Crisis

Because shame is often presented as contagious (Lewis, 1971; Livingston & Farber, 1996) and because there are so many opportunities for shame in trauma therapy, it should not be surprising to learn that shame was a major factor in most of the premature terminations among the clients surveyed in the Trauma Countertransference Study. Some were examples of the blame boomerang, and others were reactions to another perceived betrayal by the therapist that led to a breach in the sense of mutual respect.

A common reaction to shame for traumatized clients is "humiliated fury" (Livingston & Farber, 1996). In this case, rather than presenting despair and self-criticism, the client angrily attacks the therapist for creating the circumstances for shame—often through exposure of weakness or encouragement of dependency. In Livingston and Farber's (1996) research, in which taped clients were presented to therapists, self-admonishment and criticism (internally directed shame) brought reassurance from the clinicians. Humiliated fury was more likely to produce a confrontation reaction.

When anguish combines with a sense of utter worthlessness, the client is likely to lash out at the therapist, making exaggerated statements about blame. Fighting back, and particularly engaging in a debate over who is right (e.g., who is trying to manipulate and control whom), shame the client further. In the midst of the fury, however, one can hear in the client a wish to connect, to relocate the sense of mutual respect and real relationship.

Listen to Ms. M as she berates me below. She was a recent victim of rape and assault who also had a history of parental neglect and had witnessed parental violence and drug abuse. I had promised her that I would be available for a telephone call in the afternoon in my office if she needed me (after a police interview). Unfortunately for both of us, I then forgot to unplug my fax machine. She tried to call me for several hours and was unable to reach me.

> *Ms. M:* I can't believe you could be that cruel, so heartless. You knew I was going to call. This was so . . . not right for a doctor to do. I feel like you just betrayed me, you just threw me away, and I was nothing, nothing, like a piece of dirt, like I didn't matter. I needed you, I really needed you, and you were not even thinking of me. I don't know if this . . . I think I have to leave. I don't think I can even talk about this.

Kate, a participant in the Trauma Countertransference Study, also had such a crisis with her therapist, Dr. G. She had informed him that she was attending a public event at which he was to receive an award and make a speech about his methods of therapy. The therapist had said nothing, although he was not looking forward to this event or to his client's attendance. The week before the event, he told her that she could not attend, and that if she did, he would refuse to speak. She left in humiliation, and stayed away from therapy for several weeks, leaving tearful messages on his recorder about his betrayal. During this time, at the suggestion of her therapist, she visited a consultant, who suggested the compromise that the therapist record his speech for the client. Dr. G agreed to this but then left a message for Kate that he had changed his mind, stating that he did not believe that he could honor the request.

At the moment that I was listening to Ms. M, I had already had the opportunity to speak to both Kate and her therapist. Dr. G is a talented psychiatrist who suffers from some speech anxiety; he did not wish to aggravate this nervousness through allowing his patient's presence, but he had a great commitment to her welfare. Sadly, his indecision led him to seem uncaring to his client. His initial approach to the breach was to attempt to correct her misperception of him, asking her to trust their years of experience together as a source of information that he did care.

I learned from Kate, and from several others, that humiliation becomes the price for reconciliation in these circumstances. The client might feel that he or she must accept the therapist's statements that the client is "over-reacting," "seeking misery," or "engaging in repetition compulsion." Some clients return, apologize for their actions, and accept the interpretation. Others simply drop the subject and cede the argument implicitly to the therapist. Relieved, therapists commonly follow suit and do not bring up the subject again. A few clients are unable to overcome their sense of shame in their therapists' presence, and they drop out of treatment.

Kate and her therapist led me to examine my own anger at being misjudged and to consider putting it aside as a secondary issue—important to the therapy at a later date. Sigmund Freud repeatedly noted that interpretations—summaries of the client's contribution to the dilemma—must be offered in periods of positive transference. Thus, defensive use of interpretations should be avoided during the period of the patient's humiliated fury. Instead, the therapist is advised to self-examine and attempt to honestly apologize for his or her role in the matter without requesting a reciprocal apology. Rebuilding the interpersonal bridge (Kaufman, 1992) is the first priority.

I told Ms. M that she was right that my carelessness was cruel and deserved her anger. I told her that I might have been unwilling or unable to hear her on that day, just as she feared, but that it did not represent my overall commitment to her. I asked what I could do to show her that my apology was genuine. She replied that our relationship was forever damaged. I felt and showed sorrow then but did not tell her she was overresponding to the situation. Instead, I searched for ways that I could honor her needs and wishes ethically, mentioning the incident when I did so as a past that I had to overcome. Echoing many participants in the Trauma Countertransference Study, Ms. M eventually stated that it was the process of watching me take responsibility and communicating my care for her, rather than any specific action, that eventually healed the breach.

Summary

Conflicts over shame and blame are extremely likely in trauma therapy. Predispositions of trauma clients combine with shame-enhancing aspects of trauma therapy to maintain these symptoms and produce a more entrenched problem for the client.

Therapist shame is frequently denied, but it occurs for reasons akin to those that affect the client—shame over inadequacy in facing pain, shame at one's unacceptable feelings and limitations, and shame produced by an enhanced awareness of a harsh and cruel world.

Examining and highlighting situational causes for shame, differentiating accusatory shame and the shame of the just, and containing angry responses to the clients humiliated fury can help minimize the harmful consequences of shame-related countertransference.

6

Countertransference Responses to Repetition Compulsion

What can I give her,
what armor, invincible
sword or magic trick, when that year comes

How can I teach her
some way of being human
that won't destroy her.

(Atwood, 1987)

The above stanzas from Margaret Atwood's "Solstice poem" to her daughter touch on the anguish of caregivers for those they love and wish to protect, and suggest a recognition of human potential for self-destruction. Many forms of self-destruction, including self-mutilation and suicide, appear to be related to trauma history. The focus of this chapter is on countertransference precipitants to and reinforcers of these repetitions.

Bryant and Range (1997), for instance, found elevations on the Scale for Suicidal Ideation (Beck, Steer, & Ranieri, 1988) for those with severe sexual abuse or severe physical abuse (in comparison to those without physical or sexual abuse history). For those with a history of both physical and sexual abuse, the mean for suicidal ideation was almost two standard deviations higher than the mean for the no-abuse group. Multiple trauma appears generally to contribute to the severity and resistance to treatment of suicidality (Bayatpour,

Wells, & Holford, 1992; G. Brown & Anderson, 1991; Bryer, Nelson, Miller, & Krol, 1987). Similar patterns emerged for a Suicidal Behavior Scale (Linehan & Nielson, 1981).

Self-mutilation, defined by Walsh and Rosen (1988) as "deliberate, non-life-threatening, self-effected bodily harm or disfigurement of a socially unacceptable nature" (p. 10), also is commonly associated with trauma and abuse history. Briere and Gil's (1998) research linked severity, intensity, and number of self-mutilating behaviors to physical abuse, incest, and psychological abuse. Cutting and burning of the arms or legs appears to be the most common form of self-abuse.

Revictimization is another phenomenon often put in the category of self-endangerment. Here, the literature supports the enhanced likelihood of adult trauma in those who experienced truama as children (van der Kolk, 1989). Battered women, rape victims, and spouses of molesters all appear to be more likely to have childhood trauma histories than would be expected in the general population (Fromuth, 1986; Pettigew & Burcham, 1997; Weaver & Clum, 1996). Burgess, Hartman, and McCormack (1987) found more frequent illicit drug use, prostitution, delinquent or criminal behavior, and physical fights with friends and parents among sexually abused boys who had been involved in sex rings than they found in a matched control group. Although the trend is at times associated with the concept of masochism (pain in pursuit of pleasure) in older theoretical literature, masochism is rarely the focus of more recent work (cf. Caplan, 1987).

Finally, reenactment of trauma-related issues in therapy and in personal relationships is another common problematic theme. Again, the client engages in patterns that produce self-endangerment—this time endangerment of the stability of the client's support system. In some ways, this category of self-destructive behaviors enhances the likelihood of the others. By straining the empathy of the support system, a client is more likely to find himself or herself in an alienated and isolated position.

Suicide attempts, self-mutilation, hostile reenactments, and self-endangerment affect the therapist greatly, as we might expect. Pope and Tabachnick (1993) found that 80% of therapists of male clients and 50% of therapists of female clients at times felt so afraid (for a variety of reasons) of or for their clients that it affected the therapists' sleeping or eating. Attempting a relationship with someone whose attitudes toward authority have been "deformed by the experience of terror" (Herman, 1992, p. 136) is frustrating and frightening, producing a type of helpless dread in the therapist that can lead to defensive avoidance of the client's material in thought either within or outside of the session. Finding our way through this experience with our clients is difficult, and much has been written on these related phenomena. Much of the research has used Sigmund Freud's theory of "repetition compulsion."

The Theoretical Concept of Repetition Compulsion

Repetition compulsion was described by Freud in his paper, "Beyond the Pleasure Principle" (S. Freud 1920/1955, p. 18):

> The patient cannot remember the whole of what is repressed in him, and what he cannot remember may be precisely the essential part of it. . . . He is obliged to *repeat* the repressed material as a contemporary experience instead of *remembering* it as something in the past.

Although Freud was writing in this passage about the repression of instinctual conflicts rather than actual trauma, it is normative today to speak of the repeating or reenacting trauma within the transference–countertransference field (Chu, 1991; van der Kolk, 1989). Therapists write of being thrust into roles (perpetrator, victim, rescuer) that are relevant to their clients' traumatic experiences as the therapists unwillingly participate in the reenactments (Briere, 1996; M. Davies & Frawley, 1994).

Following again the empirical finding that both theoretical knowledge and countertransference awareness mediate adequate countertransference management (Latts & Gelson,

1995; Robbins & Jolkovski, 1987), it is worth spending a bit of time attempting to understand why clients "repeat the trauma" in the external world and in the transference. There appear to be nine major explanations offered. Five of them are motivational:

□ the effort toward mastery
□ the seeking of punishment for imagined or actual crimes
□ a dissociated repetition to facilitate integration of the memories or make sense of the trauma
□ addiction to the arousal state
□ producing pain to facilitate the avoidance of trauma memories

Thus, the individual is consciously or unconsciously seeking mastery, absolution, integration, or arousal. Other explanations are nonmotivational—that responses to trauma might produce replication despite this end not being explicitly desired:

□ habit and learning of roles
□ response to conditioned stimuli
□ replication attributable to dissociation from internal and external warning signs
□ biologically based preferences for the known over the unknown in dangerous circumstances.

As we examine countertransference reactions to the phenomenon we label as repetition compulsion, it is important to acknowledge that the clinical literature typically underemphasizes nonmotivational explanations for repetition and self-endangerment while it overemphasizes motivational theories. This could arise from the well-documented likelihood for observers to blame the disposition rather than the situation for others' behavior (Jones & Nisbett, 1987). In two role plays before workshop audiences, when I asked the assembled clinicians why a client might feel compelled to self-mutilate, 84% of one audience and 72% of another offered either the self-punishment or the mastery explanation, often as a sole theory for the behavior. The clinicians often added (with a prompt about the goals of therapy) that treatment should offer "better" ways to deal with mastery, or that they would try to convince the client that he or she did not deserve such self-harming behaviors.

Countertransference Reactions to Motivated Repetition

It is plausible that the same self-endangering or repetitive behavior serves different functions for different people. In Briere and Gil's (1998) self-report sample, self-mutilating clients endorsed a variety of motivational explanations for their behavior. Seventy-one percent stated that the self-harm enhanced feelings of power and self-control over the body, supporting a mastery motive. A slightly larger group (83%) cited the conscious wish to self-punish or cause pain. (Participants could give more than one reason.) Most patients (80%) also believed that self-mutilation facilitated the avoidance of painful feelings, helped them manage stress (77%), or broke them out of their obsession with trauma-related memories (58%). Importantly, the majority (77%) felt a *decrease* in negative affect after the self-harming behaviors. The reporting of a sense of relief after the self-harm by 68% of the sample supports the "compulsion" concept.

At times the repetitive and ultimately damaging behavior is clearly related to an adaptive childhood response to trauma. Mr. J, for instance, came to see me about his "over-reaction" to criticism. In the initial interview, he told me terrifying stories of his psychotic father's effort to purge the devil's influence from his sons. The father began by outlining the accused's sins, then escalated to beatings, day-long prayer vigils spent in awkward and painful positions, and verbal lashings. Mr. J told me that he went to sleep in these periods with the helpless certainty that he would not survive the night. In constant search of a way to protect himself, he finally did discover a strategy that worked. When his father began to speak of the devil in a way that signaled that an episode was imminent, Mr. J learned to preempt his father by screaming out Bible verses until he was hoarse, pounding wildly on the furniture, and beating himself for his sins. As an adult, impending criticism brought on a rageful response that twice had led to jail time. He would not let the other individual speak, shouting and cursing the person into frightened silence. This extremely bright and talented man was employed in a field in which he needed to have little contact with other people, and fortunately, he seldom received poor evaluations.

Mr. J came to me with a very poor prognostic label attached to his chart. Apparently, more than one of his prior therapists eventually saw his behavior as repetition compulsion, wherein he either identified with and imitated his psychotic father or produced an enraged response in a more powerful other. His therapists believed that he was seeking mastery over the traumatic experiences as well as provoking punishment for the murderous feelings that he harbored toward his father.

Unfortunately, the implication that he was seeking the replication, even unconsciously, was noxious to Mr. J. Because the interpretations themselves felt like unbearable criticism, he had twice precipitously discontinued therapy—the second time after a mutually hostile exchange with the therapist that apparently was barely shy of a physical fight. The referral sheet referred to Mr. J as an "impossible" client who was "actively hostile" and who engaged in "constant efforts to suck [the therapist] into a battle."

The first relevant issue here is that the therapist's felt urge to react to a client in a given way does not mandate the existence of the client's overt or hidden wish that the therapist engage in this way. I agree with Mr. J's previous therapists that this pattern of behavior was repetitive and compulsive. I came to disagree that he was trying unconsciously to force his therapists (including me) into battle. Instead, it seemed that his behavior was his best effort to distract his critics and to prevent an even more dangerous confrontation. As I stated in chapter 2, I had to take responsibility for my own behavior and affect (i.e., that his behavior angered and frightened me) and acknowledge that I was *misreading* him, albeit in a way that would occur for many others: I was misreading his behavior as an attack rather understanding it as a defense. In parallel, I was hoping that he would come also to see me as less dangerous and acknowledge that he often misread me. Both of us would be facing difficult tasks.

More specifically, in Mr. J's past, mild criticism had been a sign of impending physical injury and psychic attack. Thus, in learning terms, criticism had become a discriminative stimulus. For me (and for many of us, I believe) being shouted at by a man who is pounding on furniture also is a discriminative stimulus of impending danger. The following is one episode of several similar ones that helped to break the cycle. Mr. J is referring to my statement that his negative reaction to my receptionist, who had not immediately informed me that Mr. J had arrived, was stronger than would be true for most people:

> *Mr. J:* I will not be abused by you. I will not pay for this. You hire incompetent little . . . [expletive deleted]. I am expected to just sit back and not play, play along. What is this? [Referring to a picture on my wall.] This is out of a cheap hotel. [Continues angrily for 9 minutes, without a break, standing, pacing, and punching at the wall and at various objects. Other than repeating his name, I do not say anything during this time.]
>
> *Therapist:* Sit. Sit. Mr. J, you are scaring me. You're being scary. Sit down.
>
> *Mr. J:* Look. I'm not dangerous.
>
> *Therapist:* I know. Well, this is really important. Sit down. [Sits.] Mr. J, you're not dangerous. You're not going to hurt me, but what you do makes me feel like you will. It's me now that I'm talking about. I feel scared.
>
> *Mr. J:* [You are] reading me wrong just like//
>
> *Therapist:* [Interrupting] Exactly, exactly. I am reading you wrong. You do something, and I think it means something it doesn't. I get scared, I start fighting back or trying to justify myself, and I make you more mad. You're not dangerous. But listen. I'm not that dangerous either.

You're doing exactly what I'm doing. You think my comment about [the receptionist] means something that I don't think I meant. Right?

Mr. J: Right. It was abusive.

Therapist: Let's hold off, just for a minute, on who's right. I'm willing to concede that you may be right. But look. I criticized you, and you reacted. Right so far?

Mr. J: OK. Right so far, but//

Therapist: Wait, just one minute. I promise. I know it felt bad. I know I did wrong. I didn't put it well. I criticized you, and you reacted. But I'm sitting here thinking, "He's got me wrong. I didn't mean to be mean. I'm not that bad." But then you start shouting and pounding things, and I get scared. And this time it's you that thinks, "She's got me wrong. I'm not that dangerous. I don't mean to be scary." It's really hard, this thing we're trying to do.

Mr. J: This thing we're trying to do?

Therapist: Trying to break free, to break free of automatically feeling something. You're not dangerous to me, OK? And I get in trouble with you by acting like you are. But I'm not so dangerous to you either. And you get in trouble protecting yourself from me.

Mr. J: I think I understand a bit.

One problem with verbatim transcripts is that they do so eloquently illustrate one's weaknesses as a therapist. I am interrupting this client, no doubt trying to move us toward cooperation more quickly to calm my fear. Nevertheless, I was trying to make the point then and to highlight it now that, to the extent that Mr. J could be labeled as "forcing" me to assume a role (by creating an "irresistible" transference prompt), I was placing him in exactly the same situation. My criticism also was "irresistible" to him. By acknowledging to Mr. J that my compelling sense that he would hurt me when he shouted and waved his fists could be wrong, I opened the possibility that some of his compelling emotional interpretations of my behavior also could be wrong. These inaccuracies are not the definition of "craziness," present only in the client. Rather, they are human failings that we all must struggle against. As Russell (1998, p. 9) wrote,

> The patient focuses on those aspects of us that in fact do recapture the past, real parts of ourselves that do, to some degree, prove their point. However odious, this aspect needs to be located in us, and for us to try to disown or disavow it, to ascribe it all to "transference," is to sever the patient's emotional connection with us. The only thing that works is negotiation, namely a negotiation around whether things have to happen the same way this time.

The literature on borderline personality disorder, a diagnosis highly associated with childhood trauma history (Murray, 1993; Perry, Herman, van der Kolk, & Hoke, 1990; Sabo, 1997), is particularly laden with examples of frustrated confrontations between therapists and clients over reenactments in therapy. In the classic example, the patient "overreacts" (as Mr. J did) to a perceived slight from the therapist. A variety of examples can be presented from published case histories. I have chosen the following from Masterson's (1983) unusual and important contribution, in which he offered detailed descriptions (through continuing dialogues with several supervisees) of the evolution of transference and countertransference throughout analytic therapy. The client in the excerpt was a victim of paternal beatings who had recently experienced two of the more frightening symptoms that often co-occur with therapeutic confrontation of the past in those with diagnoses of borderline personality disorder. First, she was feeling increasingly frightened by the feeling of connection with the therapist, aware that closeness implied danger. Second, she had experienced the emergence of vivid images of her father's presence, along with a sense that her father's ghost was trying to engineer her suicide. Her therapist tried to solidify her reality-testing and to persuade her to continue in therapy:

Therapist C: The next day she came in with a small painting for me. When she handed it to me, I asked her what
it meant. She said that it was for me. I repeated, "Come
on now, why are you bringing me this?" I have represented everything from a bitch to a devil, an angel, a
good mother, and I thought we both needed to know
what had motivated her to offer me this painting.

She looked at me, picked up her coat and pocketbook
and stormed out of my office into her car, where she
stayed closeted for about a half hour. I then heard the
front door open. She had left a note stating that she had
been trying to do something nice, but that now she felt
rejected and hurt. She had wanted to make contact with
me by sharing the painting, but maybe we aren't meant
to have this.

Dr. Masterson: . . . You should acknowledge to her that
the painting was an effort to move closer, despite her
trouble, and that she felt rejected by your comment. You
should correct this with: "My effort to understand why
you wish to do this is not a rejection, etc." . . . She cannot
distinguish between feelings and reality, which is a con-
dition for this kind of treatment (Masterson, 1983, pp.
251–253).

Authors of anecdotes such as this typically are making several related points. First, traumatized patients in general, and
clients with borderline personality disorder in particular, are
likely to have episodes of misdirected rage. Second, the therapist's offering of benign reasons for therapist behavior that
might shame the client is crucial. Third, the reenactments
center on the client's inability to distinguish emotionally between reality and perception. The therapist thus wishes (a)
to attempt to stay out of the escalation of hostilities so that
a more thoughtful and evaluative relationship can be rein-
stated, (b) to react to the behaviors without shaming the client, and (c) to aid the client in the task of discriminating
between the past and the present.

On the last point, a simple declaration by the therapist is
unlikely to convince the client that the therapist differs from
other authority figures. I would not have told Therapist C's

client above that "my effort to understand you is not rejection," because "rejection" is not a simple function of the therapist's intent. As Therapist C began to be a true presence in the client's emotional world, he simultaneously began to fuse with key players in the client's past within her mind. She treated the therapist accordingly and interpreted his behaviors as the behaviors of these important others might have been appropriately interpreted. Certain of the client's behaviors "called forth" hostility or rejection from the therapist, because the client expected and attempted to prevent the rejecting behavior. It is upsetting and dissonant with therapist self-image to be treated as a hostile agent; sadly, it also is likely to produce occasional hostile rejections of the client as an effort to reject the client's image of the clinician. Such hostility commonly takes the form of shaming the client for his or her overreactions and misinterpretations of the innocent therapist. This might have been what happened to Lisa, a participant in the Trauma Countertransference Study:

> *Interviewer:* Was there ever a time that you felt your therapist was ashamed of you?
>
> *Lisa:* Oh yes, once when she canceled, she had to cancel. I called her on her machine, and I really did go overboard. I really did. And she was just disgusted with me. "When will you ever act like a normal person?" "Why do you have to be so dramatic?"

To short-circuit the shameful reaction of Mr. J, the client I presented earlier in this chapter, as he reacted to his "overreaction" and my own, I spoke to him about analogous individual differences between people. He agreed that my friend, who has an allergic reaction to bee stings that could lead to death, is not "overreacting" by taking extreme precautions in the presence of bees. Nor was my neighbor's child "overreacting" when she recoiled from her parents' touch while she was recovering from a painful sunburn. To say that criticism (or a bee sting, or a touch) is "no big deal" and that it should be tolerated by the client ignores the presence of the psychic allergy or sunburn.

It is important that the therapist not join the client in over-estimating the degree of conscious control over emotional evaluation and reaction. Changing an affective conditional response is work, and it typically involves "dosing" the patient with affective experience in a graduated way (Courtois, 1988). There are good biological and developmental reasons for development of the human organism in a way that produces fear in the presence of a benign feature related to impending life threat.

The therapist's countertransferential fear and disgust over client self-endangerment and self-mutilation can produce pompous and unhelpful statements about what is "best" for the client. The message that the therapist knows, without investigating, that the client's behavior is ill-chosen is the antithesis of the message championed by Briere (1992) in his descriptions of trauma therapy. "The solutions you've found for the fear, emptiness, and memories you carry represent the best you could do in the face of the [trauma] you experienced," he wrote to a hypothetical client (p. 83). Such an approach does not shame the client for his or her choice.

The clinician does try, of course, to avoid falling blindly into the repetitious interaction with the client that constitutes this particular person's primary problem in human relationships. One can respect the client's choices, admitting that this solution might be the best the client could fathom, and continue to reach for an alternative with less pernicious side effects. One also can recognize that behavior of this emotional significance calls out for motivational explanation when none might be applicable.

Countertransference Reactions to Nonmotivated Repetition

There often is no need to "explain" repetition of noxious interaction. As analyst Paul Russell (1998) has remarked, "our repetitions are what we are" (p. 1). As he pointed out, life is repetition, from cell division to the learning of multiplication tables. It is no more surprising that we repeat our trauma-related behavior than that we repeat our grammatical mistakes, drive our cars in a characteristic manner, or walk day-to-day with a similar gait. The counterargument that these latter analogies are not self-destructive stumbles over the realization that trauma-related behavior also was not necessarily self-destructive in its former context. Changes in the rules of the client's social world can turn self-protection into self-endangerment, just as someone obeying the traffic laws of the United States could surely precipitate an accident in Great Britain.

Reenactments and revictimization can occur without the client's motivation or compulsion to repeat. An interesting example of this phenomenon in our laboratory was offered within a dissertation by Dr. Stacy Hoyt (1998). Hoyt showed a film to female clients with and without an adult or child trauma history. In the film, a female actress engaged in increasingly self-endangering behavior, culminating in a scene that suggested that rape by one or more men was imminent. At several points within the scenario, the female character turned to the camera and asked her friend (the study participant) to tell her what to do. Participants commented into a tape recorder or in writing, and then they rated their own emotions and their perceptions of danger in the environment to that point in the story. We were interested to find that the women did uniformly see the elements that we would consider danger signs. However, the trauma subgroup did not feel the emotions (or at least, did not report feeling them) that would have triggered self-protective behaviors. Perhaps because of their dissociation, the participants felt mild excitement at early signs of danger rather than fear and anger.

Another series of studies in our laboratory yielded powerful support for the hypothesis that dissociation mediates repetition. In the Participant-as-Teacher series, the study participant is to "teach" an unseen "child" to spell through an interactive computer program. Varying experimental manipulations were used to examine the willingness of the individual to punish the "child" with white noise for the child's provocative behavior (such as swearing at the "teacher" online). In the three studies using this paradigm conducted to date (Aransky 1996; Eldeam, 1998; Stammen, 1999), those with a childhood trauma history tended to act out against the "child" only if they had received high scores on a dissociation inventory. The participants who engaged in this generational repetition were those who did remember at least fragments of their abuse history but claimed to feel no conscious anger.

Dissociation can operate in several ways to facilitate repetition. It can block awareness of emotions that would otherwise hamper self-harm or other-harm, such as fear or shame. Dissociation also may block awareness of other-destructive emotions, thus eliminating the opportunity to soothe or otherwise address them. This implies that the trauma therapist must target dissociation for treatment, a topic beyond the scope of this text (see Briere, 1992, 1996; M. Davies & Frawley, 1994). Relevant to this discussion, the likelihood of dissociative symptoms accompanying compulsive repetition applies both to client and therapist. The dissociative therapist will more easily fall into compatible repetition cycles offered by the client, trading the role of sadistic attacker and innocent victim back and forth with the equally unwitting partner. Both therapist and client in these instances are likely to blame one another, claiming that each is compelled to action by the other's behavior.

Susan, another participant in the Trauma Countertransference Study, was another client who allowed me to talk to her therapist about her case. Susan has a borderline personality disorder diagnosis, has twice attempted suicide, and has three times been raped by strangers whom she met in bars. She saw her therapist for 12 years before the therapist terminated treatment because the therapist did not believe that Susan was making sufficient progress. Both Susan and the therapist (Dr. T) reported multiple instances over the 12 years in which they escalated to shouting at each other in session, typically ending in Susan leaving the session early.

Interviewer: So Susan reports that you and she had some angry moments.

Dr. T: Yes, she can really make me lose it. I admit that.

Interviewer: Why do you think that is?

Dr. T: You know borderlines. I kept it up for 12 years, and I just couldn't do it anymore. She was in constant crisis for 12 years, calling me at all hours, dragging me to hospitals and police stations.

Interviewer: Yes, I know. Could you go back to losing it, though? When did you find yourself getting angry?

Dr. T: When she would say, after she kept me up all night, that I didn't care about her. It was as if I had to shout at her to show her I cared about her. I really believe that. I would finally say something like "Shut up, [Name]. You know perfectly well that I care about you. Stop wasting my time."

Interviewer: Which part of that? . . . I hear two mechanisms there. One is that you were probably tired and stressed, and the other is the content of the charge, that you didn't care. Which one do you think was more important? Which one led you to lose it?

Dr. T: That I didn't care.

Interviewer: You don't have to answer this. It's a little intrusive, but I'm trying to understand these patterns better. I just wondered whether the pattern was an old one for you, too. Does the request to prove you care ring any bells for you?

Dr. T: Oh, good question. I hadn't really thought about that one. I had a mother who was forever telling me that I didn't prove to her enough that I cared about her. I didn't buy her an expensive enough birthday present—you know the drill. That's interesting. I hadn't thought of that connection.

The therapeutic dyad above had met for 12 years. Dozens of times this talented therapist, sophisticated in her understanding of psychoanalysis, had raged against her client for the client's lack of acceptance of care. Dozens of times the patient had repeated her self-endangerment, claiming that the therapist's offers of care were insufficient or ingenuine or that she needed the repetition of the therapist's statements.

With increasing resentment, Dr. T continued to offer the client the requested statements, silently signaling her mixed emotions. With increasing suspicion, Susan questioned the sincerity of Dr. T's statements, feeling and misinterpreting the presence of her resentment. The denouement of this relationship occurred when Dr. T was forced to cancel several sessions in a row, and Susan felt that Dr. T's claims of inflexibility in her schedule were exaggerated. Susan broke a vase and cut her wrists superficially, leading to another call from the hospital to Dr. T. Dr. T came to the hospital and told her patient that she could no longer work with her.

There is no real substitute for the presence of another compassionate person (e.g., a consultant) in sorting out these patterns. However, I offer the following set of questions for the therapist to use in self-evaluation of the countertransferential component to a repeated interpersonal dynamic in therapy.

Self-Evaluation of Therapeutic Repetitions

I have found the set of questions below helpful myself and for my students in analyzing repeated client–therapist interactions that could represent repetition compulsion on the part of the client, the therapist, or both. The questions are designed to target the therapist's role in the repetitions.

What Sets Off the Repetitions?

- Does the client behavior that is repeated appear to be instigated directly by a therapist behavior, or is it independent of therapist behavior?
- In what way might the therapist affect the power or frequency of the instigation of the repetition?

If the client repetition appears to the therapist to be independent of therapist behavior, it is worth speaking to the client during a positive period in therapy about the client's perception. At times, the client will state that the behavior is indeed related to therapist actions, even though this position had not been disclosed earlier.

When participants in the Trauma Countertransference Study tied their self-destructive actions to therapist behaviors, by far the most common perceived instigator was therapist "coldness." Clients feared that they had "worn out their welcome," which might have been partially true (see chapter 8). Unfortunately, the repetitive behavioral response to coldness typically backfired in the long run, further alienating the therapist. Other common therapist behaviors related to self-destructive client repetition (limited in this study by the client's ability to consciously notice the therapist behaviors) were perceived criticism, idiosyncratic likeness in behavior to that of the perpetrator of the trauma, and symbolic or real abandonments.

If the behavior is therapist related, the therapist might ask the client, again during a nonvolatile period, what he or she might do to make the client's reactivity less strong. For instance, the therapist might unknowingly be giving too little warning for vacations or treating his or her absences too casually. Such behavior can be taken by the patient as a sign that the therapist is uninvolved. If neither therapist nor patient believe that the repetition is triggered by therapist behavior, the patient still can be asked about what types of behaviors might be more useful for the therapist to employ to prevent the dynamic from unfolding or to minimize damage as it unfolds.

What Reinforces or Maintains the Repetition?

☐ In the first stage of the repetition, when the client engages in the self-endangering or relationship-endangering behavior, what does the therapist feel?

☐ Is the therapist's response after the client's initial "provocative" behavior a reinforcement of that behavior?

The therapist may feel frightened, angry, incompetent, ashamed, or alienated from the patient at the time of the reenactment. Interventions that flow from these feeling states could be in keeping with the therapist's overall philosophy, or they could be self-evaluated as mistakes. If the interventions appear to be mistakes, perhaps generated by the urgency of the therapist's feelings, the focus of the self-evaluation should be on methods of reducing the strength of these feelings. This process can be accomplished jointly with the client.

Suicidal or physical self-endangerment, for instance, tends to produce either fear or alienation (which is at times a defense against fear) in the therapist. Both interfere with therapy progress. Several writers have recommended that therapists tell their clients that little progress is made when the therapist is terrified. Negotiations should include clear statements about what the clinician intends to do to protect the client in various circumstances.

Therapist anger also is a common response both to client self-endangerment and to client revictimization and reenactment within therapy. Here, self-evaluation should include examination of the flexibility of the therapist's boundaries. It is not uncommon for therapists to assure their clients that they wish to be called whenever suicidal impulses seem overwhelming but then to resent the client's dependence on such calls. It is crucial in trauma therapy not to promise a degree of availability or encourage a degree of dependency that is in fact beyond the therapist's capacity to deliver in the long term.

Furthermore, it is a paradox that the problems associated with repetition compulsion can involve both the therapist's reinforcement of a behavior and his or her lack of attention to it. Kate, a psychologist and client participant in the Trauma Countertransference Study, explains it well:

> *Interviewer:* Was there anything that your therapist did that made it more likely or less likely that you would engage in roulette [her label for placing herself in danger]?
>
> *Kate:* I would say that his compassion made it less likely. I wanted to see him again week to week.

Interviewer: Anything make it more likely?

Kate: It's hard to explain. There were times when I would just ache to feel this intensity from him. I needed his compassion, and usually got it. But sometimes I would think that if I was really in trouble, if I scared him—and myself, because the danger was quite real—then he would come closer. All of this is a lot more conscious now than it was then.

Interviewer: Did he come closer?

Kate: Periodically. Sometimes he did nothing, and I would feel totally abandoned, as if he didn't care at all. Other times he would really be so moving that it would reverberate in my mind, and I felt better for a while. But then I wanted that again, and it seemed like the only way to get it was to stay in pain. I very much respect my doctor, and he was helpful to me. With the roulette I made him part of it whether he wanted to be or not.

Discussions of the trauma client's great need for holding and the ambivalent reaction to it are ubiquitous in the trauma literature (Briere, 1992, 1996; Courtois, 1988; Davies & Frawley, 1994). Shamed by the magnitude of their need, it is not unusual for trauma clients to try to trick or force the therapist into more involvement. Self-endangerment is a reliable way to achieve this, in most cases, because few therapists will ignore a·suicidal client's call. Although the level of conscious awareness of this motive clearly varies, I was surprised to hear how often participants in the Trauma Countertransference Study stated that they were fully aware of their behavior and yet never honestly discussed it with their therapists. (Kate above was an exception.) Notice the parallels in Kate's treatment and that of Elizabeth below:

Interviewer: Was there anything that your therapist did that made it more likely or less likely that you would self-mutilate?

Elizabeth: I did it, I think, when I was frustrated, at the end of my rope. I felt a kind of push to do it, and then as soon as I did I would call her.

Interviewer: What did she do or say?

Elizabeth: She was angry at me, but she also got sort of gentler in the next session. She felt guilty about being a jerk on the phone. I sometimes took extra bandages to therapy because when I redid the bandages she would offer to help me. It was the only time she ever touched me.

Interviewer: That sounds like a powerful experience to me.

Elizabeth: It was.

Interviewer: Do you think you were ever thinking of that when you did the cutting in the first place?

Elizabeth: Oh, definitely. That wasn't the only reason, but I did . . . we had a rule that I was not to call her at home except during emergencies. So I sort of wanted emergencies for a while, until I had so many that she just gave up on me.

Elizabeth did not discuss with her therapist her conflicted sense of being punished and rewarded for the repetition. The escalation and bad feeling that grew between the two was one saddening outgrowth of that failure to communicate. The therapist can and should (in my view) share with the client his or her understanding that the process of therapy can exacerbate the client's regressive neediness (Gunderson, 1996). When and if this occurs in a client whose childhood caretakers were not immediately available to meet intense need, repetitive self-endangerment can occur in response to the overwhelming fear of aloneness. If countertransference fear and concern lead the therapist to increase the intensity of the connection after suicidal or self-endangering behavior (both understandable and potentially necessary), the reinforcing nature of this therapist behavior must be understood and negotiated without blaming the patient for "making" the therapist act.

How Might the Repetition Operate Within a Therapist Blind Spot?

- □ Is the feeling engendered by the client's initial behavior in the repetition reminiscent of a prior unresolved concern or a present concern on the part of the therapist?
- □ With whom can the therapist honestly discuss the client and his or her dynamics?

The therapist's emotional reaction to repetition compulsion tends to follow predictable patterns both in published case studies and in my own research. In general, the most frequently reported responses are (a) fear that the patient will be harmed or killed; (b) fear of the professional consequences of failure to control the client's self-destructive behavior; (c) anger at the patient for jeopardizing the therapist, the therapy relationship, and himself or herself; (d) panic, guilt, and turmoil over the patient's degree of involvement with the therapist; and (e) shame and felt incompetence. In general, therefore, it is worth the therapist's time to think through the following set of questions about the past:

- □ Did you ever live for a period in fear that a person important to you (particularly in childhood) would be harmed or killed?
- □ Is there someone in your past or current support system whom you believe was or is on a path of self-destruction?
- □ Did you ever come unexpectedly on the knowledge that a loved one had been engaging in self-destructive actions, particularly suicidal behaviors?
- □ Have you seen a colleague treated badly for failure to prevent a client's self-harm or self-destruction?
- □ Do you fear being manipulated by those who claim to love you? Have you been harmed by this behavior in the past? Or, alternatively, do you automatically doubt intense expressions of feeling toward you?
- □ Do you feel generally comfortable with the extent of your knowledge about self-endangerment in particular? Do you feel competent in general?

> ☐ Do you have a trusted colleague with whom you can discuss therapeutic concerns without shame?

Focusing on the last point, it is important that we believe the message that we send to our clients. That is, it is useful to have an "outsider" to help one think through a repetitious process. This could be a therapist, a colleague, a supervisor, or a peer support group. Periodic discussion with a valued supervisor or colleague is especially important for trauma therapists. If the therapist finds himself or herself ashamed to share the problem, this is probably the most reliable sign that such supervision or discussion should be sought.

I have at times found myself saddened and concerned at the degree to which psychotherapy is a private profession. In a related sense, I do not believe we have thought through adequately as a profession how we might teach students to use supervision well. As an example, because most graduate programs give students multiple supervisors, it could be useful to divorce supervision from evaluation for one supervisor–therapist pair per student. For this supervisor, bound by confidentiality to keep both the client's and the therapist's secrets (barring legally and ethically defined misconduct), the therapist's more personal concerns about countertransference can be shared. I note that, in the current structure, most students report that, for the most part, they do not share their shameful concerns about their competence with their supervisors. Instead, they make an effort to present themselves as thoroughly competent paractitioners.

Although I feel at risk of bullying the reader over a particular point, I would argue that access to consultation is critical to conducting effective trauma therapy. Participation in repetition compulsion is not avoidable in long-term therapy, nor in fact does one wish to completely avoid it. However, the failure to recognize one's own escalating participation in repetition compulsion within psychotherapy places the therapist in a dangerous position. Repetition that is unexamined can transform suddenly into a distortion of the therapist that can be fairly labeled as a psychotic version of the transference, in which the therapist truly becomes (rather than partially symbolizes) the perpetrator in the eyes of the client (Hedges et al., 1997). Therapy with this population cannot be conducted without risk, but the risk to client and therapist is minimized by continuous self-evaluation and openness to learning.

Countertransference Reactions to Traumatic Play

Lenore Terr's clinical and theoretical discussions (Terr, 1981, 1990a, 1991) have immeasurably increased our understanding of the nature and quality of traumatic play. The rigid, grim, and repetitive form of traumatic play alienates the therapist and at times frightens him or her. Terr (1990a) described children's repetitions of a traumatic kidnapping in the form of repeated burials and simulated kidnappings, as well as more dangerous simulations presented as "play." The obvious symbolic nature of the play almost shouts for interpretation by the therapist; the countertransference press that most student therapists have reported to me has been the urge to pull the child away from the deadly symbol by explaining to the child his or her effort to master. "I bet that boy is very frightened," a therapist I supervised said to her client as he was threatening one doll with another (in an exact replication of an event in which he had been injured). "He's being scared by the big boys, just like you were." "No," the boy replied. "He's not scared. And these are not like those big boys. They're just dolls."

Just as the therapist for adults can use the transference-countertransference matrix and the replications that occur within it to allow the client to rethink and master complex emotional dilemmas, the therapist for traumatized children can allow the play to serve the same function. This is more safely done, however, if the symbolic nature of the play is not interpreted. For instance, I have spent many fruitful hours discussing Hansel and Gretel's father (and why he left them in the woods) with neglected children, read the "Ugly Duckling" hundreds of times to rejected children, and raged against the Wicked Witch and empathized with the Little Mermaid's fears with abused children. Biting your tongue when obvious parallels arise ("I bet you felt just like the Little Mermaid when . . .") allows the child to freely discuss and process unacceptable and murderous feelings within the protection of play.

The therapist's countertransference in such situations is best contained by parallel play, in which the therapist allows the child to see, in as engaging a manner as possible, a form of play that is one step closer to life than is the child's current pattern. One example of the phases of such play is shown below, as Client A, a 6-year-old boy, works through repetitions of a car crash that permanently paralyzed both of his parents. We had up to this point repeatedly engaged in a play sequence in which we built a structure with blocks, hurtled our cars (each containing a doll) toward the structure (thus destroying it), rushed the dolls to the hospital, declared them dead, and rebuilt the block structure to begin again. Approximately three months into the therapy, in the "hospital," this sequence occurred:

> *Client A:* Now our guys are dead.
>
> *Therapist:* Wait, wait.
>
> *Client A:* What?
>
> *Therapist:* I think my guy's alive. I'm going to get a doctor.
>
> *Client A:* He's not alive. They're dead.
>
> *Therapist:* Your guy's dead, but my guy is just barely alive, but he might die. I'm going to get the life-saving equipment. [I rushed frantically about to retrieve and apply aid to my "patient."] I hope he'll live.
>
> *Client A:* OK, he can be a little bit alive.

I did not force life onto Client A's doll, but prayed for life for my own, resorting to as many interesting maneuvers to save him as I could cook up, playing off the minimal sparks of interest that at times occurred to guide my play. For the next months, my valiant efforts to save my figurine from death were always defeated, although he clung to life for a greater and greater proportion of the hour. Once my figurine's death was a perfunctory afterthought at the end of the session, I began modeling in the next sessions an increased emotion in my character, still allowing his character to play the more uninteresting early scenario.

Client A: Is your guy dead yet?

Therapist: No, my guy is going to make it. Oh, he is very mad and sad.

Client A: Why?

Therapist: Because the stupid car steering wheel broke. Stupid steering wheel.

Client A: My guy just died.

Therapist: Oh, no.

Client A: Did yours?

Therapist: No. He's just mad and sad. So I guess he will cry because your guy's dead. We better plan the funeral.

When Client A's character leaped into life again with me, he did so carrying immense magical and self-protective powers. Below is his rebirth:

Therapist: OK, so now they're in the hospital.

Client A: So in comes this doctor and gives us a pill.

Therapist: OK.

Client A: And then we are fine.

Therapist: We are?

Client A: And we can fly.

Therapist: We can?

The countertransference press I felt here was to join Client A in the safety of magic. However, just as the compassion naturally drawn from therapists by self-endangerment can reinforce repetition in adults, the shared relief from pain provided by fantasy can draw therapist and child client away from the more distressing real world and toward evasion and repetition.

The experimental literature on trauma treatment is convincing in its conclusions that the fear memory must be activated to make it available for modification (Foa, Steketee, & Rothbaum, 1989). Foa and her colleagues found, for instance, that positive results for exposure therapy are found only for those who showed a fearful countenance during treatment (Foa & Kozak, 1986; Foa, Riggs, Massie, & Yarczower, 1995). Working through the trauma in play or through creative acts can be highly effective, and it can heighten the creative skills (Terr, 1987, 1989, 1990b). However, trauma also appears to be one route to a dissociative, suggestible, and fantasy-prone adult style (Lynn, Pintar, & Rhue, 1997). Therefore, the clinician is urged to consider that this highly enjoyable resistance can still be resistance and that the therapist could be the only hold that the child has on a more reality-based interaction.

> *Therapist:* Ouch, my guy's hurt.
>
> *Client A:* He can't be hurt. He has the magic in him.
>
> *Therapist:* The magic's wearing off. It's temporary. You know, like in "Incredible Hulk." Do you watch that?
>
> *Client A:* Yeah.
>
> *Therapist:* So my guy can fly, but then suddenly he's like a regular guy again.
>
> *Client A:* The Incredible Hulk can't fly.
>
> *Therapist:* He gets big and strong though.
>
> *Client A:* And green.
>
> *Therapist:* He does. True. He gets big and strong and green, and then it wears off and he's that man again.
>
> *Client A:* "Don't make me angry. You wouldn't like me when I'm angry."

Therapist: Right. You sound just like him.

Client A: So your guy falls out of the sky because he can't fly.

Therapist: No, I don't want him to fall out of the sky from way up there. He has to land just in time and be a man again. Sometimes he's a man and sometimes he's a superhero, OK?

Client A: OK.

Therapist: OK.

Client A: My guy's crying.

Therapist: Oh, how come?

Client A: He fell out of the sky 'cause he's just a man again.

Although these phases of traumatic repetition in therapy are common, the grim and concrete repetition, tolerance of the therapist's play as the holder of hope, and magical avoidance of pain may alternate for a given child. Countertransference disclosure with children is often best expressed through play, as the therapist's play character is frightened, saddened, and angry at the events that he or she confronts. Expressing these emotions for the child can be a therapeutic mechanism, allowing modeling of affect, and a useful way to express the strong emotions that working with traumatized children can provoke. The day that Client A's character was hurt falling out of the sky, Client A cried for him, and so did I. The recordings of our play after this point reflect much less rigidity in character exchanges and more of the creative expression of trauma imagery.

Summary

The concept of repetition compulsion is the trauma therapist's theoretical equivalent to George Santanyana's (1905/1954) most famous line: Those who cannot remember their histories are condemned to repeat them. Repeating, however, need not mean wishing to repeat, either on a conscious or an unconscious level. Nonmotivated repetition, mediated through habit or conditioning, also can lead to unwanted repetitive outcomes. In discussing repetition compulsion and repetitions within the transference, I hope to have underlined Russell's (1998) point that the most important resistance in the treatment process is not the client's resistance, but the therapist's resistance to what the client is trying to express. The way out of self-endangering repetition is through the therapist's willingness to tolerate the client's rage, terror, disgust, hatred, and longing, while hanging onto and championing a more human and humanizing world.

7

Countertransference Responses to Anger and Perceived Manipulation

> I do not love thee, Doctor Fell,
> The reason why I cannot tell;
> But this alone I know full well,
> I do not love thee, Doctor Fell.
> —Thomas Brown

The majority of trauma specialists note that anger and hostility is a major problem in traumatized populations and a major counterreaction in trauma therapists. The National Vietnam Readjustment Study, for instance, found that 40% of combat veterans (sampled in the late 1980s in a nationwide epidemiological study) reported engaging in violent acts three or more times during the previous year (Shay, 1994). The number reporting one or more violent acts per month was five times higher in the combat sample than in the civilian control group. Briere, Woo, McRae, Foltz, and Sitzman (1997) found that childhood sexual abuse was significantly correlated to homicidal ideation, arrest, and violence against others. Similar results have been noted for victims of physical abuse and neglect (Egeland, 1989; George & Main, 1979; Reidy, 1977), an effect that appears in studies of very young abused children (Howes & Eldredge, 1985). Anger and rage appear in general to be major problems across traumatized populations (Adshead, 1994; Kendall-Tackett, Williams, &

Finkelhor, 1993), particularly among those whose trauma has involved physical mistreatment (Briere & Runtz, 1990).

As an introduction, it should be noted that the clearest countertransference pattern in the literature that is linked to patient hostility and anger is counterhostility. Therapist anger, hatred, and hostile response to clients form one of the two emotional reactions that gain most attention in the literature on countertransference and transference in trauma therapy (the other being love and sexual feelings). In some respects, the therapist's or client's hatred or anger are seen as more acceptable in the literature—less as a sign of a problem in the relationship—than are strong positive or sexual feelings in either individual (see chapter 8). Nevertheless, the therapist's anger is a problem from the perspective of the client, as participants in the Trauma Countertransference Study noted. Eighty-six percent stated that they experienced at least one instance in which the therapist directed angry responses to them that one or both members of the dyad later considered inappropriate. Thirty-eight percent stated that their therapists "lost control" at least once during therapy and engaged in a behavioral act of cruelty. A greater percentage (48%) stated that, although their therapists never acted out maliciously, the therapists did make comments to their clients that the therapists later reported regretting.

In the well-known Vanderbilt Psychotherapy Project (Strupp, 1980), a major predictor of poor outcome was a tendency for therapists to respond to client's verbal aggression and hostility with counterhostility. In fact, Strupp noted,

> We failed to encounter a single instance in which a difficult [client's] hostility and negativism were successfully confronted or resolved. Admittedly, this may be due to peculiarities of our therapist sample and the brevity of therapy; however, a more likely possibility is that therapists' negative responses to difficult patients are far more common and far more intractable than had been generally recognized.

Strupp noted that this "negative complementarity" was manifested by subtle hostile responses to the therapist to client provocations. Furthermore, he provided evidence that such interactions were measurable in the initial sessions of therapy. Hostile interactions between therapists and clients, even in experienced therapist populations, were predictive of poor long-term outcome.

This depressing conclusion is in part supported by the large number of papers on hatred, rage, anger, and violent feelings of therapists toward clients found in the literature on countertransference (L. Epstein, 1977, 1979; Lion & Pasternak, 1973; Nadelson, 1977; Poggi & Ganzarian 1983; Searles 1965, 1979; Spotnitz, 1976). Winnicott (1949) was among the first to argue that the client has an active need to be told of the therapist's "hateful" feelings, stating that such disclosure was necessary to establish the genuineness of the therapist's more positive feelings. He was also clear that disclosure might be necessary for the therapist to go on treating such a client. Changes in the therapist's responses once hostility is turned toward the clinician also have been recorded in the empirical literature (Berry, 1970; Gamsky & Farwell, 1966; Russell & Snyder, 1963). Most commonly, the responses include counterhostility and withdrawal.

L. Epstein (1977) outlined four reasons for disclosing anger or hatred to the client that parallel (in part) the arguments made here in chapter 2. First, agreeing with Winnicott (1949), Epstein stated that disclosure demonstrates the therapist's credibility and genuineness. Second, the therapist's countertransferential feelings are important sources of information for the client regarding his or her effect on other people. Third, disclosure of anger or hostility can diminish the client's guilt and paranoia by making apparent the actual (as opposed to fantasized) impact of his or her own behavior. Finally, such disclosures are thought to diminish the client's envy (and establish the therapist's humanity), because the client need not feel alone in his or her susceptibility to hostility.

Certainly we can simultaneously agree that these are reasonable arguments for anger disclosure and note that they can be used inappropriately to justify acting out of the therapist's annoyance, anger, and general sense of being martyred by the continuous strain of the relationship. The therapeutic environment itself in trauma treatment can provide many reasons for the therapist to feel anger at the patient apart from or in addition to more specific hostile provocations from the client. As a partial list to prompt further thought in the reader, several structural sources for anger might be considered.

Structural Sources for Countertransferential Anger

Although we often (and quite fairly) speak of therapy as depriving for the client, we less often note the deprivation experienced by the therapist within the hour. Traumatized clients can appear to be holding the therapy hostage with threats of incapacity to handle anger or distress in their therapist. Their expectation of tolerance seems at times (to the therapist) to be more fairly descriptive of saints than human practitioners. Compassion fatigue (Figley, 1995) results in part from the strain of inhibiting strong and pressing emotion. This fatigue often is manifested as irritability or hostile interpretation. An honest appraisal by Dr. O, the therapist to Michael (a participant in the Trauma Countertransference Study), is illustrative here:

> *Interviewer:* Did you ever get angry at Michael and later think it was not fair of you?
>
> *Dr. O:* Many times. Many times.
>
> *Interviewer:* Any themes?
>
> *Dr. O:* It was answering the first call, OK. Answering the second call, OK. And then answering the third call, not so OK. I just thought he would get a clue here that he was asking too much. I held onto my stress as long as I could, and then finally, when he called me in the middle of dinner twice in one week, I just had it. I told him off in session.

From the perspective of the participants in the Trauma Countertransference Study, trauma therapists (and perhaps all therapists) have a tendency both to hide their feelings from their clients and to blame the clients for failure to adequately assess and respect these feelings. Again, the structure of therapy, a situational factor, is transformed into a dispositional characteristic of the client by both parties, as therapists blame clients for not knowing when the clients are "asking too much."

Michael, Dr. O's patient whom she is describing above, told a story that gave a perspective that I heard often in the course of this research. Michael is a victim of physical abuse who had had a recent traumatic loss before therapy began. Below he describes the same incident that Dr. O reported:

> *Interviewer:* Was there ever a time that your therapist got angry at you for something that either one or both of you later thought wasn't your fault?
>
> *Michael:* Yes. There was one time, it took us a long time to get over really. There was one time that she really let me have it.
>
> *Interviewer:* What happened?
>
> *Michael:* This was at the very beginning, and I was, I suppose this is hard to believe . . . Let me start from the beginning. You see, I really had a hard time opening up, and then when I did, and she was pushing me to do it, I started calling and telling her my thoughts and my emotions, got me?
>
> *Interviewer:* Got you.
>
> *Michael:* I'm telling her this, and she is praising me for opening up, and I am starting to call her more and more, and then really suddenly, she says, "You are taking advantage of me, [Michael], and we have to reevaluate our relationship."
>
> *Interviewer:* That sounded like a quote.
>
> *Michael:* Oh, yeah. And you could have knocked me over

I was so surprised by the whole thing. I had barely gotten to the point where I could have called this thing a "relationship."

Interviewer: Sounds like she thought you were taking advantage, and you were completely surprised by that.

Michael: There was no warning, and suddenly she's pissed. I have to say, I still think she had no right.

The mechanism for this source of countertransference anger is the therapist's misjudgment of his or her own tolerance for a specific phase in patient dependency or disclosure. Very few therapists live well in a martyr role; they are thus well-advised not to offer a degree of extended care that is difficult to bear over time. (I remind the reader of the story of Atlas, who was tricked into carrying the world on his back forever by the sly companion who asked him to take over for a few moments.) My own approach to availability is spelled out in my informed consent document, a personalized statement that others are free to use as they wish. As can be seen, I prefer to avoid legalistic language in favor of a clear, understandable, compassionate and, I hope, even therapeutic message:

Availability: I am not a full-time clinician. I teach, travel, and testify, all of which consume blocks of time that lead me to be unavailable for periods during each week. If I plan to be out of town for more than a day, I will tell you about it even if it does not affect your appointment. If I am in town, I check my voice mail a few times each day. I will return your call.

I know that it is difficult to imagine at the beginning of therapy, but hopefully there will be a time that you will be bursting to tell me some new thought you have about what you are discovering about yourself. Your pain or your excitement or your pleasure at discovery may be so great that you will wish immediacy from me. It will feel like we need to talk *now*. This is part of the work, and it can be a great part, but from the beginning we need to negotiate it.

Keep me informed about what you need.

My purpose here, given my target population, is to signal from the beginning that our compromise on availability will be imperfect. Respecting and legitimizing the wish to speak immediately thus might be combined repeatedly with recognition of human limitations.

A related source for countertransferential anger that was noted by several of the clinicians whom I interviewed was the feeling of jealousy associated with the therapist's sense of being expected to serve as the all-giving parent figure. Several explosions between patient and therapist occurred after clients showed strong reactions to changes or inconveniences that therapists viewed as minor—a change in office location, a need to reschedule, the forced absence due to a death. The therapist's retaliatory fury—understandable on one level—appeared to be greater than the situation typically merited. In speaking to these therapists in depth, they repeatedly linked their anger to their sense of the unfairness of the relationship. "After all that time, I thought I deserved a little consideration," one therapist stated. "I had bent my schedule out of shape for her so many times, it just galled me that she could make such a big deal out of my doing it one time for myself," said another. "I could have shot her right then and there," said a third. "There's a limit to how much of my life I will give up to someone who does not [care] about what we are doing." The statements reduce to a very simple point. Therapy often does not feel emotionally fair to the therapist experientially. And it is not emotionally fair. This is one reason that financial compensation is required for the therapist's presence.

Trauma experts and analytic experts on treatment of difficult clients typically urge therapists to contain their anger, pointing out the harm that can be done by "dumping unmodified anxiety [or anger] back into the [client] before [the client] was ready to handle them" (Gabbard & Wilkinson, 1994, p. 77). Interpretation or confrontation can "force [the affect] back down the [client's] throat" (p. 77). Summit (1987, p. 7) wrote,

> The most minor failings from the therapist can trigger torrents of misplaced fury and fledgling righteousness

> [in the client]. The need to either apologize or to punish
> ignores the meaning of the primary betrayal. While the
> client has every right to enrage or provoke, the therapist
> must attenuate angry or hurt reactions into supportive,
> optimistic responses.

I believe that it is easy for the therapist to forget the confusion inherent in the enactment of the client role. On one level, the therapist typically emphasizes to the client the ways in which the relationship is not reciprocal. The therapist does not talk out his or her problems, does not disclose everything that is on his or her mind, and takes care not to burden the client. Clients often are assured that their anger, fear, and shame will be tolerated. On the other hand, as we self-examine, most of us discover certain hidden rules of required reciprocity that we expect from our clients. I will bend to your last-minute changes in schedule, as long as you are grateful for it. I will work to understand you, as long as I feel that you too are working to change. I will bear your anger, as long as you do not attack my competence, my commitment, my integrity. Each of these expectations of reciprocity is common in the world at large, and therapists often do not feel that it is necessary or therapeutic to discuss them with clients. However, leaving solely to the client the complex task of discovering when reciprocity is expected and when it is not is likely to produce (sooner or later) an instance of felt betrayal.

In managing this source of countertransference anger, I am urging therapists to consider the context of an instance of client failure to give reciprocal consideration to the therapist. Has the therapist been complicit in creating an environment in which reciprocal consideration is not typically offered? Is the therapist verbalizing to the client a lack of need for emotional reciprocity and then responding angrily when the client behaviorally accepts this offer?

Another source of countertransference anger is the therapist's frustration with the slow pace of trauma therapy. Effective short-term treatments of trauma are becoming more available to the well-read clinician (Echeburua, de Corral, Sarasua, & Zubizarreta, 1996; Foa & Rothbaum, 1998; Stein & Eisen, 1996). However, such treatments are less effective with the chronic client who presents with a complex history of childhood and adult trauma. Such clients often stubbornly resist our most compelling enticements toward change, leaving us feeling not only impotent but at times even invisible. Ms. K, for instance, the daughter of a wealthy and abusive alcoholic couple, would tell me that she found my words life-changing, inspiring, and compassionate. How lucky she was, she told me in Session 9, that she had met me after years of working with ineffective and incompetent professionals. Happy that my point (a suggestion of a change in her behavior) had been so well taken, I suggested in Session 10 that we go back to the issue and explore further how she could pursue self-change. She said, "Oh, I have been thinking about that. You really have me wrong on that score. I mean, I realize that you don't know me all that well yet, but that was just really off base."

Session discontinuity of this type, characteristic of dissociative clients, can frustrate and shame the therapist. Not only have we failed to "cure," but we have been misled or seduced by the client's response into overestimating therapeutic change. As noted in chapter 5, shame can easily transform into anger.

The process of interpretation within psychotherapy is another structural source for transference and countertransference anger. Goethe wrote in *Sprüche in Prosa*, "Die Mängel erkennt nur der Lieblose; deshalb, um sie einzusehen, muss man auch lieblow werden, aber nicht mehr als hierzu nötig ist." ["Only the unkind recognize deficiencies; therefore, in order to understand them, one must also become unkind, but not more than necessary" (cited in Racker, 1968, p. 33)]. Structurally, it is important to remember that interpretation and confrontation are unkind by the standards of normal interpersonal exchange, and sometimes these crucial statements are offered in a way that is more unkind than necessary.

Structural Sources for Countertransference Anger in Short-Term vs. Long-Term Therapy

In part, the job of the therapist is to provide expert assistance in symptom management and relief, for example, by providing an environment for controlled reexposure to the traumatic stimuli and encouraging and facilitating the effective use of this environment. Use of more short-term strategies elicits anger in the client most commonly through the client's belief that the therapist is treating too casually the client's fear of revisiting the trauma. The therapist's corresponding anger is most often linked to the clinician's belief that he or she is being attacked for doing a difficult job well.

Judith, for instance, participated in a research study in which she was given 10 sessions of therapy based on a controlled-exposure theory. In her interview for the Trauma Countertransference Study, Judith told me that she felt that the therapist did not warn her about the depth of feeling that would accompany the reexposure. She felt "pushed" into participation. It is important to note that Judith apparently benefited greatly from the therapy, as evidenced by her report that her symptoms of posttraumatic stress disorder diminished markedly. However, upon completion, she wrote an excoriating attack on the therapist to the researcher in charge of the project, citing a lack of compassion. The therapist then called her, and again by patient report chastised her for her ingratitude and personality failings. Judith's fury in repeating this story to me vacillated greatly, at times replaced with a self-mocking monologue about her lack of ability to sustain relationships.

In longer-term therapy, symptom relief is typically a less central theme. Instead, more complicated patterns of self-destruction and alienation from others are targeted, most commonly through interpretation and confrontation. The goal here is to increase client self-knowledge and conscious self-control through interpretation and rational discussion; i.e., "where id was there ego shall be" (S. Freud, 1930/1961, p. 73). Of course interpretations are rarely flattering to their recipients, and they are understandably resisted. The content of the most significant interpretations is uncomfortably close to the substance of the critiques thrown in the client's face by others. Albeit with the trappings and jargon of the trade, we agree with one client's girlfriend that the client fears commitment, with another's husband that the client is self-absorbed, and with another's colleagues that the client is uncooperative in the workplace. The importance of giving such interpretation tentatively rather than authoritatively (Steingart, 1995) has already been mentioned. The point here is that we often struggle to build a gift of enhanced understanding out of the fragments of history that we are given, together with information deduced from the transference, only to have that gift crushed or treated with disdain.

A useful method that I have found to offer interpretation in a manner that prevents my acting out countertransference anger is a change in phrasing from the classic interpretation format. Ms. G, for instance, had been neglected as a child and had come to therapy after a race-related crime. She had been out on a date with her fiancé, a light-skinned biracial man who was perceived to be white by a gang of white thugs. The attackers separated my African American patient and her date, taunting and frightening them both with racial epithets and explicit obscene threats of violence. My client's fiancé allowed the group to assume that he was white, fearing more violent retaliation. The two later married, but Ms. G had been unable to forget the incident (in which she felt that her fiancé had failed to protect her).

In speaking with Ms. G, I learned that her husband felt that she was angry and withdrawn. My patient denied this, and claimed to be reacting to accusations by her husband that were based on his guilt. As I began to feel her anger and dismissal within the transference and felt the seeds of countertransference retaliatory withdrawal, I told her about it. Rather than tell her that I believed that she was pulling away from me, however, I told her that I thought I too experienced what her husband had misunderstood to be rejection. True, I felt that Ms. G was pulling away, but I also believed her when she stated that this was not her conscious wish, a statement supported by her behavior in remaining in therapy and in her marriage.

By offering negatively toned interpretations in the context of misunderstandings, I attempted to affirm Ms. G's surface understanding of herself while providing an interpretation that might have had greater depth. It has been my experience that this framework accurately depicts the phenomenology of the client; that is, the experience of being previously empathically misunderstood by loved ones. Acknowledging that misunderstanding from the start, I presented the dilemma to the client as centering on discovery of what I might have been seeing that led me to this misunderstanding, agreeing from the start that both of us wished to have me to see her more accurately and more as she wished to be seen.

This effort is in keeping with the general analytic recommendation to monitor "distance from the surface" in an interpretation (Glover, 1955; Levy & Inderbitzin, 1990; Loewenstein, 1951, 1954) and to interpret from surface to depth. I also believe that it is fundamentally true that I often misunderstand the client at one level when I react only to the client's anger and rejection and not to the client's terror.

Countertransferential Anger Stemming from Perceived Patient Manipulation and Adversariality

The difficult client (most commonly, the client with a diagnosis of borderline personality disorder) is now often presented as "needing" the therapist's anger. Gabbard and Wilkinson's (1994) valuable text contains the following analysis (pp. 237–238):

> One study of the therapeutic alliance in the psychotherapy of borderline patients (Frank, 1992) indicated that certain hostile reactions by the therapist may even help the patient work more effectively in therapy. In studying the first 6 months of psychotherapy with borderline pa-

tients, Frank found an unexpected correlation between therapists' perceptions that they were making negative contributions to the therapeutic alliance and symptomatic improvement in the patient. Frank reflected on some of the therapists' behaviors, including the therapist's being overly active and directive; exclusively pursuing his/her own agenda in the session; being critical of the patient; displaying intolerance of the patient's need to perpetuate problems; and conveying disappointment, annoyance, or frustration because the patient was not making sufficient progress. For some patients, these actions may indeed impede the formation of a good alliance and have a negative impact on outcome. For hospitalized borderline patients, these same interventions may be just what is needed to limit regressions, anchor the patients in reality, make maladaptive behaviors ungratifying, and otherwise enable a solid alliance to evolve and structural change to occur.

The foregoing may well be an example of a causal misinterpretation of a correlational result. Gabbard and Wilkinson (1994) argued that the unexpected correlation between the therapist's sense of making negative contributions to the therapy and the client's symptomatic improvement were the results of the positive value of conveying annoyance, disappointment, or intolerance to the client in appropriate instances. This could be the case, but it is also plausible that therapists' awareness of these contributions—present to some extent in virtually all such therapies—and perhaps their subsequent taking of responsibility for their contributions is the ameliorative factor here. Thus, it is not the presence of therapist anger that is corrective, in my view, but the opportunity to experience anger within connection, that is, to have the experience of another human being who is willing to care despite his or her anger and to negotiate a better relationship.

For trauma clients in general and for child abuse victims in particular, anger can be so threatening that therapist annoyance is immediately met reactively. The client may immediately change his or her behavior (at least superficially), or might avoid the situation or refuse to discuss the incident —reactions that might initially seem positive to the therapist. Alternatively, clients might take control of the situation by dismissing the therapist's anger or matching it and escalating the hostilities. If the therapist can model anger within connection, the client could learn that relationships that contain but that are not ruled by hostility are possible.

The traumatized client's retreat from anger and distrust in the relationship combine to produce a pattern recognizable to any trauma therapist. John Briere (1992) called the pattern *trauma-induced adversariality*:

> By virtue of childhood experience, former abuse victims tend to assume that the world is a hostile environment, where nothing is inherently deserved and thus nothing is ever freely given. From this perspective, the survivor may conclude that the only way to gain needed things or resources is to trade other things for them, or to trick someone into providing them. . . . The child who discovers that servile attention to his or her abuser's various needs can forestall impending violence or elicit rare praise or affection is likely to conclude that powerful ones should be groomed and catered to, in exchange for love or forestalled abandonment. (pp. 54–55)

The potential for countertransference explosion is so high in the case of a highly manipulative or distrustful client that discussion of the issue is critical to therapeutic success. Whether this discussion is initiated through interpretation (Kernberg, 1975), confrontation (Gabbard & Wilkinson, 1994; Masterson, 1983), or education and countertransference disclosure, most authors agree that it should be a discussion topic of well-conducted trauma therapy (Briere, 1992, 1996; Courtois, 1988; M. Davies & Frawley, 1994).

This discussion should include a chance for the therapist to help the client give words to the depth of his or her anger and the profound terror associated with it. I have at times given to clients a list describing the "berserk state," a rage reaction associated with war experience as articulated by

Shay (1994). Below is Shay's list, taken from his volume on treatment of Vietnam veterans (p. 82). The list helps both client and therapist avoid minimizing the client's anger.

- □ beastlike
- □ godlike
- □ socially disconnected
- □ crazy, mad, insane
- □ enraged
- □ cruel, with restraint or discrimination
- □ insatiable
- □ devoid of fear
- □ inattentive to own safety
- □ distractible
- □ indiscriminate
- □ reckless, feeling invulnerable
- □ exalted, intoxicated, frenzied
- □ cold, indifferent
- □ insensible to pain
- □ suspicious of friends.

Participants in the Trauma Countertransference Study at times complained that their therapists encouraged anger in therapy without realizing the power and sense of loss of control with which anger is associated. When anger at the therapist is finally expressed by the client who is beginning to feel safe, the therapist can be unprepared for the lack of reason and control. Aaron, a participant who had lost his entire family in a traumatic accident, stated,

> [The therapist] said, go ahead, be angry with me. I can take it. And I thought "Oh yeah, you can take it if I break everything in your office. You can take it if I rip your heart out. You can take it if I explode."

In general, traumatized patients need to be aware both that their strategy is off-putting and that their therapists understand the source of this behavior and are working to counter their own reactivity to it. The therapist's anger at perceived manipulation is an expression of humanity and involvement as well as insensitivity and rejection, at times in equal measure. Expressing this complex set of emotional reactions in toto is the task of effective countertransference anger disclosure.

The antithesis of effective countertransference anger disclosure is therapist countermanipulation. In the interviews conducted in the Trauma Countertransference Study, the most common pattern of countermanipulation was a form of withdrawal. Here, therapists punished their manipulative clients by withholding normal social connections. The conscious rationale, interestingly, might be to "refuse to be manipulated."

Susan, for instance, a victim of traumatic loss and multiple childhood trauma, would frequently call her therapist and cancel when her therapist had been slightly less intimately connected to her during the previous hour. The tearful messages implied that the client might not return to therapy and that it was the fault of the therapist. Dr. T remembers one message as, "I won't be coming in to therapy Thursday. I guess that will please you. I'm sure you agree that it does not seem worth it. Have a nice life. I know I won't."

Susan recognized that the form of her messages was often cruel and dismissive, but Dr. T came to realize only during our discussions that her response (or nonresponse) also might be seen as cruel and dismissive. Dr. T stated that it was her personal policy to try to reschedule if a client called and canceled a session and that she knew that Susan was waiting by the telephone for her return call. Failure to return the call with an expression of sorrow at the client's need to cancel and a clarification of how long the appointment might be kept open (if the client wished to change her mind) was an expression that the client was right that the cancellation "pleased" the therapist. Nonparticipation in the pattern of manipulation includes not only attempting not to be pulled into forced interactions that are nontherapeutic, but also attempting not to be pushed away from a position of support for a client who distrusts the therapist and fears abandonment.

Hostile Disclosure as a Response to Patient Anger

As therapists attempt to manage this discussion of their anger, there can be instances of what I would label as "acting out of the countertransference." A typical case is one in which a therapist has been pushed to the breaking point by a difficult client. Ehrenberg (1992) presented such a case, in which she was forced to cancel a session on short notice with a woman whose previous relationships had been "destructive and sadomasochistic":

> She was unwilling to accept my apology and, despite my efforts to open this for discussion, she was absolutely unyielding, unwilling to consider anything I might say, and self-righteous about her position. . . . I insisted that on the basis of our work so far, though she seemed to feel she had the "right" to now wipe the floor with me, I had at least earned the right for her to consider that my canceling the session might not have been frivolous or uncaring or irresponsible. Furthermore, if she felt she couldn't give me the benefit of the doubt, and even forgive me, then I felt I had as much right to be angry at her as she had to be angry at me.

There is a plausible case to be made for this intervention, and there is no reason to doubt that it was appropriate for this client. On the positive side, Ehrenberg is modeling the expectation that both members of the dyad would be treated with respect; in this way she could be preventing further escalation. However, there is a minimization of the client's need in the equation being presented. If the client had been in dire physical pain, and a physician's emergency delayed potentially ameliorative treatment for days or a week, I wonder whether the anguish and anger might be seen as more understandable (no matter how valid the therapist's excuse).

As we encourage deep and at times regressive and dependent relationships to develop, to facilitate transference and therefore deeper change, we also implicitly agree to honor the depth and felt life-saving quality of that attachment. When forced to abrogate our contracts temporarily, therapists are typically expected by trauma clients (as part of the felt agreement) to tolerate anger. This does not mean that Ehrenberg, for instance, should ignore her life needs and self-sacrifice in each case for this patient. It might mean that she not so strongly negate the right of the client to "wipe the floor" with her when she returns.

In Ehrenberg's example, however, there is a final line to the case study: "At this point I told her that I had actually canceled to go to the funeral of a friend" (p. 71). Why "at this point"? If this specific information were not disclosed earlier, at the point of cancellation, perhaps because it was judged too personal, why would it be disclosed later? Drawing on instances in which I have behaved similarly, I wonder whether the disclosure was meant to accuse the client of having wronged the therapist.

> "Do you not know I had a good reason for my actions? You dare to doubt me? Well, not only was my reason acceptable, it was one that would be judged so by almost anyone. Take that. I hope you now feel guilty for having misunderstood me."

In my view, periods of strong countertransference anger are not appropriate moments either for the pithy interpretation or the metaphor that comes to mind or for disclosure of information about the therapist. The time is better spent modeling for the patient the ability to manage anger without transforming it into hostile behavior and in discussing or disclosing the anger itself in a modulated form. Furthermore, it should again be emphasized that the distress of the trauma victim easily translates as manipulation to the therapist, even when manipulation was not the conscious purpose of the client disclosure. Suicidal ideation, for instance, provokes anger and frustration (in addition, one hopes, to concern and sorrow) in most therapists (Maltsberger, 1994; Maltsberger & Goldblatt, 1996; Watts & Morgan, 1994). Yet disclosure of suicidal thought is not necessarily meant solely as a threat to the therapist. Clients attempting to play by the therapeutic rules can be placed in a perceived double-bind, because their true feelings about the therapist (distrust, lack of faith in the process, sexualization, fear of perpetration) can insult or degrade the therapist. Ideally, one must convey both acceptance of the client's negative feelings and sorrow at the alienation that such feelings engender. One participant of the Trauma Countertransference Study described such an example.

Interviewer: So what did your therapist do with your distrust?

Sandra: You mean how did she fix it?

Interviewer: Well, I'd be interested in that next. But right now I mean how did she react to it.

Sandra: It made her sad, I think, then mad eventually. I was real guilty.

Interviewer: Did you tell her that?

Sandra: Oh, I had to. That's how I lived through it, I think. She said . . . I can't remember what she said. I'll just tell you what I felt when she talked, OK?

Interviewer: OK.

Sandra: Well . . . now I don't know how to say it because it wasn't simple.

Interviewer: Just talk around it for a while.

Sandra: She was kind of mad at me for not trusting her because she was like a really nice person.

Interviewer: Yeah.

Sandra: But the thing that saved it was that she would just fight against being mad, and I could see it. It really helped me. It really helped me . . . kind of feel like my husband's being mad was not hate it was . . . you know . . .

Interviewer: Pain?

Sandra: Yeah, it was pain. Whenever [the therapist] didn't like me for a minute, it gave her pain.

This therapist managed to convey anger in connection, to teach her client that anger can be an expression of that connection. As Sandra stated, it is not a simple task, but it can be a therapeutic one.

Therapist as Perpetrator

Few therapists fully escape the propensity to return anger and hostility with like responses. Clients thus frequently report feeling that their therapists are indeed their perpetrators. Projection also plays a part, as innocent actions by the therapist are transformed into acts of cruelty by their symbolic value for the traumatized client. This dynamic crosses many subgroups of traumatized clients for different reasons, the most generalized of which is the wish of many clients to find an enemy on whom to vent their rage at the unfairness of life. Identification with the aggressor or with the parent perpetrator can lead the client to be abusively penetrating of the therapist's boundaries, making entitled demands for time and attention.

Typically, given the client's legitimate and great need, the therapist initially responds by meeting the demands. Gradually, however, as M. Davies and Frawley (1994) noted in describing this pattern, "the therapist begins to feel used, furious, but helpless to extricate himself [or herself] from what has become a regular way of relating with the patient" (p. 173). In the Trauma Countertransference Study survey sample, the descriptions of therapist behaviors during such periods often involved breaches or modifications in the frame or boundaries of therapy. The therapist then presented the modifications to the client as "poisonous gifts," offers of time or affection that are not freely given. The client might then be treated punitively as retaliation for the perceived manipulation, even though the modifications themselves might have stemmed more from the therapist's guilt and wish not to feel abusive than from any client trickery.

Davies and Frawley (1994) go on to call this dynamic as "another dramatic recreation of an early relational matrix within the transference-countertransference of the treatment" (p. 173). I agree, but note that the countertransference side of this matrix has been neglected. The client too often feels furious, used, and helpless and experiences the therapist as a powerful person who is withholding a needed resource. Rage at the therapist's failures alternates with shame at the realization that the valued therapist is being mistreated. The therapist's refusal to acknowledge mistakes (similar to the parent who will not take responsibility) and shaming responses to perceived client attempts at manipulation maintain and escalate this pattern. Davies and Frawley also recommended that the therapist attempt to appreciate during these scenarios the terror, paralysis, hopelessness, and impotent rage of the victim of trauma, particularly the child victim.

Therapists also can feel placed in the role of perpetrator as they participate in the recovery or processing of memories of abuse. Even if not accused of the causing distress by the frightened and angry client (cf. Courtois, 1988, 1999), the therapist commonly reports guilt and shame for triggering this painful period. The crucial treatment element in this situation is for the therapist to hold on to the hope of a better life for the client, even as the latter may insist on the hopelessness of further work. Several examples in the Trauma Countertransference Study sample suggested countertransferential anger explosions in the therapist as they lost hope in their future work with the client, blaming the "impossible client" for the failure.

Anger as an Attachment Strategy

As we revisit angry client interactions in an effort to generate useful clinical interventions, it can be helpful to realize that anger itself can be an attachment strategy for some clients, particularly those with insecure attachments. Such anger is most likely to surface at times of great distress, as insecurity becomes anxiety over abandonment. Anxiety over abandonment has in turn been empirically linked both to high emotional expressivity (Bartholomew & Horowitz, 1991) and to the use of coercive strategies to attempt to block abandonment (Bartholomew & Horowitz, 1991; Feeney, Noller, & Callan, 1994). Although the above research is focused on romantic relationships, the patterns would logically extend to the intimate setting of therapy.

Anxiety and anger are natural processes used to protest the disappearance or temporary unavailability of an attachment figure (Bowlby, 1988) that appear as general patterns in primate species. Given the primate dependence on the parent for moment-to-moment survival, there is good reason to build into the organism a press toward proximity in dangerous times (Bowlby, 1973, 1988). Attachment theorists thus understand and predict an anxiety response when the relationship is threatened. Given recent empirical work, it has become possible to argue strongly that anxiety is "a biologically wired-in form of feedback on potential danger to the organism" (Safrin & Segal, 1990, p. 61).

Some chronically traumatized patients—battered women, child abuse victims, and those with prolonged imprisonments or war experiences—thus respond in an exaggerated fashion to the therapist's mild anger or annoyance, either becoming disabled by anxiety or disengaging, dissociating, or shutting down. Research has shown that those with histories of difficulty in maintaining close relationships (Bartholomew & Horowitz, 1991; see the "dismissing" category, Exhibit 7.1) are particularly likely to overuse dissociation (Coe, Dalenberg, Aransky, & Reto, 1995). Insecure teens show more avoidance of issues under discussion (and more anger) than do secure teens in conversations with their mothers (Kobak, Cole, Ferenz, & Fleming, 1993). Bartholomew and Horowitz (1991) have written extensively on the subject, and have developed the category system described in Exhibit 7.1.

The anxiety of the young child in the presence of a needed but inaccessible attachment figure moves predictably toward anger. For some, anger then becomes (through learning) the preferred mode of response to the perception of risk of abandonment in a relationship. This bypasses the opportunity of the well-intentioned partner to respond compassionately to the fearful person and confronts him or her with the much

Exhibit 7.1

Adult Attachment Styles

Secure Attachment

Securely attached adults report the ability to develop and maintain close intimate relationships without feeling a loss of autonomy or control. Their descriptions of their close relationships show "thoughtfulness and coherence" (Bartholomew & Horowitz, 1991, p. 228).

Insecure Attachment

☐ *Fearful.* Fearful adults distrust others and therefore avoid close relationships. Intimacy, although desired, leads to discomfort and concern about rejection. Their unease is related to a distrust both of others and of the self, due to their sense of personal inadequacy and insecurity.

☐ *Preoccupied.* Preoccupied adults are overinvolved and overly dependent on others, relying on others for a sense of personal well-being. Others are idealized and relationships are described with "incoherence and exaggerated emotionality" (Bartholomew & Horowitz, 1991, p. 228).

☐ *Dismissing.* Dismissing adults typically claim to be comfortable without close personal relationships. Bartholomew and Horowitz (1991) described this subtype as showing "restricted emotionality, an emphasis on independence and self-reliance, and a lack of clarity or credibility in discussing relationships" (p. 228).

more difficult job of meeting anger with connection. Many trauma clients become angry almost simultaneously with their realization of their need, expecting rejection and the need to demand satisfactory treatment. Such an interpersonal style is self-fulfilling in general, as others react negatively to interpersonal opening gambits that cast them in the villain's role. The emotional feel of the request for aid in many of these relationships would translate this way: "I know you won't be there unless I force it upon you. I know you will offer help grudgingly, if at all. But love me, damn you! Prove yourself."

Ms. W, who had been neglected and physically abused, spent five years in therapy with me attempting to move out of such a relationship style. Here is her description of why she was late for a session nine months into our work.

> *Ms. W:* I'm sorry I'm late. This woman made me stand in line behind her for ten minutes when I just had to make one copy. She's such a bitch.
>
> *Therapist:* That would make me angry too, I'm sure. Did she know you only had one page?
>
> *Ms. W:* Oh yeah. I told her.
>
> *Therapist:* Can you show me?
>
> *Ms. W:* Show you what?
>
> *Therapist:* How you told her.
>
> *Ms. W:* I explained. I said "Look, [name], I need to get out of here fast, and I just have one sheet of paper. I don't suppose you could get out of the way for a minute, instead of hogging the machine. You have all day to do that and I have to go."
>
> *Therapist:* That's the first thing you said?
>
> *Ms. W:* Yeah. Why?

A description from Bowlby (1973, pp. 208–209) is apt here:

> For some the very existence of caretaking and supportive figures is unknown; for others the whereabouts of such figures have been constantly uncertain. For many more the likelihood that a caretaking figure would respond in a supportive and protective way has been at best hazardous and at worst nil. When such people become adults, it is hardly surprising that they have no confidence that a caretaking figure will ever be truly available and dependable. Through their eyes the world is seen as comfortless and unpredictable, and they respond either by shrinking from it or by doing battle with it.

Building attachments to those who had insecure attachments to their parents is an arduous process. Crittendon (1997) suggested that the type of insecure caregiving also is important in the child's and adult's development, and differentiates between "ambivalent" and "avoidant" caregiving. Children with avoidant attachments have been punished consistently for the expression of negative affectivity, and they learn to inhibit anger, desire for the caregiver, and anxiety over abandonment. The "ambivalent" group are raised by caretakers who are unpredictable in their responses, a pattern shown in the behavioral literature to produce intense affectivity that is resistant to extinction. In therapy, the avoidant group attempts to prevent rejection by inhibiting affect, and the ambivalent group feels constantly in danger independent of therapist behavior.

Crittendon (1997) stated that coercive or manipulative behavior is likely particularly in the ambivalent group, because the client can attempt to force predictability on the relationship. A parental response, perhaps also likely for therapists involved with this population, is to increase the frequency of "false cognition." False cognition is the effort to hide from the ambivalent child or client any expression of feeling that might be upsetting. When the child client finally relaxes his or her guard, the parent–therapist sees an opening to tell the individual the truth; thus, relaxation of defense and honest expression of connection are punished.

The unique setting of therapy provides repeated opportunities for a "clash in worldviews" (Crittendon, 1997) that can produce "earned" security of attachment. For those who have experienced both the abusive avoidant environment and the chaotic ambivalent environment—Crittendon's Type A/C—she argued that

> their personalities sometimes contain the essential ingredients of creative genius. For there is no profound art that does not have shadows and a vanishing point, nor great music without counterpoint and minor keys, nor exquisite dance without the distance that makes closeness poignant.

Summary

There are several structural reasons for anger that can be expected in the treatment of trauma, including therapists' misjudging the degree of strain that such treatments produce, therapists' failure to respect the difficulties and confusion of the client role, and therapists' frustration at the slow pace of therapy. Even as therapists attempt to control and moderate their hostility, communications of anger can occur through mistimed disclosure or subtle withdrawal. Countertransference explosion from a clinician stretched to his or her limits of compassion is also a real danger in such treatments. The goal of countertransference management and disclosure of anger is to model *anger in connection*—the ability to feel and disclose anger without indirectly expressing that the relationship has suffered an irreparable injury.

Amery, Rosenfeld, and Rosenfeld (1966/1980) wrote that, after the Holocaust, "a person who could no longer say 'we' and who therefore said 'I' merely out of habit, and not with the feeling of full possession of myself" (p. 380). Therapists in relation with those who are so distinctly uncomfortable with the concept of "we" can feel rejected, angered, and humiliated by client behavior. Understanding that the angry howl of the aggrieved client can be a wounded cry might help the therapist to resist responding with counterhostility.

8

Therapy as a Unique Human Interaction: Management of Boundaries and Sexual Countertransference

> There exists in most of us a tendency to avoid or deny countertransference feelings. This is based on several factors. Primarily, it is due to the nature of the issues themselves. What we repress in relation to our patients are the same incestuous, perverse, envious and vengeful desires that we prefer to not see in ourselves in any case. But also this denial is tolerated because it accords with certain highly unrealistic, but socially accepted images of what a psychotherapist is or should be—calm, without anger or desire, mature, only a little neurotic. . . . (Hunt & Issacharoff, 1977, pp. 100–101)

The intensity and ferocity of transference love in traumatized populations is a phenomenon that draws comment from virtually all experts in this complex field (Briere, 1996; M. Davies & Frawley, 1994). As the power of these emotions decimates what is left of the trauma therapist's belief in the stereotypical picture of therapist equanimity that Hunt and Issacharoff paint above, clinicians turn to each other to frankly admit their confusion about adequate responses. The published discussions poignantly illustrate the therapist's recognition of the potential both for countertransference and for transference-based debacles, as one or both members of the therapy dyad become incapable of continuing under the strain of unfulfilled desire. Therapists pressed for more obvious signs of their care at times give in and then regret their statements or acts. Alternatively, they hold up the law and code of ethics like a shield against the dangers of being pierced by the clients' painful requests, sometimes embedding a guilt-producing statement within the refusal ("Holding your hand would be unethical. Do you want me to lose my job?").

Occasionally, we see more complex and frankly conflictual discussions appearing in the literature. Baur (1997) presented Father Walsh, a Catholic priest discussing his pastoral counseling duties with women who at times feel intimately connected to him. He spoke of his continuing struggle with his sexuality:

> "A vow is not taken once," he explained. "It is lived out every day. It is grown into, like a marriage or a title. It is not an answer, but a tension among forces that pull me in different directions. It suspends me between desires, and leaves me vulnerable. Every day there's the possibility that your heart—my heart—will be stolen or broken. With this job," he concluded, looking me straight in the eye, "comes a characteristic ache of the heart." (Baur, 1997, p. 215)

Baur presented the argument that Father Walsh's vow of celibacy was no more a solution to the priest's problem of sexual attraction and transference love than is our code of ethics: "Both vow and code merely announce to candidates the particular kinds of tension that come with the job and must somehow be tolerated. Like good priests, good clinicians do their work suspended between conflicting desires" (p. 215). Again, like Father Walsh, the clinician's dilemma is best managed through the "counterweight" of a greater love—the love of truth, for some (e.g., S. Freud, 1937/1964, p. 238), a passion for healing for others.

Although agreement has most certainly emerged on the nature of the problem, the solutions offered in many cases seem unsatisfactory. Glen Gabbard (1996, pp. 1–2) described a series of reactions to the disclosure of sexual transference that sounds familiar to most of us:

Ms. S., a shy young woman about my age, stared intently at me and blurted out, "I think I'm in love with you."

With masterful poise I responded, "What do you mean?"

Ms. S. looked at me incredulously, "What do I mean?! Just what I said! I think I'm in love with you. Look, don't make this any harder than it already is. My sister's in therapy, and she said I should tell you." . . .

I contemplate my options carefully. I could, of course, run out of the office screaming (a course of action that seemed most in keeping with my affective state). I could be silent and mysterious in the same way my analyst was with me. I could explain to her that her feelings were a form of resistance to the therapy and tell her to stop having such feelings. I could fake a nosebleed and tell her I'd be right back after tending to it (that would at least buy some time to think).

I leaned back in my chair (trying to get a bit of distance from the patient's intensity), and I tried to look as thoughtful and accepting as I could. In a reassuring way I said to the patient, "Well, this sort of thing happens quite frequently in psychotherapy."

The emergence of sexual feelings does "happen quite frequently" in therapy with trauma survivors, and it often leaves in its wake the tumultuous reactions that Gabbard so vividly described. Other questions in regard to boundaries between client and therapist also predictably arise. Ethical quandaries and difficult clinical questions abound:

- Should a clinician with an abuse history disclose this history?
- Is nonerotic touch harmful to clients?
- Is transference love "real"?
- Should the therapist who feels sexual attraction to a client refer the client?
- What "should" a therapist feel toward a patient?

Such questions lend themselves poorly to the development of easily applicable guidelines. Although relevant to any therapeutic encounter, however, they are more often encountered in trauma therapy for several reasons:

1. As therapist and client discuss great adversity, the painful events can become a shared burden. The members of the dyad often become bonded through their (possibly secret or illicit) knowledge of the trauma and at times through their joint identification with this trauma. The latter effect might occur through numerous mechanisms, such as demographic or background similarity (both are women, war veterans, children of Holocaust survivors, Jews) or commitment to the importance of the trauma (mediated through the client's experience and the therapist's expertise). The telling of the story intensifies this connection in cases in which the members of the dyad have good empathic connection. The clinician's press for knowledge of the client often feels very much like *love*, which has been defined by Menninger (1942) as the experience of "a pleasure in proximity, a desire for fuller knowledge of one another, a yearning for mutual identification and personality fusion" (p. 272).

2. When clients offer externally generated trauma rather than intrapsychic conflict as therapy content, it is likely that the therapist will respond with empathy, support, and concern rather than confrontation, defense clarification, and interpretation (cf. Josephs, 1995). The former, more supportive, tools also are less distinctively associated with the therapeutic relationship and more characteristic of any intimate relationship. Thus, trauma therapy can begin to have more similarity to friendship or loving partnership, leading to loving feelings on the part of therapist and client.

3. The idealization presented by many trauma clients to the sympathetic therapist can be gratifying. Because authorities can be dangerous to those who have had interpersonal trauma, victims can respond with exaggerated deference and efforts to please. These efforts take pleasant as well as problematic forms, including the offering of small gifts, overaccommodation of the therapist, and collusion to hide the therapist's contribution to therapy obstacles or stalemates. Such positive

transferential behaviors, together with the vulnerability of the client, can produce feelings of friendship or love in the therapist.

4. Some types of childhood abuse, most notably sexual abuse, lead the traumatized individual to fuse sexualization and affection, such that virtually any positive relationship comes to have strong sexual overtones (cf. Briere, 1996; M. Davies & Frawley, 1994; Pearlman & Saakvitne, 1995). Other types of chronic childhood abuse can lead to a fusion of aggression and attachment, culminating in a connection to the therapist that feels both hostile and sexually toned. Understandably, sexualization by the client can be a trigger for sexual countertransference in the therapist. Most therapists (85% in the sample of Rodolfa et al. [1994], and 71% of the clinicians in the study by Pope, Keith-Spiegel, and Tabachnick [1986]) believed that their clients were not typically aware of the sexual countertransference when it occurred; however, over two thirds of the clinicians in each study believed that the attraction was mutual. In fact, the tendency to discuss sexual material in therapy was the third most frequently named descriptive characteristic of clients to whom therapists were attracted (Pope et al., 1986).

5. A by-product of the neglectful environment in which chronic trauma can occur is a general loss of strength in the individual's sense of self. We have found in our laboratories that at-risk populations (e.g., children of alcoholics) show great instability in their self-descriptions (Drozd & Dalenberg, 1994). In therapy, such individuals might wish to merge with those who appear stronger and more centered, attempting to take on the therapist's core sense of self.

The reader will note that three of the reasons above refer to the structure of trauma therapy rather than simply to personality characteristics of the traumatized client. As such, they will be likely to affect therapist and client alike. Although I have only anecdotal data to support this contention, it is my belief that therapists are most likely to have strong negative and positive countertransference reactions to their traumatized clients than to other clients of similar ages and backgrounds. These positive feelings, in particular sexual feelings toward clients, are disconcerting to many therapists (Pope et al., 1986). Yet, referring to the tension of love and desire referenced earlier, clinicians from diverse perspectives typically agree that positive transference or positive feelings are important to successful therapy (cf. Mays & Franks, 1985). This was Freud's justification for his statement that the first aim of treatment was to "attach [the client] to it and to the person of the doctor" (1913/1958, p. 139). Freud considered positive transference to be the major force inducing cooperation with the treatment (S. Freud, 1937/1964), although sexual transference was considered a resistance to the treatment (S. Freud, 1915/1958).

Therapist Responses to Sexual Transference

The ambivalence of therapists to the experience of sexual transference was apparent from the time of Sigmund Freud's early writings on the subject. Warning therapists not to assume that transference love had anything to do with the clinician's "charms," Freud (1915/1958) outlined several arguments to dissuade the (female) client from her belief in the reality of her passionate feelings. First, he suggested that the client be confronted with the "unmistakable element of resistance in the love" (p. 167), because genuine love would make the client docile and obedient to the physician in resolving the problems in her case. Second, he noted that the love "exhibits not a single new feature arising from the present situation, but is entirely composed of repetitions and copies of earlier reactions, including infantile ones" (p. 167). It is interesting that a page later he retracted his arguments, noting that "the genuineness of the phenomenon [is not] disproved by the resistance" and that the blend of new and old components in transference love "is the essential character of every state of being in love" (p. 168). Still, modern writers also warn against "mistaking the transference as real" (Celenza, 1991, p. 501).

The defensive function of generally labeling strong negative and positive feelings as transference and "unreal" has been noted frequently (Bauer, 1993; Szasz, 1963), but nowhere is the phenomenon so ubiquitous as in the literature on countertransference love. Gorkin (1987, p. 108) wrote: "One does sometimes have the impression that it is more comfortable nowadays for a therapist to fantasize throwing a patient out of the office than it is to imagine joining the patient on the couch." Therapist reactions to sexual topics in therapy range from titillation and arousal to shame, guilt, and concern (Pope et al., 1986; Rodolfa et al., 1994). Case studies and theoretical papers also frequently mention hostile responses in both therapist and client when sexual issues begin to dominate the transference–countertransference matrix (Celenza, 1991; Gabbard, 1996). Survey studies suggest that anger toward the client could be disclosed in such situations, but that the sexual countertransference typically is not shared (Stake & Oliver, 1991). Stake and Oliver found that slightly more than 18% of the clinicians they surveyed (n = 320) had disclosed sexual countertransference to the patient; 22% had referred a client for this reason. Simon (1989) also raised the issue of the appropriateness of termination and of the possibility that a clinician might choose not to "burden the client with the truth" by disclosing the reason for a referral. Despite the vast literature on the sensitivity of the involved client to therapist moods and desires, most therapists believe that their clients do not know when the clinician experiences sexual countertransference (Rodolfa et al., 1994).

To supplement the material on sexual transference and countertransference provided by participants in the Trauma Countertransference Study, my colleagues and I have conducted a series of studies specifically related to sexual countertransference. In addition to empirical laboratory research (discussed later), the Sexual Countertransference Study project included a survey of 60 former clients solicited through the Internet. Participants replied to a posting on several Internet boards requesting e-mail responses from those who had completed psychotherapy and who had experienced "sexual feelings toward [their] therapists" during the therapy process. Three versions of the posting were used—a general request, a request for responses from those who believed that the issue had been handled poorly, and a request for responses from those who believed that the issue had been handled well.

Ellen, a participant in the Sexual Countertransference Study, and Carol, a participant in the Trauma Countertransference Study, were two of the participants who were terminated after they raised sexual issues with their therapists. Neither client was "burdened with the truth" about the termination, and both were disturbed about the referral years after the fact. Ellen, who completed a written questionnaire offered over the Internet, stated that she had disclosed her wish for sexual closeness to her female therapist and had asked if, had the two met in another way, therapist and client might have been friends. She was referred without explanation two weeks later. Carol had engaged in blatant (verbal) seduction of her therapist, and her therapy had been terminated by letter. The brief memo, which she showed to me, stated that the therapist was "unable to continue your treatment given your inappropriate responses toward me."

In one of our laboratory studies of sexual countertransference, beginning and doctoral level therapists (n = 51) watched realistic tapes of professional actors playing clients who expressed sexual interest in their therapists (Dalenberg, Aransky, & Dunkerley, 1996). After disclosure, the tape stopped, and clinicians audiotaped their responses to the client. Clinicians were asked to assume that this was a long-term client and that this topic had occasionally arisen during therapy. The scripts were developed by editing actual client requests made in therapy taken from my files and from those of a student assistant (who used the tapes for a graduate training project in her dissertation: Steres, 1992). They were directed in a manner of affective display that was consistent with the clients who had inspired each vignette. Two of the clients requested a spoken sexual statement from the therapist; two requested a form of physical contact. Examples of each type are given here, and readers are encouraged to imagine and consider what their own responses would be.

Tape 2: I've been in therapy with you for four years now. I've really changed a lot in that time. We've worked long and hard together, and I feel comfortable with us beginning my termination phase. You know we've talked about my strong sexual feelings for you, and I'm not worried that we're going to sleep together. I'm more worried that you don't want to, even just a little. I'm worried that you don't respond to me as a whole worthy adult, all of me, my sexuality, too. Do you understand what I'm saying? I guess all I want is for you to tell me that you're frustrated too, that we can't have what we can't have.

* * *

Tape 4: Unless you prove to me that you care about me, how can I trust you? You talk about my parents not giving me everything I need. You are repeating that abuse by not giving me the human contact that I want and need. If you want to tell me that you don't find me attractive, fine. Saying that a sexual relationship between us is unethical is ridiculous and disrespectful of my feelings. We could work this through. Why is this different? Be honest with me. I want us to do what we honestly want to do. This is very frustrating and humiliating for me. I have to leave unless we can be real with each other. If you want me to sign forms, then fine. If you want me to see another therapist to discuss our intimacy, I will. But I will not continue therapy if you don't give me what I know is right for you and me. I want to be as close to you as possible. I need to know that you care about me. All I want now is a hug. Is that against your ethical standards?

An average of 18% of the clinicians who listened to each of the four clients disclosing sexual attraction responded punitively (as rated by both client and therapist raters). When the disclosure included a direct request for touch or sexual contact, however, an average of 39% of the clinicians punished, referred, or terminated the hypothetical client. One

•

therapist in this study responded this way to the client on
Tape 2:

> What would you do if I asked you to go out and come
> in again and we'll just start our sessions over. Let's start
> the session one more time without you going over things
> that we've been over before, asking for things that you
> know you can't have. OK? Let's do it.

Another therapist responded this way to the client on Tape
4:

> It would be inappropriate to even think about having a
> personal relationship. I wonder if this is how you interact
> with other people and what the reaction is that you re-
> ceive from them. I think that if you choose to stay in
> therapy this is an area that needs to be explored. How-
> ever, if you choose to terminate, I would be happy to
> give you referrals.

More than 70% of all clinicians and more than 50% of the
doctoral level clinicians reported moderate to extreme anxiety. When the client made a direct request, more than 50% of
the clinicians in both groups were angry.

Table 8.1 shows the verbal responses given by clinicians to
the hypothetical clients. The verbatim responses were transcribed and shown to client participants who had completed
psychotherapy. Each client participant rated five responses in
each category on the degree to which he or she felt the response would be harmful, tolerable (neither harmful nor
helpful), or helpful. More than 70% of the therapist responses
to sexual material were rated by clients as harmful (a mean
score under 5 on a 10-point scale). The category with the
most positive rating, the statement of care, included a boundary statement for about half of the clinicians. Among the clinician statements in this category that were rated helpful and
respectful were the following:

> □   I think you are an attractive person, but it's going to
>   have to stay a thought and not an action.

Table 8.1

Responses to Sexual Transference Cues

Response	Disclosure Alone (%)	Disclosure and Request (%)
Punitive response	18	39
Request for discussion	21	17
Avoidance	13	7
Transference interpretation	25	23
Statement of care	22	13

Note: n = 102 responses in disclosure and disclosure plus request group.

- □ Yes, sometimes I am frustrated by some limitation of this role, but some of what makes it frustrating also makes it work. It makes us therapist and client instead of family or friends.
- □ I think you are really asking several questions. Do I care? Yes. Do I recognize that you are a sexual person and an attractive person? Yes. Will anything happen between us. No, it really can't. Do you want to talk about any of that?

The generalizability of the laboratory responses was supported by the results of the clinical survey studies. Of the 84 Trauma Countertransference Study participants, 40 (48%) reported a sexual transference to their therapists at some point during treatment. (An additional 21 stated that they did feel some sexual feelings occasionally but did not develop a strong sexual transference.) Fourteen of the 40 individuals did not share this information with their therapists, and most of the 14 believed that their feelings were not known. Ten of the 14 thought that their therapists would not have accepted the sexual feelings and might have referred them or reacted punitively. Of the remaining 26 former clients, 12 stated that their sexual feelings were adequately addressed, 7 stated that the subject was avoided, and 7 believed that the issue was handled poorly.

Several unexpected features of the Internet portion of the Sexual Countertransference Study also underlined for me the need for further clinical discussion of this issue. In 1993 and 1994, when this study was completed, I posted a request for volunteers on several Internet discussion sites. As stated earlier, I asked to hear from individuals for whom sexual feelings had arisen during therapy and who had experienced either negative or positive resolution of those issues. I asked to confer only with former clients, those who had completed psychotherapy. Over the course of the two years, 60 clients self-identified in one of these categories, 21 of whom had positive experiences. In contrast, in one month I received 164 e-mails from persons who did not fit the criteria (they were still in psychotherapy), 97 of whom had not yet shared their feelings with their therapists. Most were upset, and some were almost desperate for advice on what to say to their psychiatrists, psychologists, and social workers that would not lead to the termination of a valued relationship. The experience strongly reinforced my belief that our standard methods of addressing the issue are inadequate.

The 40 participants in the Trauma Countertransference Study who reported sexual transference, the 60 Internet contacts specifically recruited to discuss sexuality in therapy, and 22 participants who responded to a newspaper advertisement requesting general positive and negative responses to psychotherapy were combined to produce a sample of 122 persons who had experienced sexual transference. Of this group of volunteers, 33% shared their belief that the situation was handled well and resolved positively. It thus is of interest to discuss in some detail the differentiating features of these groups.

Given the focus of this book, it might not surprise the reader that the key aspects that statistically differentiated the successful from unsuccessful resolutions were aspects of the countertransference reaction of the therapist. Those clinicians who were part of a dyad successfully resolving a sexual transference were more likely (by report of their clients) (a) to normalize the feelings, (b) to acknowledge positive reactions to the sexual material, (c) to disclose that they too felt some sexual attraction, and (d) not to make a distinction between "real" love or attraction and feelings that arose in therapy. Although the issues of disclosure are complex, it is particularly interesting to note that none of those in the successful resolution group failed to disclose some aspect of their countertransference reaction to the client (characterized by the patient as either conflicted or positive). In contrast, in the cases of unsuccessful resolution, 33% of the therapists made no statements about their own feelings about the issue. I should add, however, that the disclosures of the successful therapists were not always (or even generally) sexual in content.

We know from Pope et al. (1986) and Rodolfa et al. (1994) that most therapists report guilt and anxiety when they feel themselves responding sexually to a patient. Our own research participants (Dalenberg et al., 1996) responded similarly in the laboratory. Most also reported that, in the typical case, they did not share any feelings of sexual attraction toward the client. The attitude toward disclosure in the professional literature is predominantly negative. Pope, Sonne, and Holroyd (1993), the most widely read authorities on the matter, concluded that "in some rare cases, it may be clinically useful and appropriate to disclose to the [client] one's sexual attraction." However, they warn, "such disclosure is so fraught with potential risks that it should be done only after particularly careful consideration" (p. 90). Gabbard and Lester (1995) reported that such disclosure almost invariably collapsed the analytic space by replacing the symbolic with the concrete. In a case study, Gabbard and Lester presented a client who was told that her therapist was sexually attracted to her. "The [client] told me that she held on to those words for many months and could think of nothing else." Despite the fact that the therapist also had assured the client that boundaries would be respected, "as far as she was concerned, the analytic work stopped at that moment" (Gabbard & Lester, 1995, p. 133).

The reports of the clients in our surveys and the anecdotal responses within the literature can be combined usefully by noting that the typical negative response to clinician disclosure of attraction comes when this disclosure is not dictated or guided (apparently) by client need. Turning back to Maroda's (1991) general guidelines for countertransference disclosure, such disclosure must be in service of the treatment rather than in pursuit of an unrelated personal goal of the therapist.

Client descriptions of therapist disclosure of sexual countertransference in my own case studies of successful resolutions involved a clear statement of boundaries and an acknowledgment of the normalcy of the human sexual response in intimate settings. Successful resolution also involved a clear understanding on the part of the client about why the topic was being discussed—typically direct client inquiry, response to client discussion of sexual feelings, or response to general client concerns about how he or she is viewed by others. Examples of a successful and an unsuccessful resolution are presented in Exhibits 8.1 and 8.2, respectively.

In three-quarters of the unsuccessful resolution cases that we studied, the therapist response to sexual material was an intellectualized and jargon-laden offering. Like the example given in Exhibit 8.2, most unsuccessful resolutions involved use of the concept of transference in a distancing rather than in an illuminating way (from the client's perspective). Most clients within both groups discussed transference, but unsuccessful outcomes were highly associated with the clinician's claim of the "unreality" of the experience. A few clients felt protected by the claim of unreality (as did, presumably, some clinicians), but most felt demeaned and misunderstood by this interpretation. As discussed in chapter 4, one effect of trauma is to undermine clients' faith in their own perceptions. As the dyad works toward a situation in which the client can trust self-perception, the introduction of the idea that one does not really feel as one believes one does is threatening.

Exhibit 8.1

Successful Resolution of Sexual Transference

How did it come up?
I told him about it after about a year in therapy. He had kind of warned me earlier.

How did he react to it?
He was very sweet. He said that this was a hard part of therapy and that two good people like us were bound to feel warmly toward each other after all this intimate time together. He said that it could be a positive for us, so that we felt good and attractive in each other's company, and the only negative would be if either of us decided to focus on changing the basic goals of the relationship we were in.

How did you feel?
Well, I was scared to bring it up, but he was so . . . I don't know, kind of gently worried about it, like of course we would both feel that way, but we have something important to defend. I was so glad that he could accept me as a sexual person but that that wasn't the most important thing in his life. It was probably the most important interaction we had.

The most provocative description of this client position that I have seen was offered by Baur (1997), as she related a skit written by a client who was distressed at her therapist's frequent allusions to transference in discussing their shared experiences. The skit places her therapist in the role of a clerk at an ice cream store where the client had gone in search of peppermint ice cream, her favorite:

> Initially, the psychiatrist–clerk claims that the pepper-mint ice cream is frozen solid and thus not available. He tries to give her a substitute, and when she holds out for what she really wants, he insists that her desire is a case of transference. "You don't want peppermint, that's a transference from strawberry," he says. No, she tells him, even as a child, I cut the strawberry off the Neapolitan and traded it for vanilla. "You like the peppermint for

Exhibit 8.2

Unsuccessful Resolution of Sexual Transference

How did the issue come up?

He kept asking me again and again whether I had any sexual feeling toward him. He interpreted my dreams as veiled sexual statements, which I didn't agree with. Finally, I just agreed with him and convinced myself that I felt it. I was really pleased when I began to feel it. I thought it was progress.

How did he react to it?

He immediately said that I should know that there would be no sexuality between us no matter how provocative I was and that this was transference.

How did you feel?

I was pretty humiliated. I asked him how he felt about me, whether he was angry or thought less of me, and he said his feelings were not really relevant, but that we might talk about what I expected him to feel. I've never felt so alone and humiliated in my life.

its healing properties," says the clerk. "It's a transference from Pepto-Bismol." No, no, says Barbara, that's not it either. "You want to be young again," counters the clerk, reminding her that she ate peppermint ice cream with hot fudge sauce in college. No, she insists, she doesn't want to be twenty years old. Finally, Barbara asks the crucial question. "Why do you have the peppermint here if you can't sell it?" To this question—which asks the doctor why he seems to be offering love when clearly he cannot deliver—the clerk says weakly, "To study your reactions." "Unfair," snaps Barbara, "You're driving me nuts . . . I'm getting out of here." "Wait!" says the clerk. "Maybe the peppermint will thaw. Wait . . . wait." (Baur, 1997, p. 193)

One client for whom I managed the sexual transference very poorly myself was a lesbian client, Ms. F, who strongly confessed her positive feelings and love for me from early in the treatment. While I discussed her assumptions about me, I did not correct them (e.g., by telling her that I am heterosexual). I no doubt minimized the importance of her feelings in this area. Both her sexual orientation and her other personal characteristics led her to be so far away from my own categories of sexually interesting individuals that I did not treat her sexual interest seriously in my own mind—I was treating it as "unreal." I now believe that my almost casual acceptance of feelings as transference was betrayal, partially explaining why she became increasingly angry at me without being able to pinpoint the reason for her anger. Finally, she confessed to me that the man whom she was accusing of rape at her workplace had not in fact touched her, and she asked me to keep her secret during my testimony at her trial. Shortly after I told her that I could not legally or morally do so, she left therapy, stating that I had been emotionally dishonest with her by not standing by her in this way. Had I disclosed my sexual orientation, and further discussed honestly with her what I did and did not feel, I believe that she would have been able to use the foundation of support that I could have given.

Without dismissing the depth of the sexual feelings and self-experiences, successful therapists have highlighted the powerful positives of the therapist's role, such that the client can come to believe that the relationship is more than a false offer of love for dubious purposes. Such therapists perhaps used interventions similar to one proposed by John Briere (1992, p. 93):

> I understand your desire to have a special relationship with me, one that meets your needs for connectedness, rescue, protection, even love. But our relationship isn't for those things. It's better, because it's based on you and your continued learning and growth—not on a fantasy that could be blown away in a second (as undoubtedly it has many times in your past). Because it is real, you can count on it, on me. The good news is that although I am not your fantasized savior/parent/lover, this relationship is a place where you can feel safe, supported,

and optimistic, and where you can examine things that you otherwise might not. All of these things are based upon what is actually present, right now, right here.

Briere's statement did not deny either the reality or the appropriateness of the client's feelings. Instead, he clearly identified purposes that the relationship would not serve and purposes that it could serve. He simultaneously emphasized the clinician's faith and belief in the client and the client's process. This message minimizes the possibility that a client will feel betrayed by the discovery that therapy is not a substitute for parenting or marriage.

I wish to emphasize here that successful therapists in the Sexual Countertransference Study walked a very difficult line. They did not privilege the sexual material, and they did not leave their clients feeling that sexual discussion was the purpose or goal of therapy. However, neither did they run from sexual content or punish client sexual discussion. Sexual discussion is laced with shame for many patients, but particularly for those with sexually assaultive pasts. Many of my research participants felt that it was fair to treat sexual feelings between therapist and client as a common "side effect" of therapy; that is, as an aspect that must be accepted, understood, and carefully monitored but not encouraged. Participants in the Trauma Countertransference Study who came to believe that their therapists wished sexual content to dominate the therapy often fulfilled this perceived wish, but little other therapeutic work seemed to be completed.

The most reasonable position to take on the issue of disclosure of sexual countertransference at the moment thus would consider the empirical and clinical literature, including its seeming contradictions. It is fair to state with some confidence that even sophisticated clinicians are at times discomfited by sexual countertransference, and that they therefore could benefit from supervisory input when relevant circumstances arise. The results of the Sexual Countertransference Study make it clear that sexual content need not remain unspoken; however, the discussions are fraught with danger for the well-meaning therapeutic pair. My own tentative modifications to the common advice to suppress sexual countertransference feelings and withhold disclosures is in part a distrust in the clinician's ability to entirely hide such powerful emotions.

It is likely that more benign countertransference responses to client sexual transference will await the profession's creation of arenas for safe discussion of sexual feelings. The frank admission of the problem of client–therapist sexual involvement is a recent phenomenon, and sexual countertransference responses (or even admission of client sexual transference) can lead to therapist fear of "guilt by association" (Pope et al., 1993). In the area of trauma treatment, I believe the discussions are even more crucial, as clients with sexual trauma often believe that their sexuality is dirty and unspeakable. Open professional discussion inevitably will lead to more clarity and sophistication in the appropriate intervention methods in these situations.

At present, trauma therapists are urged to self-examine regarding the role of sexual feelings in their own treatments. A more thorough list of related questions is offered in Pope et al.'s (1993) indispensable text on sexual feelings in psychotherapy. However, here I would suggest self-assessment along at least three dimensions:

1. As you think about each of your clients, ask yourself at which moments you feel great warmth, the desire to touch them, or the desire to tell them that you care.

The Dr. Peppermint ice cream story illustrated the frequent client assertion that therapy often seems to be a seduction of the patient. It is love and not love, care and not care, protection and not protection, all in combinations that can seem arbitrary. The issue I raise here is to urge respect for clients' communication of their perceptions of the arbitrary negotiation of closeness on the part of many therapists. Is closeness being offered according to an invisible schedule dictated solely by the clinician's personal needs or theoretical assumptions?

Naturally, one feels closer at some times than at others to

any given client. The countertransferential question here is whether these times give information that is about the client, about the clinician, or about the two individuals in combination, which is most typical. The spontaneous and unexpected wave of sympathy or closeness in the clinician can be a sign of a new and important clinical change in the client—a new openness or vulnerability in an individual who is typically rigidly defended. Such feelings are worthy of examination, first silently, and then, if the information appears useful, as part of the transference–countertransference discussion. It also is not unusual for seriously ill patients to become more sexually interesting to the clinician as they change, perhaps due both to the therapist's self-congratulatory pleasure in the process and to the awakening of a more mature and reciprocal type of love. In the Trauma Countertransference Study, such stories from successfully treated patients were not unusual. They were told to me with the pleasure similar to a teenage daughter's description of a first public dance with her proud father.

   2.   How would you respond to a statement by a client that he or she found you attractive? How would you respond to an overt request for sexual contact from a patient?

If we judge by the clinical literature, our laboratory studies, and the stories from the Trauma Countertransference Study, the answer often will be, "probably not that well." Clients in our samples understand, at least in retrospect, that boundary statements should be offered at such moments. However, clients need not be bludgeoned with such statements, and a sensitivity to the injury that can occur in such situations is critical. Successful therapy patients who believe that their therapists managed these situations well all mentioned disclosure of the countertransference, and many specifically mentioned that the therapist was both flattered and a little frightened by the events. As the client in Exhibit 8.1 stated, however, they managed to communicate that there was something important to protect in the nonsexual therapeutic relationship, something of deep and significant value. My students tell me that they were well served by thinking about the actual words that they would use in such an instance and by discussing alternatives in supervision groups.

3. Why is it inappropriate to have sexual contact with a patient? Is it simply illegal, or does it feel wrong to you at a visceral level?

I do not wish to suggest in any way by raising the above question that sexual contact is not wrong or that it should not be illegal. In fact, there are multiple moral and empirical foundations for our current ethical stance in the helping professions. Instead, we should be brought back to Father Walsh's comment about the inherent tension between desires in clinical work. Using the law or the code as an easy way out of the discussion of "Why can't we?" leaves both clinician and patient without a foundation on which to continue their work.

Other classic responses to the reality of client–therapist sexual abuse, such as "it is like incest" and "patients have no power to consent," have some symbolic truth, but they can be used to infantilize the client and to remove the possibility of respectful and egalitarian discussion. Client ratings in our laboratory research and participant experience from the Trauma Countertransference Study suggest that affirmative reasons for nonparticipation in sexual contact and sexualization of therapy (protection of the transference, protection of the safe environment, preservation of distance to preserve neutrality) are more effective than are warnings or defensive reasons ("Because you cannot choose." "Because I symbolize your parents." "Because it is against the law").

Therapist Responses to Requests for Touch

In Pope, Tabachnick, and Keith-Spiegel's survey of professionals (1987), only 13% of respondents stated that they had never hugged a patient. We found similar results in our Standard of Care Study interviews of 59 clinicians conducted in person (a random sample recruited by telephone with an 87% agreement rate) (Dalenberg, Dunkerley, & Collopy, 1997). For trauma clients, most therapists also stated that they have used touch (a) as a connecting event as the patient leaves the office, (b) to calm or reassure of presence in cases of reality disturbance, and (c) to ease fear of disclosure or facilitate the telling of a traumatic incident. Nonetheless, a fairly large minority (5–13%) of therapist interviewees thought that each type of touch was unethical. Sixty-seven percent of our sample responded affirmatively to the general question "Can you remember a specific example of the use of touch when you felt later that it was not the best choice?" Eighty-four percent also answered affirmatively to the question "Can you remember a specific example of the use of touch that had a powerful positive effect on the therapy?" In each instance, when the therapists were asked for a free description of an example in each category, the most likely diagnosis of the client was trauma related (posttraumatic stress disorder or dissociative disorder).

Thus, professional reaction to the use of touch in therapy is fraught with concern. Yet, at the same time, many therapists across orientations suggest that touch plays some role in their work, and they warn others not to be pathologically rigid in their decision making. The final decisions are important to patients, who frequently mention the therapist's use or nonuse of touch in their descriptions of their therapies in our studies. Roazen (1995) noted that Freud's patients also spoke of the special significance that his handshakes held for them.

There are several reasons to expect the issue of touch to emerge in trauma therapy. The frequency of discussion of the topic in the clinical trauma literature attests to the likelihood that touch will arise as an issue in therapy.

1. *Facilitation of disclosure.* Frozen in fear by the unspoken trauma memory, the client often perceives a need for physical evidence of the therapist's safety and connection. Experimental evidence is fairly clear that touch

facilitates self-disclosure in general (Pattison, 1973; Woodmansey, 1988). This could be more true if the material to be disclosed is such that the client feels shamed and fears therapist withdrawal.

2. *Reality contact.* Both the experience of trauma itself and the dissociative aftermath of some traumatic experiences can leave the client feeling "out of touch" in a concrete sense. Touch can hold the client to the world in a physical sense. Recognition of the clinical need to touch clients with a psychosis to reestablish reality contact is common (Woodmansey, 1988). The same needs can arise in the extreme states associated with trauma.

3. *Clinical treatment of shame.* The pervasive feeling of ugliness and untouchability experienced by chronic child trauma clients is much discussed in the literature (Courtois, 1988; Dolan, 1991). Experiences in therapy that include some touch can combat this sense, allowing the client to be more open to internal change.

4. *Establishment of therapist humanity.* As I argued earlier in the sections on reasons for countertransference disclosure, there are times when refusal of a request for touch is so inhumane as to be a retraumatization of the client. When one of my clients grabbed my hand at the door, after a session containing initial disclosure of the loss of his family in a tragic accident, it was rather hard for me to imagine the positive therapeutic benefit of a "don't touch the therapist" speech.

Descriptions in the clinical literature generally describe an impulsive touch or acquiescence to a request for touch by a client, followed by positive client response. McLaughlin (1995) described a session in which an impulsive client grabbed her therapist's hand for a few moments as a breakthrough and believed that it helped the client understand that she was not untouchable. Dolan (1991) wrote about similar instances of the communication of the client's worth by acquiescence to requests for touch. Most common is presentation of the clinical sense that touch can be a more believable sign of therapist good will than anything he or she might say (Balint, 1968; Little, 1966) and that the refusal to touch is likely to be a narcissistic injury that is more damaging to therapy than acceptance of touch might be in most instances (Maroda, 1991).

Nevertheless, conclusions of most authors range from cautious acceptance to general rejection of the role of touch. Gutheil and Gabbard (1993, p. 195), for instance, stated,

> Patients who deliberately or provocatively throw their arms around the therapist despite repeated efforts at discouragement should be stopped. An appropriate response is to step back, catch both wrists in your hands, cross the patients wrists in front of you, so that the crossed arms form a barrier between bodies, and say firmly "Therapy is a talking relationship; please sit down so we can discuss your not doing this any more."

Two texts on countertransference come to more cautiously positive conclusions:

> I have had both good and bad outcomes as a result of touching patients. The types of touching I have used include hand-holding and a hand on the shoulder. I have also accepted, but not initiated hugs. I generally am not enthusiastic about hugging, but have found that the narcissistic injury involved in refusing the spontaneous gesture of a patient's hug can have a far worse outcome than accepting it. My preferred type of physical contact is touching the hand of the patient. (Maroda, 1991, p. 150)

* * *

> There is one other small but meaningful aspect of the last session that is often anxiety-provoking for patients, and sometimes for therapists too: the manner in which the two parties physically part. I think many therapists attempt to manage this anxiety—the patient's and their own—by demonstrating a certain ritualized form of physical leave-taking, like a firm handshake. For several years that is what I did. More recently, though, I have found myself allowing a more spontaneous and personal

response . . . This may result in no physical contact being made at all, or a shaking of hands, or a firm hug. (Gorkin, 1987, pp. 284–285)

The findings from the Trauma Countertransference Study confirm some of these clinical impressions, although the role of touch was more powerful than I might have anticipated. Some of the more interesting touch-related findings are as follows:

- Of those trauma clients who self-labeled their therapies as successful, 94% ($n = 56$) stated that their therapists would have unequivocally refused to have sexual contact with them had the question been posed directly.
- Nine participants (11%) had directly requested and been refused sexual physical touch. Four went on to resolve these issues to their satisfaction, two were referred, and three left therapy in frustration. Two of the three who left therapy believed that the sexual transference issues could have been resolved without physical contact but felt that the disclosure of sexual feelings led to a distancing and withdrawal by the therapist that was intolerable to the client. Such an overall pattern of results suggests that sexual transference and the necessary refusal of requests for sexual touch need not dictate referral and can be resolved by a sophisticated clinician (preferably with consultation).
- Ninety percent of all trauma clients in the study (76 of 84 participants) had touched or been touched by their therapist beyond a handshake.
- Nineteen clients (23%) had been refused all physical contact. The initial request had typically been to ask to touch the therapist on the arm during the hour, to hold the therapist's hand during a trauma story, or to hug the therapist after a significant event. Members of this group were much less likely to resolve the issue. Eight left therapy; eight continued but felt that the events significantly damaged their capacity to make use of the verbal material. Three felt that the issue was resolved. Importantly, all three who successfully worked through the refusal to touch reported that their therapists strug-

gled with their painful reaction and took responsibility for developing alternatives to touch that would meet client need. This nonphysical expression of care apparently does not always succeed, but it can be one of the few viable alternatives for clinicians who are uncomfortable with nonerotic touch. The conclusion that should be drawn, then, is that requests for touch are often highly charged, deeply important, and emotionally complex events. Refusal should not simply be offered in the context of "keeping our boundaries," and attention must be given to ensuing client shamed responses (see below).

□ Fifty-seven clients had requested and at times received a form of nonerotic touch without verbal processing of the event. The level of intensity of touch was low, and the frequency of touch was typically rare. Fifty-one study participants (89% of the requesting clients) evaluated the unprocessed touch events as positive in all cases. Only 8 individuals had neither requested nor received nonerotic physical contact beyond a handshake.

Minimizing the Damage Stemming From Touch Refusal

Although I seldom refuse all physical contact, I have had many experiences of refusing touch in a specific instance with a trauma client. Refusing sexual touch rarely creates major difficulties, because it is the rare client who cannot understand how a sexual relationship would undermine the safety of the setting and the capacity of the therapist to stand both inside and outside of the interaction (to clarify and interpret it). Among therapists who did not punish the client raising sexual content, there were many instances of resolution in the Trauma Countertransference Study that left clients feeling helped and respected. Negative resolutions more often appeared to be due to referral, avoidance, or hostile countertransference behaviors.

As Celenza (1991) noted, persistent demands for sexual touch are a rejection of the therapy as potentially useful in and of itself. It is understandable and even expected that a lonely client with a connection solely to the therapist could wish to substitute the richness of an extratherapeutic friendship or love relationship for the benefits of a once-a-week treatment. If the client is convinced (for delusional or reality-based reasons) that the therapist shares the wish to trade in the therapy for friendship or romance, the problem is more intractable. However, as stated earlier, the introduction of a sexual relationship is an abandonment of the therapeutic one and thus an abandonment of a promise made both professionally and personally. This reasoning is typically convincing, albeit not emotionally comforting in some circumstances. The resolution hinges on the therapy's adequately meeting other needs for the client.

Refusing to allow clients to grasp the therapist's hand on occasion, to touch the therapist on the arm, or to engage in the limited forms of physical contact appropriate to nonintimates is much more problematic. It is difficult to argue that therapy will automatically be undermined by therapist agreement to some forms of touch, given that this is not the result reported in most of the clinical and experimental literature. Respect for client boundaries, allowing client as opposed to therapist initiation of touch, and nonparticipation in any form of touch that appears sexualized are principles that are advanced by most trauma therapists and general commentators on the use of touch (Briere, 1996; Dolan, 1991; Maroda, 1991).

My argument here is less for automatic refusal or agreement to use touch and more for a principled approach to such decisions. In fairness to clients, the first tenet of such a principled approach is to acknowledge when refusal is an expression of countertransference discomfort with touch and when it is based on perceived client best interest alone. In the Trauma Countertransference Study, clients often viewed therapists as claiming the latter ("This is bad for your therapy.") when they meant the former ("Your request frightens, arouses, or disturbs me."). One could argue, of course, that arousal of these negative feelings in the therapist undermines therapy, but presentation of these boundaries as unexplained rules of the game ("It is wrong to ... in therapy.") often is unconvincing to clients, at least in my clinical and research samples. Other writers, however, have disagreed. R. Epstein (1994) stated that trauma patients are often reassured by refusal to touch, even if they do not understand or accept the reasons, because "it is a clear message that the therapist has thought this matter out before hand and takes his or her professional role very seriously" (p. 210). His sample refusal reads

> It's a nice and friendly custom for people to shake hands when they say hello or good-bye, but since our relationship involves a special way of working together to help you with your problems, and since treatment works best if all of our communications are put into words, I advise against our shaking hands until your treatment is completed. (R. Epstein, 1994, pp. 209–210)

Epstein stated that in his experience the patient's offer of a handshake can be an unconscious testing of the therapist to see whether he or she will be exploitative. However, he acknowledged that at other times, the offer could be an indication of attachment or relief.

Many of the Trauma Countertransference Study participants had experienced a touch refusal by the therapist. Although overall refusals to touch were rare and difficult to overcome, individual instances were commonplace. Dr. O and Michael, the therapeutic dyad discussed in chapter 7, fought their way through one such episode successfully. During one session in which a very frightening episode was being discussed for the first time, the client sat up (from a prone position on the couch), moved to the end of the couch, and took the therapist's hand, still agitated, crying and talking. He gripped the therapist's hand tightly as he told his story and then dropped it and returned to his prone position. Subsequently, he told her that he thought he would have been unable to tell his story without the touch and asked for permission to engage in this form of touch in the future.

Dr. O declined. She stated that she was unable to concentrate well when she was holding the client's hand. She told

Michael that, although she did not believe he experienced the event in a sexual manner, she was wrenched from her self-experience as a doctor when holding hands with her attractive client. She was concerned for further "slippery-slope" behaviors if the client sensed her discomfort and became more aware of the behavior, and she thought it best not to allow a form of touch that felt to her to be outside professional boundaries. Michael was able to accept this, he said, because his therapist labeled the issue as her own. He also believed that he did not move toward certain intrapsychic issues from that point on, because he feared being unable to contain his wish for contact. However, he was able to make use of his therapist in other ways, and he judged his therapy to be helpful overall. Dr. O reported that she worked to develop acceptable substitutes with Michael, and believes that the process made obvious her commitment to work to ensure that her personal limitations and preferences did not unduly harm the therapy.

There have been times in my practice that touch seemed to be a substitute for working through and an obstacle to the process, and I have shared this (with reasonable results) with my clients. I allowed Ms. M to periodically touch and grip my arm as she told me the details of her rape. Later in therapy, however, when she requested touch as she discussed the same incident, I said,

> You know, [Ms. M], I really understand your wanting to do that. It actually feels soothing to me too, the two of us holding hands when we're so scared. But you know how sometimes when you're in an auto accident and they won't give you morphine at first until you can tell them where it hurts? [She nods.] Well, I think of touch like that sometimes. It soothes us so it doesn't hurt so much, and it can make you less able to really explain what's happening inside. I'm right here. I won't go anywhere. But I want you to just try to talk about it without holding my hand.

She did so, and she did so more frequently in subsequent sessions. At times she would speak for a while and then stop and say, "Morphine, doctor," outstretching her hand, or "I'm taking an aspirin break" and touch my arm or grip my pillows. In this way, we tried to negotiate an agreement that, although requests for touch are not wrong or immoral, they were not our goal and in some ways might circumvent our goals.

Therapist Responses to Intense Need for Availability, Closeness, and Boundary Flexibility

Perhaps the reader will recall Samuel Taylor Coleridge's poem "The Rime of the Ancient Mariner":

> Since then, at an uncertain hour,
> That agony returns,
> And till my ghastly tale is told,
> This heart within me burns.

This stanza has always reminded me of the agonizing desire of the trauma patient for a witness to interpersonal trauma. Increased dependence and reliance on a caretaker in the face of potential danger are well-known and well-supported effects within attachment research (Bowlby, 1973, 1988), and therapists can find themselves inadequate to the task of meeting a client's yearning for protection, safety, and care. Most important here is the therapist's awareness of societal disdain for dependency in adults and his or her willingness to show respect for client attachment.

As argued earlier, human beings are predisposed to respond with anxiety to "high-risk" situations (Bowlby, 1988). Separation from a caretaker is such a risk, particularly when the caretaker cannot be counted on to remain when the client moves away. It is a central task of trauma therapy for therapists to present themselves as objects that can be clung to, rejected, and then returned to without punishment. Fulfillment of this task requires boundary negotiation rather than simple boundary maintenance (Pearlman & Saakvitne, 1995), as therapists attempt to become constant objects for the traumatized patient (C. Cohen & Sherwood, 1991). Rigid boundaries or lack of boundaries interfere with the client's efforts to attach and yet remain separate and to internalize the therapist's benign presence.

For clients who ask for or appear to need more availability or less rigid boundaries, much has been written regarding a "boundary crossing" as opposed to a "boundary violation." The former is the relaxation of a typical boundary for a therapeutic purpose with a benign result. Examples might be increased availability (Gunderson, 1996), use of therapist-related transitional objects (Adler, 1993; Gunderson, 1996), notes or telephone calls from the therapist (Adler & Buie, 1979), the giving or receiving of minor gifts (Peters, 1991), or increased use of disclosure or nonerotic touch (Woodmansey, 1988). Freud was known to have sent postcards to patients, lent books and money, and treated clients while on vacation or during walks (cf. Gutheil & Gabbard, 1993; Roazen, 1995). Little (1990) described Winnicott as clasping her hands on occasion, as sharing his countertransference reactions to other clients, and as being offered coffee and biscuits. R. Epstein (1994) noted that common examples of minor boundary crossings by patients include failure to keep fee arrangements, use of the telephone to obtain free therapy, calling the therapist at inappropriate times, attempting to extend the hour, and "borrowing" from the therapist's waiting room.

More serious boundary violations by both therapist and clients are reported in the literature. In addition to sexual boundary violations, physical assaults on therapists are not rare. Bloom (1989) found that between 32–61% of psychiatrists had been assaulted at least once during their careers, but most assaults occurred in hospital or other inpatient settings. It is also not uncommon for sexually abused children to unexpectedly grab the therapist's genitals or to expose their own (Gabel, Oster, & Pfeffer, 1988). My own research and patient reports correspond well with the theoretical and anecdotal literature, suggesting that immediate behavioral limits with clear articulation of reasons should be offered in these situations. Adult patients who repeatedly violate physical or sexual boundaries should not be treated in office-based outpatient settings.

Boundary negotiation, however, is a viable and important part of trauma therapy and need not be sign of a problematic dyad. The therapist treating childhood trauma clients should be reminded that the neglectful mother (whose children often suffer from an attachment disorder) is distinguished from good-enough mothers by her tendency to (a) fail to look at her child, (b) fail to touch her child, (c) spend more time out of her child's sight, and (d) spend more time in silence when with her child (Bowlby, 1988). The silent therapist who spends little time in eye contact and who refuses to engage in minor nonerotic touch thus often awakens a regressive yearning in the neglected client. The intensity of this yearning, and the frequency with which it is combined with a manipulative style (to "trick" the therapist into a display of attachment), can anger the therapist and lead him or her to engage in counteraggression (R. Epstein, 1994).

Therapists who treat trauma must understand that attachment is an untrustworthy and amorphous phenomenon to many patients. A history of betrayal is likely to mean that the client will need both "therapeutic word" and "therapeutic act" to feel safe. The therapist needs to "shout" his or her attachment to the trauma client, and "whisper" his or her comments about the client's disturbing and distancing behaviors. Shouting attachment might mean a willingness to state repeatedly and without punishing caveats ("for the hundredth time") that the client is worthy of care, increasing the intensity of the interpersonal interaction, and constantly reinforcing and providing symbols of the attachment without humiliation. On the last point, clients in my survey studies have commented negatively about transitional objects that had childish connotations (dolls, teddy bears), but they have been virtually unanimously positive about the value of more adult objects that serve a similar purpose.

Increased need for therapist availability, therapist statements of care, and therapist symbols must both be accepted by the trauma therapist and treated gently over time as signs of the underlying attachment disorder. It is also crucial that the doors to availability not slam shut suddenly as therapist endurance is exhausted. Negotiation of availability should occur from the early stages of therapy, and a structured hierarchy of transitional options to therapist constant availability might be useful. Such a hierarchy is offered by Gunderson (1996), who presents initial stabilizing options (increased therapist availability), later transitional options (therapist-related transitional objects), and final steps toward the internalization of self-soothing capacities (use of external support systems or internally generated distractions).

The key to use of such a hierarchy *as* a hierarchy, however, is a discussion with the client of the advantages of being able to make use of the symbolic when the actual is unavailable and the advantages of developing the capacity to self-soothe. The therapist must be extremely involved in this growth process to facilitate its development, akin to a parent's applauding of the child's independent accomplishments. As Cohen and Sherwood (1991) stated, the child of abusive parents fears not only being abandoned, but also fears the experience of *having* abandoned the other by becoming independent. "The problem for [such a] child," they wrote, "is not whether the mother will leave, but whether she will be there if the child moves away" (pp. 12–13).

In service of these goals, the therapist's expression of care, both directly and symbolically, virtually always serves a positive purpose. Such statements further the sense of therapist warmth that so regularly emerges in regression studies of client progress, and they can be indispensable in trauma treatment. Unfortunately, however, statements of care are still regarded as less acceptable in much of the literature than are statements of anger or confrontation. Greenson (1974), for example, wrote that when asked by a client if the client was hated, he responded, "Yes, Dorothy, at times I hate you." To another who commented that she was not a pleasure to work with, he stated, "Yes, these hours of nagging and complaining are a pain." However, when a client had "begged" Greenson (1967) to say that he might feel some liking for her, that she was "not just a number," sobbing her humiliation at his silence, he commented that, although he knew his silence was difficult to bear, the analytic situation was "not an equal one. It is your job to let your feelings come out and it is my job to understand you, to analyze what comes up" (pp. 226–227). For many trauma clients, but particularly for those with a history of parental nonsupport, feelings will not "come out" unless therapist attachment is trusted.

It is my opinion that the therapist who treats trauma clients cannot afford to allow issues of availability, touch, intensity, and self-disclosure to be decided by the fluctuating pressures of the situation. Trauma clients require a more constant effort by the therapist to keep attachment issues at the forefront, to take responsibility for communicating a desire for reconciliation when alliance rupture occurs, and to shine a spotlight on their benign intentions without blaming the client for periods of seemingly paranoid search for malevolence in the "innocent" therapist.

Countertransference Responses to the Press for Therapist Self-Disclosure

A final issue in this chapter is the tendency of the traumatized client to wish to know personal details about the therapist's life. Here I am speaking not of countertransference disclosure but of disclosure of therapist lifestyle or history. Many of the Trauma Countertransference Study participants (74 of 84) reported at least one session in which they pressed the therapist for factual disclosure. Most common were requests born out of fears for the relationship, requests stemming from confusion in reading therapist signals, and requests related more directly to rendering the therapist a safer figure by knowing him or her more deeply.

Disclosure of therapist history, problems, or background is generally regarded as more risky to the therapy than is carefully thought-out countertransference disclosure. Exceptions might be made for reality factors that are needed to contain the patient's anxious fantasies about the therapist's future behavior or well-being or to explain the need for an exception to regular policy. Borys and Pope (1989) reported that 38.9% of a sample of over 2000 therapists acknowledged that they had disclosed details of current personal stresses to one or more clients, but only 7.8% (41 of 532 therapists surveyed) in the replication and expansion published by R. Epstein, Simon, and Kay (1992) stated that they had disclosed the information with the expectation or desire to gain sympathy. No participant in the Trauma Countertransference Study survey stated that he or she was negatively affected by a clinician's disclosure that an unexpected break in session continuity was due to a family emergency, but several became obsessed or distressed by repeated, sudden, unexplained cancellations.

Table 8.2 gives results for client requests for factual infor-

Table 8.2

Disclosure Requests and Outcome

Request Type	Requests Made	Disclosures Made	Refusals Made
Explanation for cancellation	41	31 (1)	10 (7)
Injury explanation	6	5 (0)	1 (1)
Health questions	14	8 (0)	6 (4)
Future plans	39	24 (0)	15 (9)
Trauma history	36	18 (3)	18 (3)
Demographics	51	40 (2)	11 (7)
General interpersonal	27	15 (4)	12 (4)
General loss	19	8 (2)	11 (3)
Financial status	5	2 (1)	3 (0)
Theory	16	9 (0)	7 (5)
Sexual orientation	9	6 (0)	3 (3)
Other patients	19	5 (3)	14 (1)
Details about therapist's partner	21	19 (1)	12 (2)

Note. Numbers in parentheses indicate the number of participants who cited a negative outcome in each category.

mation from their therapists recorded in the Trauma Countertransference Study. More than 25% of the 84 participants asked their therapists for information on the reasons for a therapist cancellation, the clinician's plans for the future, the therapist's individual trauma history, how the therapist had behaved in an interpersonal situation relevant to a problem being discussed, and demographic information regarding the therapist's family and loved ones. The overall pattern supports the conclusion that most of the patient's requests across categories eventually were answered; however, there is evidence that some disclosures are more risky than others.

Honestly addressing the patient's questions regarding reasons for cancellation, explaining an obvious injury, allaying fears regarding the therapist's health, and discussing the therapist's plans for vacations virtually never led to negative results (by patient self-report). Withholding such information, however, was perceived negatively in many cases. The sole exception in this category was a therapist who told a suicidal client that the reason for her cancellation was to attend the funeral of another client who had died. The therapist then, reportedly for reasons of confidentiality, refused to divulge any further information. The client wished that her question had either been fully answered or not answered at all, because she felt trapped in fantasies about the therapist's role in the other client's life and death.

Evaluation of these examples of disclosure with negative and positive outcomes generally led to conclusions that are supported by the theoretical literature to date. Specifically, disclosures that were seen as nonhelpful by clients were more likely not to be in response to a direct inquiry or to be anxiety provoking. In such an instance, it could be that the therapist is using disclosure to diffuse or discard some tension of his or her own. Anecdotally, a surprising number of the disclosures by generally nondisclosing therapists were made in anger, responding to pressure from the client on a different issue. One Trauma Countertransference Study participant, for instance, remembers a disclosure this way:

Interviewer: Was there ever a time when your therapist just told you something factual and personal about herself that you didn't ask about?

Sandra: No, I don't think so. Maybe something minor. Oh wait, there was once.

Interviewer: Do you remember the details?

Sandra: I was hounding her about something, I can't remember what . . . oh yeah, I was saying that she didn't return my phone calls within the day like it says on her answering machine. I kind of said it was unprofessional or something.

Interviewer: OK. Looks like you feel guilty about that.

Sandra: Yeah. I was hard on her.

Interviewer: I think she probably got over it, though. It's tough to be in therapy and never be hard on your therapist. But so what did she tell you?

Sandra: She said something like "So look, the reason I don't return your phone calls is that my son dropped out of school and is into drugs. Sometimes this just is not about you." She was sort of calling me egomaniacal. [Later context suggests that she means "egotistical."]

Therapists often report a desire to be known by their clients, particularly by clients who repeatedly misinterpret them—as can be true of the fearful and suspicious trauma client (Pearlman & Saakvitne, 1995). Perhaps this desire motivated Sandra's therapist above, who felt wrongly accused of irresponsibility by her client at the same time that she might have been feeling guilty and responsible for her son's problems. Disclosures of this type also can be last-ditch attempts to stop the client from badgering the therapist beyond his or her ability to operate effectively.

Refusals by therapists to answer questions also can serve positive and negative purposes. Refusal to answer client questions about other clients is a professional boundary issue, and acquiescence to this request led to more problems than did refusals. Refusals also can signal that the therapist respects privacy and is able to guard himself or herself in difficult interpersonal situations, a skill that the client often must learn. In general, refusals to answer questions about topics not directly bearing on an active clinical issue were well tolerated (if the client's distress was treated as understandable and underlying needs were addressed).

It is interesting that all clients who requested disclosure of sexual orientation felt positive about disclosure (if given) and negative about nondisclosure (if this occurred). The question was rarely asked, but exploration of the nine instances in Table 8.2 suggested that the question was often an effort to understand a countertransference pattern. Clients felt that they had a "right to know" sexual orientation, because subtle communication between therapist and client can be more accurately interpreted if orientation is known.

The other two categories with high rates of client dissatisfaction with nondisclosure were family demographics ("Are you married?") and theory ("Why should this process help me?"). Therapists who refuse to answer this type of question might self-examine about whether they are threatened by these requests, fearing invasion of privacy or client disdain at an inadequate answer. Refusal to answer, although possibly clinically appropriate, also can be an effort by the therapist to retain a superiority or sense of control in the session. One therapist, for instance, stated in my interview with her that she refused to answer her client's questions about her theory because she thought the client would not understand. However, she also refused to answer my questions about her theory, stating that she was not an expert in trauma and did not wish to be "on record" with her ideas about her client.

The question of the appropriate response to "Were you abused?" is controversial. I typically do not answer questions by clients about my experiences that relate to their traumas, although the questions arise frequently. For example, I am asked often by clients with similar experiences if I have been raped, assaulted, or abused. Most often, I do not answer. I explain this to the client by stating that many of us have traumas in our histories but that mutual sharing of our stories would lead naturally in a caring dyad to mutual support, drawing the center of attention away from the client. I honestly state that telling one's trauma stories to a valued other is a powerfully positive experience. Out of respect for the professional relationship, and in realization that the client is a kind and caring individual who would listen sympathetically to my own experiences, I find it best to retain the general rule that therapist trauma history is not the best topic for discussion. When this boundary is retained in the context of a more general willingness to discuss those areas of the self that bear directly on the therapeutic process, and when it is not rigidly applied in an overbroad manner—by refusing to state, for example, whether I have seen a particular movie —I have not experienced an instance of strong negative client reaction. In general, however, disclosure held less risk in our research than did nondisclosure in the situation of direct client request.

Pearlman and Saakvitne (1995) have an excellent discussion of the special disclosure issues and general countertransference themes for the survivor therapist. It should be noted that rates of child abuse history among mental health professionals are high, ranging from 30 to 66% (Elliott & Guy, 1993; Follette, Polusny, & Milbeck, 1994; Pope & Feldman-Summers, 1992). Such survivors can engage in extremes of over- or underidentification with the client for compassionate or defensive reasons (cf. Wilson & Lindy, 1994), and they can be at risk for violating client boundaries in reenactments (Kluft, 1994) or for overdisclosing in a conscious effort to avoid collusion with the incest secret (Marvasti, 1992). On the other hand, clients interviewed in research studies by those with similar trauma histories have commented positively on the degree to which their perception of similarity facilitated disclosure and inspired hope (Brabin & Berah, 1995). Clinical research also suggests that similar others can be seen as more credible and can be preferred over therapists with no personal experience with the relevant tragedy or trauma (Tedeschi & Calhoun, 1995; Wagner & Calhoun, 1991).

The survivor therapist has a challenging task in determining when the spontaneous and client-elicited therapist disclosure of trauma history is appropriate. Data on the subject are limited. For instance, only seven of the participants in the Trauma Countertransference Study knew that their therapists had experienced a trauma similar to their own. In retrospect, three of these participants wished they had not been told. However, two felt greatly helped by the therapist's disclosure, and two felt that the disclosure was largely irrelevant to the overall success of treatment. The most consensual statement that can be made based on the literature on this topic is that the discussions of therapist history must be held according to the client schedule and based on client need to know rather than on therapist press to disclose.

Summary

The negotiation of boundaries, like the negotiation of responsibilities in a marriage, can be a stressful process. It is least stressful, however, when one's "partner" attempts to understand one's needs and to make allowances for them. Successful boundary negotiation by therapists in my research involved a recognition of the enormous emptiness and terror that a perceived threat to attachment (or threat by an attachment figure) can produce. It also appeared to involve therapist attention to the countertransference, such that therapists could take appropriate responsibility for their own limitations and consider the possibility that current boundaries were overly rigid or lenient in a given case.

Sexual transference, press for disclosure, and repeated requests for touch can raise anxiety in the therapist and lead to countertransference withdrawal or hostility. Supervision is extremely useful in finding ways to allow this content to enter the therapeutic hour without taking permanent center stage in the treatment.

An important question to ask in therapist self-examination is whether therapist and client understand the purpose served in an individual case by granting or refusing a request for disclosure or touch. Often it is this purpose, rather than the disclosure or touch itself, that requires therapeutic scrutiny.

Independent of the therapist's decision, the most common error in countertransference management in this arena was a sudden and unexplained change in boundary rules, seemingly driven by compassion fatigue or therapist exhaustion. Clearly, this area is important for individual self-examination and for development of tailored approaches to boundary-related decision making.

Countertransference and Trauma Resolution

You can exert no influence if you are not susceptible to
influence. (Jung, 1933, p. 49)

The final chapter of this book, meant to discuss the final
chapter of trauma therapy, raises some of the most difficult questions of our work. What does it mean to "resolve"
trauma? How do we decide that treatment is or should be
over? Building from the discussions in chapter 8, perhaps
some answers can be found in going back to an understanding of what the treatment alliance is and what purposes it is
meant to serve.

The Life and Maturation of the Transference and Therapeutic Alliance

Beutler, Machado, and Neufeldt (1994), commenting on therapist variables in Bergin and Garfield's *Handbook of Psychotherapy and Behavior Change,* wrote that the construct of the
therapeutic relationship or therapeutic alliance has "consistently been found to be a central contributor to therapeutic
progress" (p. 244). Therapeutic alliance, however, is a state
perceived by the client, not a set of processes independent of
therapist and client. It seems to be built from the residue of
the therapist's ability to practice *indwelling* (Polanyi, 1968,

1974), the experience and belief of the client that the therapist has marshaled his or her energies to immerse himself of herself in the client's inner world. The feeling that someone truly "hears" is almost painful in its power to touch many trauma clients, who find their stories to be avoided, minimized, or exploited by many. Helping therapists find ways to protect this relationship, therefore allowing therapeutic change in a population for whom the relationship feels constantly under siege, has been a major goal throughout this text.

Traumatized clients often have limited ability to "hold on" to a therapeutic relationship (or to any other relationship). Their tumultuous transference responses interfere both with their ability to experience the transference as transference (that is, to know that their disturbing feelings about the therapist are partly based in reality and partly serve a defensive purpose) and with their ability to rest comfortably within the respect and joy of an egalitarian relationship. Therapists tire of proving themselves time and again, and they can long for a passionate and yet mutually trusting intellectual exchange where they need not monitor every syllable of their conversation.

Over time, the wild fluctuations of the feelings of a trauma client within therapy often lead to a withdrawal from emotion-related discussion on the part of the therapist. Clinicians in supervision with me speak of trying not to "set the client off." But "holding down the transference," as it is often termed, also holds down the countertransference, which often can be the unconscious or conscious point of the techniques. By calming both oneself and one's client, the therapist often hopes to produce a more cognitively mediated and therefore more effective interaction.

Unfortunately, as supported both by empirical literature and by my own experience, the most vivid learning episodes in therapy are mediated through the intensity of the client's feelings and through the immediacy of these feelings as they apply to the events of psychotherapy. High emotional involvement (Davenloo, 1978) and a high level of "patient experiencing" (Orlinsky & Howard, 1978) consistently predict positive client outcome. "To be most effective," wrote Bauer, "the psychotherapy framework must foster an emotionally meaningful experience" (1993, p. 14). And nothing is more meaningful, as Strupp (1977) argued so cogently, than present-day events discussed within emotionally charged relationships.

Trauma therapy thus requires great courage on the part of the client, and an equal measure of honesty and courage on the part of the therapist. One allows the most frightening and disturbing attachment-related beliefs to become speakable, in part by granting them a special transitional reality. "I can be treated as your father, but I am not your father," we say, either directly or by our actions. "I will not punish you for seeing me in that role. Instead, I will notice it with you— notice the times I merge with him in your mind, notice the ways in which I am like him and unlike him, ways in which you encourage me to be like him and unlike him, and ways in which you misperceive me as being like him and unlike him. I will not demand to be separated from your perceptions of me, because this you cannot do alone. But I ask you to consider that I *might be* separate and to further consider learning the ways in which you re-create your past so that you have more choice about your future."

Most often, trauma clients need a vivid highlighting of the difference between our real selves and their perceptions of us, typically through clarifying the emotional meaning of our behavior and our emotional reactions to their behavior by means of countertransference disclosure. The advantage of transference interpretations, mediated either through silent or through open countertransference examination, is that the therapist stands at the center of the problem. His or her perspective cannot easily be discounted, nor are differences in perspective as often perceived as a betrayal (as long as the nature of therapy is continuously discussed).

James Strachey (1934) wrote long ago that transference interpretations allow the therapist to hold both ends of the rope and therefore to more easily untie the knots that clients bring to a session. Untying some of the knots, however small, illustrates to the client that a relationship might serve a benign instrumental purpose. The therapist comes to be not simply a substitute for life—the only one who listens, the only one who cares—but a bridge to life. Turning back to the boundary issues discussed in chapter 8, it is not touch, or self-disclosure, or boundary crossing themselves that lead to the slippery slope to sexual misconduct or client despair, early termination, and suicide about which we hear so much. Rather, after reflecting on the case studies referenced in chapter 8, I believe it to be the desperate therapist's slip from the symbolic into the actual, his or her inability to help the client assign meaning to boundary flexibility, that creates the problem.

When clients discuss touch, self-disclosure, extended availability, or overtime within sessions, saying "this is the cure," and therapists, after a trial boundary crossing, say, "See, I told you that it would not be enough," both are making the same error. They are trying to force these acts to bear the burden of meeting the attachment needs of the patient, when they can do no more than serve as a passageway to a discussion of internalization of more benign attachment beliefs by illustrating the therapist's genuineness or involvement. Thus, feeling that some trauma clients are unable to use the care and attachment symbols that the therapist offers to steady them as they walk across treacherous territory toward a better life, the clinician can err by taking over responsibility for the client's emotional safety. More often the clinician is at fault for abrogating the responsibility to share the journey, instead of simply watching the spectacle.

Therapy seldom meets the partnership, love, or companionship needs of the isolated and misunderstood client, although our hearts go out to these individuals and we might wish to provide them respite. Therapist willingness to actively symbolize involvement is crucial in traumatic transference cases, but involvement must highlight rather than obscure the goals of therapy as a catalytic environment for client change, not (or at least not solely) as an escape from the client's current, demanding world. Ideally, the therapy moves toward the egalitarian and emotionally involving task described by Briere (1996) and by Enns, McNeilly, Corkery, & Gilbert (1995). The therapist can acknowledge both expertise and humanity and can cede to the client authority on what has transpired in the client's life, authority on what traumatic experience subjectively feels like, and authority on which treatment interventions seem to help.

As the relationship evolves, the role of the therapist predictably becomes more peripheral. Two of my clients, who are themselves writers, have brought to my attention Robertson Davies' description of "Fifth Business" as an apt metaphor. Ramsey, the novel's protagonist, is asked to identify who he is—that is, what role he plays in life. His questioner uses the metaphor of the opera, explaining that a permanent company must have a soprano (the lead female and heroine), a basso (typically the villain), a tenor (to play the hero opposite the soprano), and a contralto (typically the soprano's rival in the operatic production).

> So far, so good. But you cannot make a plot without another man, and he is usually a baritone, and he is called in the profession Fifth Business because he is the odd man out, the person who has no opposite of the other sex. And you must have Fifth Business because he is the one who knows the secret of the hero's birth, or comes to the assistance of the heroine when she thinks all is lost, or keeps the hermitess in her cell, or may even be the cause of somebody's death if that is part of the plot. The prima donna and the tenor, the contralto and the basso get all the best music and do all the spectacular things, but you cannot manage the plot without Fifth Business! It is not spectacular, but it is a good line of work, I can tell you, and those who play it sometimes have a career that outlasts the golden voices. Are you Fifth Business? You better find out. (R. Davies, 1970, p. 227)

Increasingly, the therapist will step from hero to Fifth Business, becoming a catalyst for self-directed learning. Advancing the plot is a good line of work.

Resolving Impasses in Trauma Therapy

Therapy with extreme trauma clients often produces a disheartened belief within the therapist that no resolution is possible. The volatility of the patients, the depth of yearning produced or awakened by the transference, the rigidity of repetitive patterns, and the frequency of the need for difficult boundary negotiations between therapist and client can all combine to exhaust the therapist. In the worst cases, the difficulties in reaching the client become despair, and neither therapist nor client can hold on to the hope necessary for continued work.

Elkind's (1992) book on resolving therapeutic impasses and Pearlman and Saakvitne's (1995) excellent chapter on therapeutic impasses with survivor clients are two helpful resources on this subject. Each emphasized the need for the therapist to consider his or her contribution to the impasse, both by examining possible contributions to repetition compulsion (see chapter 6) and by describing issues of client–therapist "fit":

> Traditional approaches to failed therapies or therapeutic impasses have emphasized deficits, despair, and intractability. For the most part they have underemphasized or ignored the interactive, relational process of the therapy, and therefore did not give rise to constructive interactive solutions. Thus, they provide a way out, but no way through. (Pearlman & Saakvitne, 1995, p. 215)

The "ways through" discussed by Elkind and Pearlman and Saakvitne include those discussed earlier in this text: consultation, countertransference disclosure, careful attention to countertransference urges to blame or shame the client, and commitment to listen without defensiveness and with shared pain to the client's agony (typically centering on not feeling understood). To this list I add and discuss briefly one more: the power of the honest apology.

Apology and Responsibility

A few years ago, in reading an angry exchange between professionals on the role of science in practice, I came across the following from Donald Peterson (1996, p. 18), an important scholar in this area of theory and research:

> Recently, the "professionals" and the "scientists" in psychology have not done enough [sensible discussion]. To an unfortunate degree, we have separated our forces and sniped at one another. Before McFall wrote his response to my article, I felt that I was above all that. To my shame, McFall has shown me that I am one of the culprits. When he lays out the words I used in criticizing his first corollary (demolished, indefensible, completely discredited) and describes them as "exaggerated and gratuitous" (p. 6), he is exactly on the mark, and is treating me more generously than I deserve. Hyperbolic, insulting language like that has no place in scholarly discourse. I apologize for it, promise to be more careful in the future, and hope Professor McFall will accept my thanks for pointing out this error of my ways.

Peterson's responsible and honest statement reminded me how rarely I see "true" apologies in my professional life. All too often, clients hear therapist apologies as defensive and halfhearted, or even hostile. In a hostile apology, the therapist manages to convey sorrow but implies simultaneously that the client's reaction stems from pathology. Typically, the phrasing is something like, "I am sorry you reacted the way you did. I didn't intend for you to be hurt." The translation to most clients is, "I am sorry my small and innocent action caused you to have such a neurotic fit. Any normal person would not have attacked me for it. However, since you apparently demand it, here is your apology."

A therapist who has shamed or mistreated a client in his or her care and who bears any part of the responsibility for this event needs to hold tightly to the memory of the constituents of a true apology—willingness to listen to the individual who has been harmed and to understand that harm, a display of remorse, and the commitment to learn from the mistake. Minimization of the harm done (by not empathizing, for example, with the fear of abandonment that stems from a forgotten appointment), lack of distress (which reads as indifference), or failure to commit to change insofar as this is possible all work to undermine the likelihood of resolving a rupture; and they can raise the likelihood of stalemate.

Multiple Meanings in the Resolution Process

In Littrell's (1998) review of the therapeutic benefits of reexperiencing trauma-related emotions within therapy, he noted that simple reexposure to traumatic events is insufficient for reliable prediction of successful therapy outcome. Rather, successful outcome is predicated on the reprocessing of trauma in the safe therapeutic setting. In Pennebaker's studies (Pennebaker, Kiecolt-Glaser, & Glaser, 1988), in which traumatized adults wrote or spoke about their negative experiences, it is that group of individuals who appeared to gain more complex meanings of their histories who also benefited from the disclosure process.

Several Trauma Countertransference Study participants spoke of their perception that the therapist appeared "stuck" on one interpretation of the trauma, one important feature of it, or one means of coping with it, perhaps the one that had been most successful in the therapist's own life. The research literature on growth-enhancing features of painful life experience (e.g., Tedeschi and Calhoun, 1995; Tedeschi, Park, & Calhoun, 1998), together with the popular literature on survival of life-threatening illness or trauma (cf. Rhodes, 1990; West, 1995; Wholey, 1992) provide resources for the therapist who might fall into this category. Time given to alternative meanings of trauma can open fruitful avenues for client healing and remind the therapist of the range of human interpretations of single events. A synopsis of some of these avenues is given in Exhibit 9.1.

A related issue is the ability of the therapist to avoid block-

Exhibit 9.1

*Alternative Meaning and Growth-Producing Benefits
After Trauma*

Survival of trauma as a sign of strength.
Increased appreciation for life or life blessings.
Discovery of the availability of support from friends and loved
ones.
Renewed or strengthened religious belief.
Involvement in social or political action to aid other trauma
survivors.
Change in content and complexity of philosophy of life.
Enhanced ability to be empathic to others.
Discovery of new talents or resources.
Increased perspective on minor obstacles or difficulties.
Elimination of high-risk behaviors and improvement in health.
Enhanced creativity.

ing meanings that are valuable to the client but personally
unhelpful or noxious to the therapist. Ms. T, for instance, a
client of mine who had lived through an accident that
maimed her two children, found it helpful to believe that
God had sacrificed her children to the greater good by spur-
ring her to champion drunk-driving legislation. I have seen
many clients benefit from involvement in causes, transforming their anger and sadness into creative acts of kindness.
Although I believe I am able to respond well to a range of
religious and nonreligious beliefs, I had a good deal of difficulty accepting and not undermining this fervent woman's
belief in a God who would blind a child to gain an advocate
for safe driving. I was concerned for her children, and I
feared that her beliefs would lead them to feel betrayed and
unimportant. Yet it was clear that her beliefs were helpful to
her emotionally, that she was able to support her children,
that she saw the benefits and the risks of sharing her beliefs
with them, and that she was capable of examining their defensive function for her as well.

Once I identified this issue as largely my problem, as opposed to Ms. T's wrongheadedness, I located a minister within her denomination who shared her belief, and I met with him. A planned 10-minute visit developed into six heated and table-pounding discussions, expanding to include a few other religious leaders who held other perspectives. The discussions left me morally unconvinced but much more able to see how a good and thoughtful person could hold the position that Ms. T espoused. I did not share these discussions directly with her, but during the time I received this "supervision," she became less symptomatic and reported feeling more supported by me.

Tedeschi and Calhoun (1995), both of whom have written extensively on the life-changing positive benefits that can occur after trauma, noted that "clinicians need to develop an increased tolerance for the individual's tendency to perceive benefit in suffering, even if from the clinicians' point of view this involves a certain degree of illusion" (p. 101). They argued strongly that they have never seen a case in which a client was hurt by the clinician's respectful acceptance of the client's interpretation of good that came from trauma, whereas "clinicians who, in the name of 'truth' or 'insight,' rob clients of their own understanding of good coming from the struggle with negative events increase the chances of harming individuals psychologically" (p. 102). In our study of Holocaust victims (Dalenberg & Epstein, 1999), it was the complexity of the survivors' understandings and meanings of the Holocaust, not the presence or absence of specific meanings, that predicted the sense of having "grown beyond the pain of the past."

It also should be noted that some of those who have personally experienced traumatic events write of the impossibility of assigning meaning and view the attempt to do so as an affront to the magnitude of the event. This belief relates to the "duty to the trauma" discussed in chapter 3. Similarly, both therapist and client can feel that the client's recovery lessens the magnitude of the event. Just as the surviving family members might feel that posttrauma happiness is a betrayal of a lost spouse or child, other categories of surviving trauma patients can feel that moving forward betrays their own past. If trauma can be conquered, why isn't this state achieved earlier? Many participants in the Trauma Counter-transference Study spoke of recovery as potentially signaling to the other person in the dyad that the trauma was "not that bad," and clients and therapists alike were at times reluctant to raise the possibility of relating to the trauma in a new way.

A final theme in this area was the difficulty for therapists and clients in trauma therapy to find a new vehicle for meeting attachment needs within their termination phase. After months or years of relating in an intense and volatile manner, discussing the most difficult and painful of subjects, other therapeutic work can seem superficial. Client and therapist can hold on to one another through reexperiencing the trauma material—both literally (it symbolizes that they will continue to see one another) and metaphorically (they feel more bonded during these times). It is a crucial issue in the resolution phase of trauma therapy that clients and therapists learn that they can relate with strong feeling to one another without doing so only through pain. Delores was one of the Trauma Countertransference Study participants who spoke of this theme:

> *Interviewer:* OK, here's a general one. What was the single hardest obstacle to overcome in relating well, the way you wanted to relate, with your therapist?
>
> *Delores:* That is hard. Let's see. I'd say . . . at the very end . . . I'd say that it was trying to feel connected to her when I wasn't crying.
>
> *Interviewer:* When you weren't crying?
>
> *Delores:* Yeah. She was real nice to me, kind and really what I needed, when I cried. And when I stopped feeling like crying a lot, I kind of felt like she was not really close to me anymore. So I made up stuff to cry about.
>
> *Interviewer:* On purpose?
>
> *Delores:* Well, yeah. Sorry, that probably sounds bad, doesn't it?

Interviewer: No, I'm hearing it from other folks. You wanted closeness and that's the only way you knew, right?

Delores: Yeah. That was the hardest thing for me to get. Nothing else made me feel close for a long time.

Delores did eventually find a way of relating other than through tears, but it was a pattern that was directly highlighted as a target for change by her therapist. Her therapist began to share with Delores when she herself was feeling close to her client, when she was enjoying their interaction, and so on. Without implying that the client's job was to entertain her, the therapist helped Delores achieve a more workable interactional style.

The End Point of Trauma Therapy

Menninger and Holzman (1973)—like many other therapists before and since—noted the lack of consensus on the appropriate criteria to be used for termination. Many deny having specific "rules," stating that they decide when the end point is reached on a case-by-case basis. These therapists are responding at least in part to the general paucity of literature on termination, both in the trauma field particularly and in analytic writings generally. Novick (1997), one of few scholars who has written extensively on the subject, reports that the common approach to termination might be called "a genetic defect, one we can trace back to Freud, which has been passed on through the generations of analysts right up to the present" (p. 149).

A disturbing number of the accounts of termination that I have read in the client autobiographical literature (as opposed to those by therapists) present termination as poorly handled or not discussed at all. "Forced termination" was the rule in Freud's day, compounding the problem of conceptualization for analytic therapists who base their approaches on Freud's writings. Freud apparently ended Helene Deutsch's analysis to allow the Wolf Man to return to treatment (Novick, 1997), leaving Deutsch with the impression that he had grown bored with her (Roazen, 1985). Deutsch ended Margaret Mahler's analysis the same way, pronouncing her unanalyzable and dismissing her (Mahler, 1988; Roazen, 1985). In Muriel Gardiner's (another major analyst of Freud's day) autobiography (1983), she states that in one session her analyst said goodbye with such finality that Gardiner asked "Do you mean it's the end? My analysis is over?" Her analyst smiled and confirmed that this was the case. Gardiner reports that she was overjoyed and said "Oh, how wonderful! I'm so happy!" (p. 48). Novick (1997), citing this anecdote, notes that the analyst, Ruth Brunswick, also experienced a forced end of an analysis with Freud.

Of course, the fact that many therapists do not share their reasons for termination with their clients does not mean that no reasons were held in mind. Ferenczi (1927/1955), in the earliest psychoanalytic treatment of termination that I could locate, put forth the following criteria for determining the appropriate timing for the end of therapy:

> The proper ending of an analysis is when neither the physician nor the patient put an end to it, but when it dies of exhaustion ... So long as [the client] wishes to come to analysis he should continue to do so ... The patient finally becomes convinced that he is continuing analysis only because he is treating it as a new but still a fantasy source of gratification which in terms of reality yields him nothing. (p. 85)

Other signs of client readiness for termination that appear frequently in the literature are:

- Symptomatic improvement (Briere, 1992; Herman, 1992; Jones, 1936/1977)
- Ability to treat the therapist in a more egalitarian or "real" manner (Davies & Frawley, 1994; Ferenczi, 1927/1955; Kramer, 1986)
- The therapist's "intuition" that the time is right (Firestein, 1974; Kramer, 1986)
- Conscious awareness of the conflicts or traumatic

events, a lifting of the amnesia, or a decrease in dissociation (Davies & Frawley, 1994; Freud, 1937/1964;
Jones, 1936; Rickman, 1950)

□ Less reliance on the therapist for ego support and advice or interpretation, together with an increased capacity for self-analysis (or capacity to engage in therapeutic
self-talk) (Klein, 1950; Kramer, 1986; Ticho, 1972)

The conclusions of three major texts on trauma treatment are
given here:

> Though resolution is never complete, it is often sufficient
> for the survivor to turn her attention from the tasks of
> recovery to the tasks of ordinary life. The best indices of
> resolution are the survivor's restored capacity to take
> pleasure in her life and to engage fully in relationships
> with others. She has become more interested in the pres-
> ent and the future than in the past, more apt to approach
> the world with praise and awe than with fear. (Herman,
> 1992, p. 212)

* * *

> The position taken in this book is that abuse-focused psy-
> chotherapy can be deemed entirely successful when (a)
> the abuse trauma underlying "symptomatology" and
> negative tension-reduction activity has been resolved, (b)
> abuse-relevant cognitive distortions no longer interfere
> with the client's daily functioning or reasonably positive
> self-perception, and (c) the survivor's access to self is suf-
> ficient to allow adequate self-support and a stable base
> from which to interact with others. (Briere, 1992, pp.
> 108–109)

* * *

> As such experiences of real intimacy grow in the thera-
> peutic relationship, moments of true mutuality and
> shared pleasure can be expressed despite the accompa-
> nying vulnerability of both patient and therapist. The pa-

tient is once again—or perhaps for the first time—safely able to earn, fantasize and dream; and she ultimately becomes able to bring such aspects of her self experience into an interpersonal arena where they are most risky. . . . Again, we have no illusions of compensating the patient for early parental betrayal or of recreating a childhood that was filed with nightmarish terror and betrayal. . . . Rather, we view the simultaneous unfolding of mutually pleasurable and loving feelings in the patient and therapist as indicative of the successful reconfiguration of the relational matrices that are the pathological defensive consequences of traumatic abuse in early childhood. (M. Davies & Frawley, 1994, pp. 234–235)

To add more depth to the discussion, it is also interesting to view the complementarity of the opinions of the Trauma Countertransference Study participants on therapists' models of "trauma resolution" (as mediated by client understanding) to those stated above:

Interviewer: Did you have any sense of what your therapist was looking for in order to say that your therapy was over and the trauma was resolved or integrated?

Erik [traumatic loss client]: It seems like she was just waiting for me to stop talking about it, just wind down, you know. When I didn't need to talk about it, I was done.

Barbara [sexually abused patient]: I think it was when I was less emotional about it. It didn't make me shake anymore to mention it.

Karen [survivor of a recent rape]: She told me what to expect. She wanted to see me be free to sort of toss it around in my mind without freezing on one thing. Like when I came in, I would freeze on the part of it where I offered to well . . . pleasure him . . . where I tried to [titillate] him to get him on my side. But by the end, I thought of that with more meanings and less one-sidedness.

To this I would add that the intensity of the transference and the parallel intensity of the countertransference typically lessen as therapy progresses, replaced by a less conflictual sense of collegiality and partnership or friendship. Overall, however, two countertransference-related themes that did emerge across patients and therapists deserve more discussion and exploration.

Unrealistic Expectations and Damage to Treatment

A few years ago, I presented a paper on countertransference to a professional conference. A fellow presenter was speaking about art therapy and also touched on countertransference issues. She told the story of a client who had presented her with a piece of artwork, and described her countertransference responses to the patient's gift. In telling the therapeutic story, she first disclosed that her son had a rare bleeding disorder. She told of coming on a scene in a hospital when her son appeared to be bleeding to death, blood soaking the sheets and dripping on the floor as doctors worked feverishly to stop the flow. Her client, years after that episode, had shown her a graphic piece of art with masks floating in a sea of red paint, the paint "leaking" over onto the frame, symbolizing to the client his inability to contain the trauma. The therapist described her shock at the painting, and the intrusion of the memory of her son, stating in the conclusion of her talk that she clearly had not "resolved" the trauma of witnessing the hospital scene.

During the question period, I told my colleague that I did not consider her reaction to such a potent symbol of her trauma to be pathology that spoke to her lack of "resolution." Her story reminded me of one told by a Holocaust Remembrance Study participant, Isaac, who told us that a major task he was given in the concentration camp was washing dishes. He also mentioned that after losing his son, he did not cry except while washing dishes. Certainly this is of clinical interest, as one symbol of loss appears to be releasing more general overt symptoms of grief. But is this "nonresolution" or "nonintegration?"

A serious difficulty experienced differently by clients treated by therapists who did not disclose countertransference was a belief in trauma resolution that I believe is unrealistic. Such clients believed that therapists were modeling nonreactivity and equanimity as the end point of trauma therapy. "[The therapist] told me that I would be able to talk about it eventually without being upset," said Deborah of her rape experience, "but there is a part of me that will always mourn the father I might have had. I just can't stop feeling a little sad sometimes. I know I should have gotten over it. It was so long ago."

Other authors also have written of the humiliation that trauma patients report when symptoms recur at developmentally expected points in time (Herman, 1992), and they note that it is reasonable to expect that survivors of trauma "will go through periods in which they reexperience their mourning more acutely" (Tauber, 1998, p. 256). Participants in the Trauma Countertransference Study rarely reported that they had no emotional reaction to their previous trauma; sadly, they differed more in whether they believed this human concession to the life-changing aspects of trauma to be a symptom of personal inadequacy.

In rethinking "integration" of extreme trauma, and reexamining my own biases about the subject that I might impose on my clients, I have again found the Holocaust literature helpful. Remembering that trauma is conceived theoretically and described clinically as being "outside of normal experience," it is worthwhile to consider what it means to "integrate" such an event. In one way, trauma clients are symptomatic because they *have* integrated the traumatic event, meaning that the horrific reality of the trauma is now within reach of their imaginations. The survivor of a plane crash, for instance, does not report feeling immortal but instead reports feeling mortal for the first time. Their irrational beliefs about their immortality, indestructibility, and the strength of their morality in crisis have been challenged (cf. Janoff-Bulman, 1992). Tolerable lives depend on not living in constant fear that potential rapists and abusers populate our neighborhoods and workplaces.

Charlotte Delbo (1995), a survivor of Auschwitz and a prolific author, wrote that she lives not "with" her traumatic
history, but "beside" it. Like Lifton (1980), she speaks of a
double existence, an Auschwitz self and a nontraumatic self.
In one sense she appeared to be writing about dissociation
—the inability to fully experience the feelings and memories
of one reality while living in another. But this "doubling" can
be an adaptive use of the dissociation defense, allowing the
survivor to protect the nontraumatic world from constant intrusion by the traumatic one.

When I asked the 84 Trauma Countertransference Study
participants how they felt about their trauma now, 42 used
the words "distant," "unreal," or some other synonym within
their extended descriptions. Use of these terms in the Holocaust sample was even more frequent. This descriptive tendency correlated positively with the client's perception of
success of their therapy and their general satisfaction with
their current lives. It appears that allowing trauma to recede
to a more peripheral position in the client's everyday experience can be healthy and adaptive and not necessarily a sign
of "repression" or avoidance. The continued contradictions
in living with and beside trauma also must be tolerated by
therapist and client alike—remembering and forgetting the
past, mastering trauma, and accepting its power to change
one's priorities and life view.

The end point of therapy also includes mourning the un-
mourned aspects of the trauma, the loss perhaps of a loved
one, a previously healthy state, or one's own innocence and
optimism. Lawrence Langer (1991), a professor of English
who teaches Holocaust studies, once published a paper by a
student in which these contradictions and new willingness
to mourn can be seen. The author of the passage below was
14 when the Germans invaded Poland, when she had been
picked up by Christian friends so that she might be hidden
from the Nazi forces. A half-hour later the friends went back
to rescue her parents, who had already been taken away. She
never saw them again.

Can you forget your own father and mother? . . . This
awful, awesome power of not-remembering, this heart-

breaking sensation of the conspiracy of silence is my dilemma. Often, I have tried to break through my impris-
oning wall of irrational silence, but failed: now I hope to
be able to do it. Until now, I was not able to face up to
the loss of my parents, much less talk about them. The
smallest reminder of them would set off a chain reaction
of results that I could anticipate but never direct. The
destructive force of sadness, horror, fright would then
become my master. And it was this subconscious knowledge that kept me paralyzed with silence, not a conscious
desire to forget my parents. My silent wall, my locked
shell existed only of real necessity; I need time. I needed
time to forget the tragic loss of my loved ones, time to
heal my emotional wound so that there shall come a time
when I can again remember the people I have forgotten.
(Charny, 1992, p. 202)

The evidence that trauma symptoms should be expected
to recur is even more clear (cf. Herman, 1992). Without presenting a picture that the client is forever damaged or stained
by traumatic events, the therapist is well advised to normalize the experience of occasional resurgence of symptoms at
developmental or other symbolic periods, such that the client
need not interpret these temporary events as "failure to integrate or resolve the issues." Lynn Johnson's technique (described in Dolan, 1991) of asking the client to have an "imag-
inary relapse," and to predict what caused it, what might be
learned from it, and how it might be overcome, is an interesting and useful strategy to meet this goal.

The Resistance to Saying Good-Bye

The struggle with dependency that often occurs in the traumatized patient, who so fears trusting a powerful other, leads
many clients to fear termination of therapy. The Trauma
Countertransference Study participants were asked how
much time their therapists devoted to the process of termination (average three weeks to three months) and how much
time they would recommend for the process (average two to

four months). Clients reported fearing regression after termination and a concern over losing the most meaningful relationship they had ever had. Most did not experience the feared regression, but a few did. If therapy had been self-labeled as successful, the regression passed without untoward effect, and clients viewed the process as transitional and expected. Those whose therapy had been unexpectedly terminated, however, often were still mourning and rehashing their contributions to the failure many years later.

The intensity of the therapy and the associated difficulties in ending are experienced by both therapist and client in many cases. A sense of incompleteness, to be expected in any long-term therapy (Brenner, 1976: Freud, 1937/1964; Waelder, 1960), can become powerfully salient to the therapist, triggering defensive moves to prolong treatment. I find it extremely interesting that therapists commonly consider therapeutic endings as "premature," often attributed to client resistance, even in therapies lasting one to three years or more (Bosset & Styrsky, 1986). In DeBerry and Baskin's (1989) comparison of termination in private and public clinic settings, over 75% of terminations in public clinics were said to occur (according to the 450 therapists surveyed) for reasons other than the attainment of therapeutic goals.

When I asked the Trauma Countertransference Study participants why they stopped therapy when they did, many looked at me with confusion. Twenty-two participants (26%) admitted that the decision was not primarily their own. In these cases, the therapists unilaterlly decided to end treatment. For 31 participants (36%), the reason given for termination was primarily structural—a move, a change in insurance, a change in work schedule. The remaining subjects believed that they had reached an appropriate ending point. However only 16 (19%) went through a formal termination phase; fifteen participants simply found themselves cancelling and rescheduling sessions with greater frequency and decided that the time had come to stop (typically with one to four sessions of final discussion).

In general, Trauma Countertransference Study participants still were struggling with the concept of termination when I spoke to them, often many years after the end point of their treatment. Laurie, a victim of sexual abuse who terminated after a move (for a new job) made this point:

> *Interviewer:* How did it feel when you started talking about termination?
>
> *Laurie:* Well, I suppose you're expecting me to say "sad."
>
> *Interviewer:* Not sad, then?
>
> *Laurie:* Mostly it felt odd. Not seeing this woman who was so important to me for so long—just kicking her out of my life—it's odd. Don't you think?

Yes, in fact, I do think that it is odd. What other relationship ends this way? Relationships typically end because they transform from positive to negative, or because circumstances (distance, death) force the separation. Even parent and child, who must physically separate in most cases, typically stay in the relationship and continue to physically meet. Therapist and client are supposed to take their leave of one another with therapeutic love and friendship intact, often at a very positive point in the relationship (cf. Bergmann, 1997). Is it any wonder that the therapist or client (or both) would feel the need to distance, devalue, or dismiss the significance of the other to make internal sense of the leave-taking?

Termination issues also came up frequently in the overall critique (or therapeutic obstacles) section of the Trauma Countertransference Study interview. Among the criticisms raised by clients of the therapists' handling of the termination process were:

- □ Lack of preparatory discussion of termination before its announcement or lack of discussion of termination criteria.
- □ Lack of preparation of the client (by the therapist) for the post-therapy mourning period that many client experienced.
- □ Failure to share and normalizing the conflictual emo-

tions associated with leaving, including sadness, pride, gratitude, and concern.
□ Lack of clarity as to the rules of post-therapy behavior (e.g., the ethics of calling one's former therapist to announce changes in life circumstances).

Clients interviewed within the Trauma Countertransference Study generally saw their therapists as ill at ease with termination, unsure as to the rules of the final exchanges, and lacking in a capacity to conceptualize termination in a manner helpful to the client. Again, to the extent these criticisms are fair (and I suspect they are), countertransference discomfort might stem from our lack of training and theory specifically on the issue. Other sources could include the therapist's disappointment with client achievements, the therapist's uneasiness with his or her own sadness related to the client's leaving, concern for the client's future, and discomfort with the prospect of boundary issues at termination. (Should I let her hug me good-bye? Will offering a follow-up undercut the feeling of having ended successfully?)

I recommend discussion of termination as a process far in advance of the actual event. Opportunities typically present themselves early in therapy for trauma clients, when the client mentions fear of abandonment due to therapist disgust, disdain, or boredom. At this time, I am likely to begin to speak to the client about the strange nature of our relationship—that it will end at some time despite our continuing commitment to each other and that in some sense I hope to ease my own loss by positive memories of the change we produced together. I also emphasize that the timing of the ending will not be determined unilaterally by me, and discuss some of the ways (outlined above) that we will come to know the time is right. Furthermore, while our relationship will change—become more egalitarian, more peripheral in the individual's life and so on—I do not intend to become something else (a friend or a lover, for instance). For better or for worse, I am a therapist in the lives of my patients forever. I do invite them to update me with messages by phone or mail about the changes in their circumstances, and explicitly leave the door open for the client to return to treatment briefly (or long term, although this is rare).

My clients tell me that they benefit from these early preliminary discussions. Ms. B, a victim of physical assault, called the discussions our "fire drills," meaning that they allowed the actual event to be handled with less anxiety and distress because we felt more prepared. Many of my clients (and many in the Trauma Countertransference Study) tell me that the therapeutic realtionship, despite its limitations, is one of the most loving relationships they have known. In general, the more severely disturbed the client, the more the nonjudgmental, tolerant atmosphere of therapy has been a truly unique environment.

Several of my clients have given me mementos on termination, which I have accepted with little conflict. At times they have asked for something from me, and I have given thought to a meaningful symbol. One gift I received that comes easily to mind was a small carved figure of a bear, a fetish from an Indian client who identified strongly with the Indian people. He had the figure blessed by a leader of his tribe, and then, to show his wish to respect my beliefs, took it to a rabbi to have it blessed in a way that he thought I would value. I have chosen similar types of personal symbols for individual clients. I have also participated in rituals of various types requested by clients, typically client-designed and unique to the individual. Most commonly, I then hear from the client several times a year as they update me on their triumphs, tragedies, and challenges.

In any therapy that comes to a natural end, I ask the client to critique the process with me. I ask where I have done wrong, I apologize for mistakes they point out, and I try to show my respect and gratitude for what each individual has taught me. Before the final session, I spend time thinking about our work, looking for examples that will illustrate the ways in which this individual client has helped me move more toward where I would like to be as a therapist and as a person. I find that any client whom I have greatly helped has also produced growth in me. For those who participated in the Trauma Countertransference Study and who may not have come to a reasonable ending with their own therapists, I also tried to show my deep gratitude. These clients, in addition to those with whom I have worked personally, have profoundly deepened my own understanding of the trauma therapy process. I continue to believe that the topic we have begun to examine here deserves our passionate interest and best thought.

References

Ablow, K. (1992). *To wrestle with demons: A psychiatrist struggles to understand his patients and himself.* Washington, DC: American Psychiatric Press.

Adler, G. (1993). The psychotherapy of core borderline psychopathology. *American Journal of Psychotherapy, 47,* 194–205.

Adler, G., & Buie, D. (1979). Aloneness and borderline psychopathology: The possible relevance of child development issues. *International Journal of Psycho-Analysis, 60,* 83–96.

Adshead, G. (1994). Damage: Trauma and violence in a sample of women referred to a forensic service. *Behavioral Sciences and the Law, 12,* 235–249.

Alonso, A., & Rutan, J. (1988). Shame and guilt in psychotherapy supervision. *Psychotherapy, 25,* 576–581.

American Psychiatric Association. (1994). *Diagnostic and statistical manual of mental disorders* (4th ed.). Washington, DC: Author.

Amery, J., Rosenfeld, S., & Rosenfeld, S. P. (1980). *At the mind's limits.* Bloomington, IN: Indiana University Press. (Originally published in 1966)

Aransky, K. (1996). *Dissociation, anger level, and childhood punishment history as predictors of use of punishment against children.* Unpublished doctoral dissertation, California School of Professional Psychology, San Diego.

Armstrong, L. (1994). *Rocking the cradle of sexual politics.* Reading, MA: Addison-Wesley.

Armsworth, M. (1989). Therapy of incest survivors: Abuse or support? *Child Abuse and Neglect, 13,* 549–562.

Aron, L. (1991). The patient's experience of the analyst's subjectivity. *Psychoanalytic Dialogues, 1,* 29–51.

Atwood, M. (1987). *Selected poems: II.* New York: Houghton Mifflin.

Baider, L., Peretz, T., & De-Nour, A. (1997). The effect of behavioral intervention on the psychological distress of Holocaust survivors with cancer. *Psychotherapy and Psychosomatics, 66,* 44–49.

Balint, M. (1968). *The basic fault.* London: Tavistock.

Barkwell, D. (1991). Ascribed meaning: A critical factor in coping and pain attenuation in patients with cancer-related pain. *Journal of Palliative Care, 7,* 5–14.

Bartholomew, K., & Horowitz, L. (1991). Attachment styles among young adults: A test of a four-category model. *Journal of Personality and Social Psychology, 61,* 226–244.

Baskin-Creel, R. (1994). *Countertransference and individual psychotherapy with battered women.* Unpublished doctoral dissertation, California School of Professional Psychology, San Diego.

Bass, E., & Davis, L. (1988). *The courage to heal: A guide for women survivors of child sexual abuse.* New York: Harper & Row.

Bates, C., & Brodsky, A. (1989). *Sex in the therapy hour: A case of professional incest.* New York: Guilford.

Bauer, G. (1993). *The analysis of transference in the here and now.* Northvale, NJ: Jason Aronson.

Baur, S. (1997). *The intimate hour: Love and sex in psychotherapy.* Boston: Houghton Mifflin.

Bayatpour, M., Wells, R., & Holford, S. (1992). Physical and sexual abuse as predictors of substance use and suicide among pregnant teenagers. *Journal of Adolescent Health, 13,* 128–132.

Beck, A. (1989). An interview with a depressed and suicidal patient. In D. Wedding & R. Corsini (Eds.), *Case studies in psychotherapy* (pp. 125–142). Itasca, IL: F.E. Peacock.

Beck, A., & Emery, G. (1985). *Anxiety disorders and phobias: A cognitive perspective.* New York: Basic Books.

Beck, A., Steer, R., & Ranieri, W. (1988). Scale for suicidal ideation: Psychometric properties of a self-report version. *Journal of Clinical Psychology, 44,* 499–505.

Beckett, K. (1996). Culture and the politics of signification: The case of child sexual abuse. *Social Problems, 43,* 57–76.

Bergmann, M. (1997). Termination: The Achilles heel of psychoanalytic technique. *Psychoanalytic Psychology, 14,* 163–174.

Bernardez, T. (1994). The eroticized transference: A tool for the reconstruction of childhood sexual trauma. *Journal of the American Academy of Psychoanalysis, 22,* 519–531.

Bernsen, A. Tabachnick, B. G., & Pope, K. S. (1994). National survey of social workers' sexual attraction to their clients: Results, implications, and comparison to psychologist. *Ethics & Behavior, 4,* 369–388.

Berry, J. (1970). Therapists' responses as a function of level of therapist experience and attitude of the patient. *Journal of Consulting and Clinical Psychology, 34,* 239–243.

Beutler, L., Machado, P., & Neufeldt, S. (1994). Therapist variables. In A. Bergin & S. Garfield (Eds.), *Handbook of psychotherapy and behavior change* (pp. 229–269). New York: Wiley.

Biaggio, M. (1987). A survey of psychologists' perspectives on catharsis. *Journal of Psychology, 121,* 243–248.

Bion, W. (1955). Language and the schizophrenic. In M. Klein, P. Heiman, & R. Money-Kyrle (Eds.), *New directions in psychoanalysis* (pp. 220–239). London: Tavistock.

Bion, W. (1959). Attacks on linking. *International Journal of Psychoanalysis, 40,* 308–315.

Bion, W. (1984) *Second thoughts: Selected papers on psycho-analysis.* Northvale, NJ: Jason Aronson.

Bird, B. (1972). Notes on transference: Universal phenomenon and hardest part of analysis. *Journal of the American Psychoanalytic Association, 20,* 267–301.

Bloom, J. (1989). The character of danger in psychiatric practice: Are the mentally ill dangerous? *Bulletin of the American Academy of Psychiatry and the Law, 17,* 241–255.

Bollas, C. (1983). Expressive uses of the countertransference: Notes to the patient from oneself. *Contemporary Psychoanalysis, 19,* 1–34.

Borys, D., & Pope, K. (1989). Dual relationships between therapist and client: A national study of psychologists, psychiatrists, and social workers. *Professional Psychology: Research and Practice, 20,* 283–293.

Bosset, F. & Styrsky, E. (1986). Termination in individual psychotherapy. A survey of residents' experience. *Canadian Journal of Psychiatry, 31,* 636–641.

Bouchard, M., Normandin, L., & Seguin, M. (1995). Countertransference as instrument and obstacle: A comprehensive and descriptive framework. *Psychoanalytic Quarterly, 44,* 717–745.

Bowlby, J. (1973). *Attachment and loss: Vol. 2. Separation: Anxiety and anger.* New York: Basic Books.

Bowlby, J. (1988). *A secure base.* New York: Basic Books.

Brabin, P., & Berah, E. (1995). Dredging up past trauma: Harmful or helpful? *Psychiatry, Psychology and Law, 2,* 165–171.

Breggin, P. (1991). *Toxic psychiatry.* New York: St. Martin's Press.

Brenner, C. (1976). *Psychoanalytic technique and psychic conflict.* New York. International Universities Press.

Breuer, J., & Freud, S. (1995). Studies on hysteria. In J. Strachey (Ed. and Trans.), *The standard edition of the complete psychological works of Sigmund Freud,* (Vol. 2, pp. 1–311). London: Hogarth Press. (Original work published 1895)

Brewin, C., Dalgleish, T., & Joseph, S. (1996). A dual representation theory of posttraumatic stress disorder. *Psychological Review, 103,* 670–686.

Briere, J. (1989). *Therapy for adults molested as children: Beyond survival.* New York: Springer.

Briere, J. (1992). *Child abuse trauma.* Newbury Park, CA: Sage.

Briere, J. (1996). *Therapy for adults molested as children: Beyond survival* (2nd ed.). New York: Springer.

Briere, J., & Gil, E. (1998). Self-mutilation in clinical and general population samples: Prevalence, correlates and functions. *American Journal of Orthopsychiatry, 68,* 609–620.

Briere, J., & Runtz, M. (1988). Symptomatology associated with childhood sexual victimization in a non-clinical adult sample. *Child Abuse and Neglect, 12,* 331–341.

Briere, J., & Runtz, M. (1990). Differential adult symptomatology associated with three types of child abuse histories. *Child Abuse and Neglect, 14,* 357–364.

Briere, J., Woo, R., McRae, B., Foltz, J., & Sitzman, R. (1997). Lifetime victimization history, demographics, and clinical status in female psychiatric emergency room patients. *Journal of Nervous and Mental Disease, 185,* 95–101.

Briere, J., & Zaidi, L. (1989). Sexual abuse histories and sequelae in female psychiatric emergency room patients. *American Journal of Psychiatry, 146,* 1602–1606.

Brody, E., & Farber, B. (1996). The effects of therapist experience and patient diagnosis on countertransference. *Psychotherapy, 33,* 372–380.

Brown, G., & Anderson, B. (1991). Psychiatric morbidity in adult inpatients with childhood histories of sexual and physical abuse. *American Journal of Psychiatry, 148,* 55–61.

Brown, D., Scheflin, A., & Hammond, D. (1998). *Memory, trauma treatment, and the law.* New York: Norton.

Bryant, S., & Range, L. (1997). Type and severity of child abuse and college students' lifetime suicidality. *Child Abuse and Neglect, 21,* 1169–1176.

Bryer, J., Nelson, B., Miller, J., & Krol, P. (1987). Childhood sexual and physical abuse as factors in adult psychiatric illness. *American Journal of Psychiatry, 144,* 1426–1430.

Burgess, A., Hartman, C., & McCormack, A. (1987). Pathways and cycles of runaways: A model for understanding repetitive runaway behavior. *Hospital and Community Psychiatry, 38,* 292–299.

Caplan, P. (1987). No: The myth of women's masochism. In M. R. Walsh (Ed.), *The psychology of women: Ongoing debates* (pp. 78–96). New Haven, CT: Yale University Press.

Carlson, E. (1997). *Trauma assessments: A clinician's guide.* New York: Guilford.

Carmi, T. (1977). Anatomy of a war. *Jerusalem Quarterly, 3,* 102.

Carotenuto, A. (1982). *A secret symmetry: Sabina Speilrein between Jung and Freud.* New York: Pantheon Books.

Caruth, C. (1995). *Trauma: Explorations in memory.* Baltimore, MD: Johns Hopkins University Press.

Celenza, A. (1991). The misuse of countertransference love in sexual intimacies between therapists and patients. *Psychoanalytic Psychology, 8,* 501–509.

Charny, I. (Ed.). (1992). *Holding on to humanity: The message of Holocaust survivors.* New York: New York University Press.

Cheit, R., & Goldschmidt, E. (1997). Child molesters in the criminal justice system: A comprehensive case law analysis of the Rhode Island Docket (1985–1993). *New England Journal on Criminal and Civil Confinement, 23,* 267–301.

Chu, J. (1991). The repetition compulsion revisited: Reliving dissociated trauma. *Psychotherapy, 28,* 327–332.

Coe, M., Dalenberg, C., Aransky, K., & Reto, K. (1995). Adult attachment style, reported childhood violence history and types of dissociative experiences. *Dissociation: Progress in the Dissociative Disorders, 8,* 142–154.

Cohen, M. (1952). Countertransference and anxiety. *Psychiatry, 15,* 231–243.

Cohen, C., & Sherwood, V. (1991). *Becoming a constant object in psychotherapy with the borderline patient.* Northvale, NJ: Jason Aronson.

Colson, D., Lewis, L, & Horowitz, L. (1985). Negative outcome in psychotherapy and psychoanalysis. In D. Mays & C. Franks (Eds.), *Negative outcome in psychotherapy and what to do about it* (pp. 59–75). New York: Springer.

Collins, D. (1989). Sexual involvement between psychiatric hospital staff and their patients. In G. Gabbard (Ed.), *Sexual exploitation in professional relationships* (pp. 151–176). Washington, DC: American Psychiatric Press.

Courtois, C. (1988). *Healing the incest wound: Adult survivors in therapy.* New York: Norton.

Courtois, C. (1999). *Recollections of sexual abuse: Treatment principles and guidelines.* New York: Norton.

Crittendon, P. (1997). Patterns of attachment and sexual behavior: Risk of dysfunction versus opportunity for creative integration. In L. Atkinson & K. Zuckerman (Eds.), *Attachment and psychopathology* (pp. 47–93). New York: Guilford.

Dale, P., Allen, J., & Measor, L. (1996, January). *Clients and therapists perceptions of the psychotherapeutic process: A study of adults abused as children.* Paper presented at BAC Research Conference. University of Birmingham, England.

Dalenberg, C. (1994, January). *Transference and countertransference in the long-term individual treatment of abuse survivors.* Invited workshop presented to the Responding to Child Maltreatment Conference, San Diego, CA.

Dalenberg, C. (1995, January). *Transference and countertransference in the treatment of adult victims and perpetrators of sexual abuse.* Workshop presented to the Conference on Responding to Child Maltreatment, San Diego, CA.

Dalenberg, C. (1996a). Accuracy, timing and circumstances of disclosure in therapy of recovered and continuous memories of abuse. *Psychiatry and the Law, 19,* 229–275.

Dalenberg, C. (1996b). Fantastic elements in child disclosures of abuse. *APSAC Advisor, 3,* 1:5–10.

Dalenberg, C., & Carlson, E. (in press). Ethical issues in the treatment of the recovered memory trauma victim and patients with false memories of trauma. In S. Bucky (Ed.). *Comprehensive textbook on ethics and law in the practice of psychology.* New York: Plenum.

Dalenberg, C., & Cuevas, C. (1997, January). *Common transference-countertransference crises in psychotherapy with abuse victims: Empirical evidence for efficacy of resolution strategies.* Paper presented to the meeting of the International Society for the Study of Traumatic Stress, Montreal, Quebec, Canada.

Dalenberg, C., Aransky, K., & Dunkerley, G. (1996, January). *Countertransference responses to sexual attraction in therapy with sexually abused patients.* Paper presented to the Conference on Responding to Child Maltreatment, San Diego, CA.

Dalenberg, C., Dunkerley, G., & Collopy, M. (1997, November). *Sexual/affectional transference and countertransference in the care of the sexual abuse victim: The role of touch, disclosure of caring, and sexual feelings.* Poster session presented at the meeting of the International Society for the Study of Traumatic Stress, Montreal, Quebec, Canada.

Dalenberg, C., & Epstein, J. (1999). Interviewing the survivor of the Holocaust: Lessons for the advancement of understanding of the effects of extreme child trauma. In A. Memon & R. Bull (Eds.), *Handbook of the psychology of interviewing* (pp. 39–52). London: Wiley.

Dalenberg, C., Hyland, K., & Cuevas, C. (In press). Sources of fantastic elements in allegations of abuse by adults and children. In G. Goodman, M. Eisen, & J. Quas (Eds.), *Memory and suggestibility in forensic interviewing.* Mahwah, NJ: Erlbaum.

Dalenberg, C., & Jacobs, D. (1994). Attributional analyses of child sexual abuse episodes: Empirical and clinical issues. *Journal of Child Sexual Abuse, 3,* 37–50.

Danieli, Y. (1981). *Therapists' difficulties in treating survivors of the Nazi Holocaust and their children.* Unpublished doctoral dissertation, New York University.

Davenloo, H. (1978). *Basic principles and techniques of short-term dynamic psychotherapy.* New York: Spectrum.

Davies, M., & Frawley, M. (1994) *Treating the adult survivor of childhood sexual abuse: A psychoanalytic perspective.* New York: Basic Books.

Davies, R. (1970). *Fifth Business.* New York: Penguin Books.

DeBerry, S., & Baskin, D. (1989). Termination criteria in psychotherapy: A comparison of private and public practice. *American Journal of Psychotherapy, 43,* 43–54.

Delbo, C. (1995). *Auschwitz and after.* New Haven, CT: Yale University Press.

DePaulo, B., & Bell, K. (1996). Truth and investment: Lies are told to those who care. *Journal of Personality and Social Psychology, 71,* 703–716.

Dolan, Y. (1991). *Resolving sexual abuse: Solution-focused therapy and Ericksonian hypnosis for abuse survivors.* New York: Norton.

Drozd, L., & Dalenberg, C. (1994). Self as a mediator in the psychopathology of children of alcoholics. *International Journal of the Addictions, 29,* 1878–1800.

Dunbar, P. (1993). *The collected poetry of Paul Laurence Dunbar.* Charlottesville, VA: University Press of Virginia. (Originally published in 1913)

Echeburua, E., de Corral, P., Sarasua, B., & Zubizarreta, I. (1996). Treatment of acute posttraumatic stress disorder in rape victims: An experimental study. *Journal of Anxiety Disorders, 10,* 185–199.

Egeland, B. (1989, November). *A longitudinal study of high risk families: Is-*

sues and findings. Paper presented at the Research Forum on Issues in the Longitudinal Study of Child Maltreatment, Toronto, Ontario, Canada.

Ehrenberg, D. (1992). *The intimate edge: Extending the reach of psychoanalytic interaction.* New York: Norton.

Ekman, P. (1973). *Darwin and facial expression: A century of research in review.* New York: Academic.

Eldean, K. (1998). *Attribution level, anger level, and childhood punishment history as predictors of the use of punishment against children.* Unpublished doctoral dissertation, California School of Professional Psychology, San Diego.

Elkind, S. (1992). *Resolving impasses in therapeutic relationships.* New York: Guilford.

Elliott, D., & Guy, J. (1993). Mental health professionals' versus nonmental health professionals' childhood trauma and adult functioning. *Professional Psychology: Research and Practice, 24,* 83–90.

Enns, C., McNeilly, C., Corkery, J., & Gilbert, M. (1995). The debate about delayed memories of child sexual abuse: A feminist perspective. *The Counseling Psychologist, 23,* 181–279.

Epstein, L. (1977). The therapeutic function of hate in the countertransference. *Contemporary Psychoanalysis, 13,* 442–461.

Epstein, L. (1979). On the therapeutic use of countertransference data with borderline patients. *Contemporary Psychoanalysis, 15,* 248–275.

Epstein, R. (1994). *Keeping boundaries: Maintaining safety and integrity in the psychotherapeutic process.* Washington, DC: American Psychiatric Press.

Epstein, R., Simon, R., & Kay, G. (1992). Assessing boundary violations in psychotherapy: Survey results with the Exploitation Index. *Bulletin of the Menninger Clinic, 56,* 150–166.

Esterling, B., Antoni, M., Fletcher, M., Margulies, S., & Schneiderman, N. (1994). Emotional disclosure through writing or speaking modulates Epstein-Barr virus antibody titers. *Journal of Consulting and Clinical Psychology, 62,* 130–140.

Everson, M. (1997). Understanding bizarre, improbable, and fantastic elements in children's accounts of abuse. *Child Maltreatment, 2,* 134–149.

Feeney, J., Noller, P., & Callan, V. (1994). Attachment style, communication and satisfaction in the early years of marriage. In K. Bartholomew & D. Perlman (Eds.), *Advances in personal relationships* (Vol. 5, pp. 269–308). London: Jessica Kingsley.

Ferenczi, S. (1931). *Final contributions to the problems and methods of psychoanalysis.* London: Hogarth Press.

Ferenczi, S. (1932). *The clinical diary of Sandor Ferenczi.* Cambridge, MA: Harvard University Press.

Ferenczi, S. (1949). Confusion of tongues between adults and the child. *International Journal of Psychoanalysis, 30,* 225–230. (Original work published in 1933)

Ferenczi, S. (1955). The problem of termination of the analysis. *In Final contributions to the problems and methods of psycho-analysis* (pp, 77–86). London: Hogarth. (Original work published 1927)

Figley, C. (1995). *Compassion fatigue: Coping with secondary traumatic stress disorder in those who treat the traumatized.* Philadelphia: Brunner/ Mazel.

Firestein, S. (1974). Termination in psychoanalysis of adults: A review of the literature. *Journal of the American Psychoanalytic Association, 22,* 873–893.

Foa, E,, & Kozak, M. (1986). Emotional processing of fear: Expose to corrective information. *Psychological Bulletin, 99,* 20–35.

Foa, E., Riggs, D., Massie, E., & Yarczower, M. (1995). The impact of fear activation and anger on the efficacy of exposure treatment for posttraumatic stress disorder. *Behavior Therapy, 26,* 487–499.

Foa, E., & Rothbaum, B. (1998). *Treating the trauma of rape: Cognitive-behavioral therapy for PTSD.* New York: Guilford.

Foa, E., Steketee, G., & Rothbaum, B. (1989). Behavioral/cognitive conceptualization of post-traumatic stress disorder. *Behavior Therapy, 20,* 155–176.

Follette, V., Polusny, M., & Milbeck, K. (1994). Mental health and law enforcement professionals: Trauma history, psychological symptoms, and impact of providing services to child sexual abuse survivors. *Professional Psychology: Research and Practice, 25,* 275–282.

Frank, A. (1992). The therapeutic alliances of borderline patients. In J. Clarkin, E. Marziali, & H. Munroe-Blum (Eds.), *Borderline personality disorder: Clinical and empirical perspectives* (pp. 220–247). New York: Guilford.

Freud, A. (1969). Comments on psychic trauma. In *The Writings of Anna Freud* (Vol. 5., pp. 221–241). New York: International Universities Press.

Freud, S. (1957). The future prospects of psycho-analytic therapy. In J. Strachey (Ed. and Trans.), *The standard edition of the complete psychological works of Sigmund Freud* (Vol. 11, pp. 141–151). London: Hogarth Press. (Original work published 1910)

Freud, S. (1958). Recommendations to physicians practicing psychoanalysis. In J. Strachey (Ed. and Trans.), *The standard edition of the complete psychological works of Sigmund Freud* (Vol. 12, pp. 111–120). London: Hogarth Press. (Original work published 1912)

Freud, S. (1958). On beginning the treatment: Further recommendations on the technique of psychoanalysis. In J. Strachey (Ed. and Trans.), *The standard edition of the complete psychological works of Sigmund Freud* (Vol. 12, pp. 123–144). London: Hogarth Press. (Original work published 1913)

Freud, S. (1958). Observations on transference-love: Further recommendations on the technique of psychoanalysis. In J. Strachey (Ed. and Trans.), *The standard edition of the complete psychological works of Sig-*

mund Freud (Vol. 12, pp. 159–171). London: Hogarth Press. (Original work published 1915)

Freud, S. (1960). Beyond the pleasure principle. In J. Strachey (Ed. and Trans.), *The standard edition of the complete psychological works of Sigmund Freud* (Vol. 18, pp. 7–64). London: Hogarth Press. (Original work published 1920)

Freud, S. (1961). Civilization and its discontents. In J. Strachey (Ed. and Trans.), *The standard edition of the complete psychological works of Sigmund Freud* (Vol. 21, pp. 57–243). London: Hogarth Press. (Original work published 1930)

Freud, S. (1969). Analysis terminable and interminable. In J. Strachey (Ed. and Trans.), *The standard edition of the complete psychological works of Sigmund Freud* (Vol. 23, p. 203–253). London: Hogarth Press. (Original work published 1937)

Freyd, J. (1996). *Betrayal trauma: The logic of forgetting childhood abuse.* Cambridge, MA: Harvard University Press.

Friedberg, R., & Fidaleo, R. (1992). Training inpatient staff in cognitive therapy. *Journal of Cognitive Psychotherapy, 6,* 105–112.

Fromuth, M. (1986). The relationship of childhood sexual abuse with later psychological and sexual adjustment in a sample of college women. *Child Abuse and Neglect, 10,* 5–15.

Gabbard, G. (1996). *Love and hate in the analytic setting.* Northvale, NJ: Jason Aronson.

Gabbard, G., & Lester, E. (1995). *Boundaries and boundary violations in psychoanalysis.* New York: Basic Books.

Gabbard, G., & Wilkinson, S. (1994). *Management of countertransference with borderline patients.* Washington, DC: American Psychiatric Press.

Gabel, S., Oster, G., & Pfeffer, C. (1988). *Difficult moments in child psychotherapy.* New York: Plenum.

Gamsky, N., & Farwell, G. (1966). Counselor verbal behavior as a function of client hostility. *Journal of Counseling Psychology, 13,* 184–190.

Gardiner, M. (1983). *Code name "Mary."* New Haven, CT: Yale University Press.

George, C., & Main, M. (1979). Social interactions of young abused children: Approach, avoidance and aggression. *Child Development, 50,* 306–318.

Gitelson, M. (1952). The emotional position of the analyst in the psychoanalytic situation. *International Journal of Psycho-Analysis, 33,* 1–10.

Glover, E. (1955). *The technique of psycho-analysis.* New York: International Universities Press.

Goodman, G., Bottoms, B., Schwartz-Kenney, B., & Rudy, L. (1991). Children's testimony for a stressful event: Improving children's reports. *Journal of Narrative and Life History, 1,* 69–99.

Goodman, G., Quas, J., Batterman-Faunce, J., Riddlesberger, M., & Kuhn, J. (1994). Predictors of accurate and inaccurate memories of traumatic events experienced in childhood. *Consciousness and Cognition, 3,* 269–294.

Gorkin, M. (1987). *The uses of countertransference.* Northvale, NJ: Jason Aronson.

Grand, S. (1995). Toward a reconceptualization of false-memory phenomena. In J. Alpert (Ed.), *Sexual abuse recalled: Treating trauma in the era of the recovered memory debate* (pp. 257–288). Northvale, NJ: Jason Aronson.

Greenson, R. (1967). *Technique and practice of psychoanalysis: Vol. I.* Madison, WI: International Universities Press.

Greenson, R. (1974). Loving, hating and indifference towards the patient. *International Review of Psycho-Analysis, 1,* 259–266.

Grotstein, J. (1995). Projective identification reappraised: II. The countertransference complex. *Contemporary Psychoanalysis, 31,* 479–511.

Gunderson, J. (1996). The borderline patient's intolerance of aloneness: Insecure attachments and therapist availability. *American Journal of Psychiatry, 153,* 752–758.

Gutheil, T., & Gabbard, G. (1993). The concept of boundaries in clinical practice: Theoretical and risk-management dimensions. *American Journal of Psychiatry, 150,* 188–196.

Hahn, W. (1995a). Response to McCallum and Gans. *International Journal of Group Psychotherapy, 45,* 363–366.

Hahn, W. (1995b). Therapist anger in group psychotherapy. *International Journal of Group Psychotherapy, 45,* 339–347.

Harvey, J., Orbuch, T., & Fink, K. (1990). The social psychology of account-making: meaning, hope and generativity. *New Zealand Journal of Psychology, 19,* 46–57.

Harvey, J., Orbuch, T., Weber, A., & Merbach, N., Salt, R. (1992). House of pain and hope: Accounts of loss. *Death Studies, 16,* 99–124.

Hedges, L., Hilton, R., Hilton, V., & Caudill, O. (1997). *Therapists at risk: Perils of the intimacy of the therapeutic relationship.* Northvale, NJ: Jason Aronson.

Heimann, P. (1950). On counter-transference. *International Journal of Psycho-Analysis, 31,* 81–84.

Herman, J. (1992). *Trauma and recovery.* New York: Basic Books.

Himber, J. (1994). Blood rituals: Self-cutting in female psychiatric patients. *Psychotherapy, 31,* 620–631.

Hoglund, C., & Nicholas, K. (1995). Shame, guilt and anger in college students exposed to abusive family environments. *Journal of Family Violence, 10,* 141–157.

Howes, C. & Eldredge, R. (1985). Responses of abused, neglected, and maltreated children to the behaviors of peers. *Journal of Applied Developmental Psychology, 6,* 261–270.

Hoyt, S. (1998). The perception of danger cues in traumatized and non-traumatized populations. Unpublished doctoral dissertation, California School of Professional Psychology, San Diego.

Hungerford v. Jones. (1997). Supreme Court of New Hampshire, U.S. District Court No. 97-657.

Hunt, W., & Issacharoff, A. (1977). Heinrach Racker and countertransference theory. *Journal of the American Academy of Psychoanalysis, 5,* 95–105.

Hunter, J., Goodwin, D., & Wilson, R. (1992). Attributions of blame in child sexual abuse victims: An analysis of age and gender influences. *Journal of Child Sexual Abuse, 1,* 75–89.

Janoff-Bulman, R. (1979). Characterological versus behavioral self-blame: Inquiries into depression and rape. *Journal of Personality and Social Psychology, 37,* 1798–1809.

Janoff-Bulman, R. (1982). Esteem and control bases of blame: Adaptive strategies for victims versus observers. *Journal of Personality, 50,* 180–192.

Janoff-Bulman, R. (1992). *Shattered assumptions.* New York: Free Press.

Janoff-Bulman, R., & Wortman, C. (1977). Attributions of blame and coping in the "real world": Severe accident victims react to their lot. *Journal of Personality and Social Psychology, 35,* 351–363.

Jones, E. (1977). The criteria of success in treatment. London: Maresfield Reprints. (Original work published 1936)

Jones, E., & Nisbett, N. (1987). The actor and the observer: Divergent perceptions of the causes of behavior. In Jones, E., Kanouse, D., Kelley, H., Nisbitt, R., Valius, S., Weiner, B. (Eds.), *Attribution: Perceiving the causes of behavior* (pp. 79–94). Hillsdale, NJ: Erlbaum.

Josephs, L. (1995). *Balancing empathy and interpretation: Relational character analysis.* Northvale, NJ: Jason Aronson.

Jung, C. (1933). *Modern man in search of soul.* New York: Harcourt Brace.

Kassam-Adams, N. (1995). The risks of treating sexual trauma: Stress and secondary trauma in psychotherapists. In B. Stamm (Ed.), *Secondary traumatic stress: Self-care issues for clinicians, researchers and educators.* (pp. 37–48). Lutherville, MD: Sidran Press.

Kaufman, G. (1992). *Shame: The power of caring.* Rochester, VT: Schenkman Books.

Kendall-Tackett, K., Williams, L., & Finkelhor, D. (1993). Impact of sexual abuse on children: A review and synthesis of recent empirical studies. *Psychological Bulletin, 113,* 164–180.

Kernberg, O. (1975). Borderline conditions and pathological narcissism. Northvale, NJ: Jason Aronson.

Kiecolt-Glaser, J., & Williams, D. (1987). Self-blame, compliance, and distress among burn patients. *Journal of Personality and Social Psychology, 53,* 187–193.

Klein, M. (1946). Notes on some schizoid mechanisms. *International Journal of Psycho-Analysis, 27,* 99–110.

Klein, M. (1950). On the criteria for the termination of a psychoanalysis. *International Journal of Psychoanalysis, 31,* 78–80, 204.

Klinnert, M. (1984). The regulation of infant behavior by maternal facial expression. *Infant Behavior and Development, 7,* 447–465.

Kluft, R. (1994). Countertransference in the treatment of multiple personality disorder. In J. Wilson and J. Lindy (Eds.), *Countertransference in the treatment of PTSD* (pp. 122–150). New York: Guilford.

Knapp, S., & Vandercreek, L. (1997). *Treating patients with memories of abuse: Legal risk management.* Washington, DC: American Psychological Association.

Kobak, R., Cole, H., Ferenz, G., & Fleming, W. (1993). Attachment and emotion regulation during mother–teen problem solving: A control theory analysis. *Child Development, 64,* 231–245.

Kramer, S. (1986). The termination process in open-ended psychotherapy: Guidelines for clinical practice. *Psychotherapy, 23,* 526–531.

Kushner, H. (1983). *When bad things happen to good people.* New York: Avon.

Lang, B. (1988). *Writing and the Holocaust.* New York: Holmes & Meier.

Langer, L. (1991). *Holocaust testimonies: The ruins of memory.* New Haven, CT: Yale University Press.

Langs, R. (1976). *The bipersonal field.* Northvale, NJ: Jason Aronson.

Latts, M., & Gelson, C. (1995). Countertransference behavior and management with survivors of sexual assault. *Psychotherapy, 32,* 405–415.

Lerner, M. (1980). *The belief in a just world.* New York: Plenum.

Levi, P. (1986). *The drowned and the saved.* New York: Vintage Books.

Levine, H. (1982). Toward a psychoanalytic understanding of children of survivors of the Holocaust. *Psychoanalytic Quarterly, 51,* 70–92.

Levine, H. (1990). Clinical issues in the analysis of adults who were sexually abused as children. In H. Levine (Ed.), *Adult analysis and childhood sexual abuse* (pp. 197–218). Hillsdale, NJ: Analytic Press.

Levy, S., & Inderbitzin, L. (1990). The analytic surface and the theory of technique. *Journal of the American Psychoanalytic Association, 38,* 371–391.

Lewis, H. (1971). Shame and guilt in neurosis. *Psychoanalytic Review, 58,* 419–438.

Lifton, R. (1980). The concept of the survivor. In J. Dimsdale (Ed.), *Survivors, victims, and perpetrators.* New York: Hemisphere.

Lindsay, S., & Briere, J. (1997). The controversy regarding recovered memories of childhood sexual abuse: Pitfalls, bridges and future directions. *Journal of Interpersonal Violence, 12,* 631–647.

Linehan, M., & Nielson, S. (1981). Assessment of suicide ideation and parasuicide: Hopelessness and social desirability. *Journal of Consulting and Clinical Psychology, 49,* 773–775.

Lion, J., & Pasternak, S. (1973). Countertransference reactions to violent patients. *American Journal of Psychiatry, 130,* 207–210.

Little, M. (1951). Countertransference and the patient's response to it. *International Journal of Psycho-Analysis, 33,* 32–40.

Little, M. (1957). "R"—The analyst's total response to his patient's needs. *International Journal of Psycho-Analysis, 38,* 240–254.

Little, M. (1966). Transference in borderline states. *International Journal of Psycho-Analysis, 47,* 476–485.

Little, M. (1990). *Psychotic anxieties and containment: A personal record of an analysis with Winnicott.* Northvale, NJ: Jason Aronson.

Littrell, J. (1998). Is the reexperience of painful emotion therapeutic? *Clinical Psychology Review, 18,* 71–102.

Livingston, R., & Farber, B. (1996). Beginning therapists' response to client shame. *Psychotherapy, 33,* 601–610.

Loewenstein, R. (1951). The problem of interpretation. *Psychoanalytic Quarterly, 20,* 1–14.

Loewenstein, R. (1954). Some remarks on defences, autonomous ego and psychoanalytic technique. *International Journal of Psycho-Analysis, 35,* 188–193.

Loftus, E., & Ketcham, K. (1994). *The myth of repressed memory: False memories and allegations of sexual abuse.* New York: St. Martin's Press.

Lynn, S., Pintar, J., & Rhue, J. (1997). Fantasy proneness, dissociation, and narrative construction. In S. Krippner, S. Powers (Eds.), *Broken images, broken selves: Dissociative narratives in clinical practice* (pp. 274–302). Philadelphia: Brunner/Mazel.

Mahler, M. (1988). *The memoirs of Margaret Mahler.* (P.E. Stepansky, Ed.) New York: Free Press.

Malin, A., & Grotstein, J. (1966). Projective identification in the therapeutic process. *International Journal of Psychoanalysis, 47,* 26–31.

Malle, B., & Knobe, K. (1997). Which behaviors do people explain? A basic actor–observer asymmetry. *Journal of Personality and Social Psychology, 72,* 288–304.

Maltsberger, J. (1994). The psychotherapist as an accomplice in suicide. *Giornale Italiano di Suicidologia, 4,* 75–81.

Maltsberger, J., & Goldblatt, M. (1996). *Essential papers on suicide.* New York: New York University Press.

Maroda, K. (1991). *The power of countertransference: Innovations in analytic technique.* New York: Wiley.

Marvasti, J. (1992). Psychotherapy with abused children and adolescents. In J. Brandell (Ed.), *Countertransference in psychotherapy with children and adolescents* (pp. 191–214). Northvale, NJ: Jason Aronson.

Masterson, J. (1983). *Countertransference and psychotherapeutic technique: Teaching seminars on psychotherapy of the borderline adult.* Philadelphia: Brunner/Mazel.

Mays, D., & Franks, C. (1985). *Negative outcome in psychotherapy and what to do about it.* New York: Springer.

McCann, I., & Pearlman, L. (1990). *Psychological trauma and the adult survivor: Theory, therapy and transformation.* Philadelphia: Brunner/Mazel.

McGuire, W. (1974). *The Freud/Jung letters: The correspondence between Sigmund Freud and C. G. Jung.* Princeton, NJ: Princeton University Press.

McHugh, P. (1993a, May 3). Procedures in the diagnosis of incest in recovered memory cases. *FMS Foundation Newsletter,* p. 3.

McLaughlin, J. (1995). Touching limits in the analytic dyad. *Psychoanalytic Quarterly, 64,* 433–465.

Meissner, W. (1996). *The therapeutic alliance.* New Haven, CT: Yale University Press.

Menninger, K. (1942). *Love against hate.* New York: Harcourt, Brace.

Menninger, K., & Holzman, P. (1973). *Theory of psychoanalytic technique.* New York: Basic Books.

Merali, N., & Lynch, P. (1997). Collaboration in cognitive–behavioural counselling: A case example. *Canadian Journal of Counselling, 31,* 287–293.

Miller, A. (1990). *Banished knowledge.* New York: Doubleday.

Miller, A., Ashton, W., & Mishal, M. (1990). Beliefs concerning the features of constrained behavior: A basis for the fundamental attribution error. *Journal of Personality and Social Psychology, 59,* 635–650.

Modestin, J. (1987). Countertransference reactions contributing to completed suicide. *British Journal of Medical Psychology, 60,* 379–385.

Murray, J. (1993). Relationship of childhood sexual abuse to borderline personality disorder, posttraumatic stress disorder, and multiple personality disorder. *Journal of Psychology, 127,* 657–676.

Nadelson, T. (1977). Borderline rage and the therapist's response. *American Journal of Psychiatry, 134,* 748–751.

Novick, J. (1997). Termination conceivable and inconceivable. *Psychoanalytic Psychology, 14,* 145–162.

Ochberg, F. (1988). *Post-traumatic therapy and victims of violence.* Philadelphia: Brunner/Mazel.

Ofshe, R., & Watters, E. (1994). *Making monsters: False memories, psychotherapy, and hysteria.* New York: Charles Scribner's Sons.

Orlinsky, D., & Howard, K. (1978). The relation of process to outcome in psychotherapy. In S. Garfield and A. Bergin (Eds.), *Handbook of psychotherapy and behavior change: An empirical analysis* (pp. 283–329). New York: Wiley.

Osherson, S., & Krugman, S. (1990). Men, shame and psychotherapy. *Psychotherapy, 27,* 327–339.

Pagis, D. (1995). Written in pencil in the sealed railway-car. In L. Langer (Ed.), *Art from the ashes.* New York: Oxford University Press.

Pattison, J. (1973). Effects of touch on self-exploration and the therapeutic relationship. *Journal of Consulting and Clinical Psychology, 40,* 170–173.

Pearlman, L., & Saakvitne, K. (1995). Trauma and the therapist: Countertransference and vicarious traumatization in psychotherapy with incest survivors. New York: Norton.

Pennebaker, J., Barger, S., & Tiebout, J. (1989). Disclosure of traumas and health among Holocaust survivors. *Psychosomatic Medicine, 51,* 577–589.

Pennebaker, J., Kiecolt-Glaser, J., & Glaser, R. (1988). Disclosure of traumas and immune function: Health implications for psychotherapy. *Journal of Consulting and Clinical Psychology, 56,* 239–245.

Pennebaker, J., & O'Heeron, R. (1984). Confiding in others and illness rates among spouses of suicide and accidental-death victims. *Journal of Abnormal Psychology, 93,* 473–476.

Perry, J., Herman, J., van der Kolk, B., & Hoke, L. (1990). Psychotherapy and psychological trauma in borderline personality disorder. *Psychiatric Annals, 20,* 33–43.

Peters, R. (1991). The therapist's expectations of the transference. *Journal of Analytical Psychology, 36,* 77–92.

Peterson, D. (1996). Making conversation possible. *Applied and Preventative Psychology, 5,* 17–18.

Pettigrew, J., & Burcham, J. (1997). Effects of childhood sexual abuse in adult female psychiatric patients. *Australian and New Zealand Journal of Psychiatry, 31,* 208–213.

Poggi, R., & Ganzarian, R. (1983). Countertransference hate. *Bulletin of the Menninger Clinic, 47,* 15–35.

Polanyi, M. (1968). Logic and psychology. *American Psychologist, 23,* 27–43.

Polanyi, M. (1974). Scientific thought and social reality: Essays by Michael Polanyi. *Psychological Issues, 8,* 157.

Pope, K. (1996). Memory, abuse and science: Questioning claims about the false memory syndrome epidemic. *American Psychologist, 51,* 957–974.

Pope, K., & Brown, L. (1996). *Recovered memories of abuse: Assessment, therapy, forensics.* Washington, DC: American Psychological Association.

Pope, K., & Feldman-Summers, S. (1992). National survey of psychologists' sexual and physical abuse history and their evaluation of training and competence in these areas. *Professional Psychology: Research and Practice, 23,* 353–361.

Pope, K., Keith-Spiegel, P., & Tabachnick, B. (1986). Sexual attraction to clients: The human therapist and the (sometimes) inhuman training system. *American Psychologist, 41,* 147–158.

Pope, K., Sonne, J., & Holroyd, J. (1993). *Sexual feelings in psychotherapy: Explorations for therapist and therapists-in-training.* Washington, DC: American Psychiatric Press.

Pope, K., & Tabachnick, B. (1993). Therapists' anger, hate, fear, and sexual feelings: National survey of therapist responses, client characteristics, critical events, formal complaints, and training. *Professional Psychology: Research and Practice, 24,* 142–152.

Pope, K., Tabachnick, B., & Keith-Spiegel, P. (1987). Ethics of practice: The belief and behaviors of psychologists as therapists. *American Psychologist, 42,* 993–1006.

Pope, K., & Vasquez, M. (1998). Ethics in psychotherapy and counseling: A practical guide for psychologists. San Francisco: Jossey-Bass. (Originally published 1991)

Putnam, F. (1997). *Dissociation in children and adolescents.* New York: Guilford.

Racker, H. (1968). *Transference and countertransference*. New York: International Universities Press.

Ramona v. Ramona (1994). Superior Court of the State of California. In and for the County of Napa. Case No. C61898.

Reich, A. (1951). On countertransference. *International Journal of Psycho-Analysis, 31*, 179–183.

Reich, A. (1960). Further remarks on countertransference. *International Journal of Psycho-Analysis, 41*, 389–395.

Reidy, T. (1977). The aggressive characteristics of abused and neglected children. *Journal of Clinical Psychology, 33*, 1140–1145.

Rhodes, R. (1990). *A hole in the world*. New York: Simon & Schuster.

Rickman, J. (1950). On the criteria for the termination of an analysis. *International Journal of Psychoanalysis, 31*, 200–201.

Roazen, P. (1985). *Helene Deutsch: A psychoanalyst's life*. Garden City, NY: Doubleday.

Roazen, P. (1995). *How Freud worked: First-hand accounts of patients*. Northvale, NJ: Jason Aronson.

Robbins, S., & Jolkovski, M. (1987). Managing countertransference feelings: An interactional model using awareness of feeling and theoretical framework. *Journal of Counseling Psychology, 34*, 276–282.

Rodolfa, E., Hall, T., Holms, V., Davena, A., Komatz, D., Antunez, M., & Hall, A. (1994). The management of sexual feelings in therapy. *Professional Psychology: Research and Practice, 25*, 168–172.

Russell, P., & Snyder, W. (1963). Counselor anxiety in relation to amount of clinical experience and quality of affect demonstrated by clients. *Journal of Consulting Psychology, 22*, 358–363.

Russell, P. (1998). The role of paradox in the repetition compulsion. In J. Teicholz & D. Kriegman (Eds.), *Trauma, repetition, and affect regulation: The work of Paul Russell* (pp. 1–22). New York: Other Press.

Sabo, A. (1997). Etiological significance of associations between childhood trauma and borderline personality disorder: Conceptual and clinical implications. *Journal of Personality Disorders, 11*, 50–70.

Safrin, J., & Segal, Z. (1990). *Interpersonal process in cognitive therapy*. New York: Basic Books.

Salter, A. (1995). *Transforming trauma: A guide to understanding and treating adult survivors of child sexual abuse*. Thousand Oaks, CA: Sage.

Sandler, J. (1976). Countertransference and role-responsiveness. *International Review of Psychoanalysis, 3*, 43–47.

Santanyana, G. (1954). *The life of reason*. Amherst: Prometheus Books. (Originally published 1905)

Savitz, C. (1990). The double death: The loss of the analyst in the analytic hour. *Journal of Analytical Psychology, 35*, 241–260.

Scaturo, D., & McPeak, W. (1998). Clinical dilemmas in contemporary psychotherapy: The search for clinical wisdom. *Psychotherapy: Theory, research and practice, 35*, 1–12.

Schulz, R., & Decker, S. (1985). Long-term adjustment to physical disability: The role of social support, perceived control, and self-blame. *Journal of Personality and Social Psychology, 48,* 1162–1172.

Searles, H. (1965). *Collected papers on schizophrenia and related subjects.* Madison, CT: International Universities Press.

Searles, H. (1979). *Countertransference and related subjects.* Madison, CT: International Universities Press.

Searles, H. (1986). *My work with borderline patients.* Northvale, NJ: Jason Aronson.

Shaffer, P. (1977). *Equus.* New York: Avon.

Shaver, P., & Clark, C. (1994). The psychodynamics of adult romantic attachment. In R. F. Bornstein and J. M. Masling (Eds.), *Empirical studies of psychoanalytic theories* (Vol. 5, pp. 105–156). Washington, DC: American Psychological Association.

Shay, J. (1994). *Achilles in Vietnam.* New York: Atheneum.

Shortt, J., & Pennebaker, J. (1992). Talking versus hearing about Holocaust experiences. *Basic and Applied Social Psychology, 13,* 165–179.

Simon, R. (1989). Sexual exploitation of patients: How it begins before it happens. *Contemporary Psychiatry, 19,* 104–112.

Silver, R., Boon, C., & Stones, M. (1983). Searching for meaning in misfortune: Making sense of incest. *Journal of Social Issues, 39,* 81–102.

Sloane, R., Staples, F., Cristol, A., Yorkston, N., & Whipple, K. (1975). *Psychotherapy versus behavior therapy.* Cambridge, MA: Harvard University Press.

Spence, D. (1982). *Narrative truth and historical truth.* New York: Norton.

Spiegel, D. (1994). *Dissociation: Culture, mind and body.* Washington, DC: American Psychiatric Press.

Spiegel, D., & Spiegel, H. (1978). *Trance and treatment: Clinical uses of hypnosis.* Washington, DC: American Psychiatric Press.

Spotnitz, H. (1976). *Psychotherapy of preoedipal conditions.* Northvale, NJ: Jason Aronson.

Stake, J., & Oliver, J. (1991). Sexual contact and touching between therapist and client: A survey of psychologists' attitudes and behavior. *Professional Psychology: Research and Practice, 22,* 297–307.

Stamm, B. (Ed.) (1995). *Secondary traumatic stress: Self-care issues for clinicians, researchers and educators.* Lutherville, MD: Sidran Press.

Stammen, C. (1999). *Prediction of child punishment: Exploring anger level, self-concept, social desirability, and provocative child behavior.* Unpublished doctoral dissertation, California School of Professional Psychology, San Diego.

Stein, E., & Eisen, B. (1996). Helping trauma survivors cope: Effects of immediate brief co-therapy and crisis intervention. *Crisis Intervention and Time-Limited Treatment, 3,* 113–127.

Steingart, I. (1995). *A thing apart: Love and reality in the therapeutic relationship.* Northvale, NJ: Jason Aronson.

Steres, L. (1992). *Sexual attraction in therapy: A professional training interven-*

tion for clinical psychology graduate students. Unpublished doctoral dissertation, California School of Professional Psychology, San Diego.

Stern, D. (1985). *The interpersonal world of the infant: A view from psychoanalysis and developmental psychology.* New York: Basic Books.

Strachey, J. (1934). The nature of the therapeutic action of psychoanalysis. *International Journal of Psycho-Analysis, 15,* 127–159.

Strauss, K. (1996). *Differential diagnosis of battered women through psychological testing: Personality disorder or post traumatic stress disorder?* Unpublished doctoral dissertation, California School of Professional Psychology, San Diego.

Strupp, H. (1977). A reformulation of the dynamics of the therapist's contribution. In A. Guerman and A. Razin (Eds.), *Effective psychotherapy: A handbook of research* (pp. 3–22). New York: Pergamon.

Strupp, H. (1980). Success and failure in time-limited psychotherapy: A systematic comparison of two cases. *Archives of General Psychiatry, 37,* 595–603.

Strupp, H., Wallach, M., & Wogan, M. (1964). Psychotherapy experience in retrospect: Questionnaire survey of former patients and their therapists. *Psychological Monographs: General and Applied, 78* (11, Whole No. 588).

Styron, W. (1979). *Sophie's choice.* New York: Random House.

Summit, R. (1987, December). *Wingspread briefing paper.* Invited paper presented at the Wingspread Symposium: Child Sexual Abuse: Recommendations for Prevention and Treatment Policy, Racine, WI.

Szasz, T. (1963). The concept of transference. *International Journal of Psycho-Analysis, 44,* 432–443.

Tangney, J., Wagner, P, Hill-Barlow, D., Marschall, D., & Gramzow, R. (1996). Relation of shame and guilt to constructive versus destructive responses to anger across the lifespan. *Journal of Personality and Social Psychology, 70,* 797–809.

Tansey, M., & Burke, W. (1989). *Understanding countertransference: From projective identification to empathy.* Hillsdale, NJ: Analytic Press.

Tauber, Y. (1998). *In the other chair: Holocaust survivors and the second generation as therapists and clients.* Jeruselem, Israel: Gefen.

Taylor, S., Lichtman, R., & Wood, J. (1984). Attributions, beliefs about control, and adjustment to breast cancer. *Journal of Personality and Social Psychology, 46,* 489–502.

Tedeschi, R., & Calhoun, L. (1995) *Trauma and transformation: Growing in the aftermath of suffering.* Thousand Oaks, CA: Sage.

Tedeschi, T., Park, C., & Calhoun, L. (1998). *Posttraumatic growth: Positive changes in the aftermath of crisis.* Mahwah, NJ: Erlbaum.

Tennen, H., Affleck, G., & Gerschman, K. (1986). Self-blame among parents of infants with perinatal complications: The role of self-protective motives. *Journal of Personality and Social Psychology, 50,* 690–696.

Terr, L. (1981). Forbidden games. *Journal of the American Academy of Child Psychiatry, 20,* 740–759.

Terr, L. (1987). Childhood trauma and the creative product. *Psychoanalytic Study of Children, 42,* 545–572.

Terr, L. (1989). Terror writing by the formerly terrified. *Psychoanalytic Study of Children, 44,* 369–390.

Terr, L. (1990a). *Too scared to cry.* New York: Harper & Row.

Terr, L. (1990b). Who's afraid of Virginia Woolf? *Psychoanalytic Study of Children, 45,* 531–544.

Terr, L. (1991). Childhood traumas: An outline and overview. *American Journal of Psychiatry, 148,* 10–20.

Ticho, E. (1972). Termination of pyschoanalysis: Treatment goals, life goals. *Psychoanalytic Quarterly, 41,* 315–332.

Tronick, E., Als, H., Adamson, L., Wise, S., & Brazelton, T. (1978). The infant's response to intrapment between contradictory messages in face-to-face interaction. *Journal of Child Psychiatry, 17,* 1–13.

van der Kolk, B. (1989) The compulsion to repeat the trauma: Re-enactment, revictimization, and masochism. *Psychiatric Clinics of North America, 18,* 389–411.

Wachtel, P. (1982). *Resistance: Psychodynamic and behavioral approaches.* New York: Plenum.

Waelder, R. (1960). *Basic theory of psychoanalysis.* New York: International Universities Press.

Wagner, K., & Calhoun, L. (1991). Perceptions of social support by suicide survivors and their social networks. *Omega: Journal of Death and Dying, 24,* 61–73.

Waites, E. (1993). *Trauma and survival: Post-traumatic and dissociative disorders in women.* New York: Norton.

Wakefield, H., & Underwager, R. (1994). *Return of the furies: An investigation into recovered memory therapy.* Chicago: Open Court.

Walsh, B., & Rosen, P. (1988). *Self-mutilation: Theory, research, and treatment.* New York: Guilford.

Watts, D., & Morgan, H. (1994). Malignant alienation: Dangers for patients who are hard to like. *British Journal of Psychiatry, 164,* 11–15.

Weaver, T., & Clum, G. (1996). Interpersonal violence: Expanding the search for long-term sequelae within a sample of battered women. *Journal of Traumatic Stress, 9,* 783–803.

Webster, M. (1991). Emotional abuse in therapy. *Australian and New Zealand Journal of Psychotherapy, 12,* 137–145.

West, P. (1995). *A stroke of genius.* New York: Penguin.

Weisel, E. (1978). *A Jew today.* New York: Vintage.

Weisel, E. (1993). Interview with Harry Cargas. In H. Cargas (Ed.), *Voices from the Holocaust* (pp. 157–162). Lexington, KY: University Press of Kentucky.

Weisel, E. (1995). A plea for the dead. In L. Langer (Ed.), *Art from the ashes* (pp. 138–152). Oxford, UK: Oxford University Press.

Weiss, J. (1993). *How psychotherapy works: Process and technique.* New York: Guilford.

Wholey, D. (1992). *When the worst that can happen already has.* New York: Hyperion.

Wilkomirski, B. (1996). *Fragments: Memories of a wartime childhood, 1939–1948.* New York: Schoken Books.

Williams, L. (1995). Recovered memories of abuse in women with documented child sexual abuse victimization histories. *Journal of Traumatic Stress, 8,* 649–673.

Wilson, J., & Lindy, J. (1994). *Countertransference in the treatment of PTSD.* New York: Guilford.

Winnicott, D. (1949). Hate in the counter-transference. *International Journal of Psychoanalysis, 30,* 69–74.

Winnicott, D. (1974). Fear of breakdown. *International Review of Psychoanalysis, 1,* 103.

Winnicott, D. (1989). The use of an object and relating through identification. In C. Winnicott, R. Shepherd, & M. Davis (Eds.), *Psycho-analytic Explorations* (pp. 218–227). Cambridge, MA: Harvard University Press. (Originally published 1968)

Wolpe, D. (1992). *The speech and the silence.* New York: Henry Holt.

Woodmansey, A. (1988). Are psychotherapists out of touch? *British Journal of Psychotherapy, 5,* 57–65

Zerbe, K. (1995). Integrating feminist and psychodynamic principles in the treatment of an eating disorder patient: Implications for using countertransference responses. *Bulletin of the Menninger Clinic, 59,* 160–176.

Appendix

Trauma Countertransference Study

The 84 clients interviewed for this text were recruited through flyers, two newspaper ads, and Internet postings. Seventy-eight women and twenty-eight men responded. Sixty-two women and twenty-two men met criteria. The final sample of 84 included 62 Caucasians (74%), 13 Hispanics (15%) and 9 African-American (11%) participants. With the exception of six pilot interviews, I conducted all interviews myself. Sixty-one of the participants were interviewed in person in California, and 23 (4 former clients from California and 19 from other states) were interviewed by phone. Participants were interviewed in person or by phone for 1–3 hours. They responded to a call for those "who had completed psychotherapy related to trauma and who were willing to give feedback to professionals about what they found helpful and unhelpful." The interview followed the needs of the client, but all clients were asked the same core questions. The final version is printed below; some early interviews did not include some questions.

After completion of a brief demographic questionnaire, participants were asked questions about the nature of their trauma, but they were not pushed to disclose any detail that seemed too personal or that they did not wish to share. The major trauma discussed in therapy was physical or sexual abuse for 49% of the sample ($n = 41$). Other participants cited rape or assault (15%: $n = 13$), traumatic loss (19%: $n = 16$), or war trauma (8%: $n = 7$). The focus of the questions was kept on their perceptions of their therapists. Positive answers to any questions below were explored, and clients were asked how the dyad solved each problem.

The final sample described throughtout this text were those clients who met three criteria. Participants must have completed psychotherapy lasting a minimum of ten weeks. All participants were at least three months post-completion. (The therapies actually ranged from three months to fifteen years, with a mean duration of 26.98 months and a standard deviation of 31.25 months). Finally, all participants must have experienced and discussed in therapy a traumatic event. The events listed included as traumas if they were rated above five on each of four 10-point scales.

1. To what degree was the event negative to you?
2. To what degree was the event unexpected for you?
3. To what degree did the event change your view of yourself and/or the world (at least for a time)?
4. To what extent did you feel fear, helplessness or horror during or immediately after the event?

Participants were asked to describe a single therapist. For those with multiple therapy experiences, the clinician chosen was the therapist judged by the client as most successful in treating the trauma issues.

Overview Read to Client

Clients and therapists in psychotherapy can become very involved in working on the clients' issues and problems. Like any two people working on important projects, they can have some difficult times. I'm going to read you a problem list now, but I want to emphasize first that some of these things won't have happened at all, and others will have happened, maybe a lot. The fact that some problems occurred doesn't mean that your therapy wasn't good for you in many ways. We really are only trying to discover how to make life and therapy easier for trauma victims, and that means trying to change bad therapy or bad techniques and to make good therapy better. OK? [Elicit understanding.] We want you to say yes if you had the problem, even if you and your therapist fixed it. Then we will go back to some of them and get more information. OK? [Answer questions.]

Demographics Questionnaire

Here participants were asked for age, gender, and other demographic information that was known about the therapist, and about their perceptions of the therapists theoretical orientations. They also were asked about the amount of time devoted to various therapeutic activities, such as listening, expressing support, interpreting, teaching symptom management, talking about the past, problem solving about the future, and so on. Using the participants' answers to these questions together with the participants' self-report of therapist orientation, 19 (23%) of the clinicians were classified as cognitive or cognitive behavioral, 33 (39%) were classified as humanistic, and 32 (38%) were classified as analytic or psychodynamic. Most of the described clinicians (58%) were female. The following question classified the therapist as a disclosing or nondisclosing clinician:

Some therapists [Type 1] have a policy of trying to withhold any expression of their own emotions, sometimes because they are trying not to burden you with their emotional reactions. Other therapists [Type 2] frequently share their emotions, thinking that therapy must be genuine and honest. Most therapists are not perfect examples of one extreme or the other, but which type would you say describes your therapist in general?

By this method, 31 (37%) of the clinicians were identified as primary nondisclosing therapists.

Specific Disclosure Questions

1. Was there ever a time that you asked for information about him or her that your therapist refused to disclose? Did you ever ask any of these things?
    - ☐ The reason for a cancellation or change in an appointment time
    - ☐ A question about your therapist's sexual orientation
    - ☐ The explanation for an apparent injury
    - ☐ A question about your therapist's health
    - ☐ A question about your therapist's future plans (for eventual retirement or vacations, for instance)
    - ☐ A question about whether your therapist had experienced a particular negative event (for example, whether he or she had been abused, raped, or divorced)
    - ☐ A question about your therapist's everyday personal life (if he or she is married, what part of town he or she lives in)
    - ☐ A question about losses in your therapist's life
    - ☐ A question about how the therapist had handled interpersonal problems in his or her life
    - ☐ A question about your therapist's financial status
    - ☐ A question about your therapist's husband, wife, or significant other
    - ☐ A question about other patients that your therapist treated
    - ☐ A question about your therapist's theory of psychotherapy

    Any positive answer was followed up with a request for the specific question, whether it was answered, and the client's subjective sense that the decision to disclose or refuse disclosure was helpful in the long run.
2. Was there ever a time that your therapist just told you something factual and personal about himself or herself that you didn't ask about?

General Questions

3. If you had to say one thing your therapist did that made it easier for you in therapy, what would you say it was? Anything that made it harder, rather than easier?

4. If you had to say that one emotion was most difficult for your therapist to experience with you, what would it be? [Prompt if necessary:being very sad or hopeless, being angry at someone, being angry at the therapist, being ashamed of yourself, being disappointed in your therapist, wanting something badly from your therapist.]

5. Did you trust your therapist?

6. What was the single hardest obstacle to overcome in relating well, the way you wanted to relate, with your therapist?

7. Would you ever go back to that therapist?

8. What would you say was your therapist's greatest strength?

9. What would you say was your therapist's greatest weakness?

10. What did you get out of therapy?

11. How did you know you were done?

12. Did you have any sense of what your therapist was looking for in order to say that your therapy was over and the trauma was resolved or integrated?

13. Do you think your therapy was successful?

Avoidance or Encouragement

14. When you told your story, did your therapist do or say anything that made it harder for you to talk about it? Easier?

15. Did you ever feel as if your therapist was avoiding a subject that he or she didn't want to talk about (in your life?)

16. Did you ever want to talk about something more deeply and feel as if your therapist was getting in your way?

17. Did you ever think your therapist was pushing you

too much to talk about the trauma? Did he or she push too little?

As with all categories, clients who indicated problems in this area were asked how they got past the problems with their therapists.

Shame and Pride

18. Can you think of anything that your therapist said or did that made you feel very good about yourself, even temporarily?
19. Can you think of anything that your therapist said or did that made you feel very bad about yourself, even temporarily?
20. Was there ever a time that you felt your therapist was ashamed of you? Did your therapist ever make you feel worse about something you were already ashamed about?
21. Did you ever feel very ashamed yourself of something in therapy?

Anger

22. Are you still angry at your therapist for anything he or she did or said?
23. Were you ever really angry at your therapist?
24. Was there ever a time that your therapist got angry at you for something that either one or both of you later thought wasn't your fault or was a little unfair?
25. Did your therapist ever get angry with you, even for a good reason, but express it in a way that you or your therapist thought was harmful to you?
26. Was there ever a time that you were angry at your therapist for something that later you thought wasn't his or her fault?

Blame

27. Did you ever feel like your therapist blamed you for something that was not your fault when you were talking about your life outside of therapy?
28. Did you ever feel like your therapist blamed you for something that was not your fault in a situation that happened between the two of you?
29. Did you ever feel as if your therapist was defensive when you asked him or her to take a share of the blame for a problem?
30. Did you ever feel as if your therapist encouraged you to blame others and then suddenly blamed you?

Dependency

31. Did you ever feel that your therapist encouraged your dependence on him or her in a way that became a problem?
32. Did you ever feel as if you got too dependent on your therapist in a way that was not healthy for you?
33. Did you ever feel as if you could not risk dependency on your therapist?

Sexual Interest

34. Did you ever have sexual feelings about your therapist? Did you ever think your therapist had such feelings about you? Did you discuss it?

Boundary Rigidity

35. Did you ever have the experience of your therapist making a very rigid rule that didn't seem to be in your best interest?
36. Did you ever have a specific experience that made you feel as if your relationship was not important and you were "just a patient"?
37. Did your therapist ever seem to change the rules on

you about when you could call, have more appointments, etc.?

Boundary Crossing and Intrusiveness

38. Did your therapist ever do anything that seemed as if
   he or she was interfering in your life in a way that
   was a problem?
39. Did your therapist ever tell you what to do in a way
   that was a problem?
40. Did your therapist ever tell you what to believe in a
   way that was a problem?
41. Did your therapist ever act as if he or she knew more
   about your history than you did?

Care

42. Did your therapist care about you? Did you have trouble believing that? How could you tell that your therapist cared?

Failure to Understand

43. Did you ever feel as if your therapist failed to understand something about you that was very important?

Other

44. Did your therapist always believe you when you
   talked about important things?
45. Did you ever lie to your therapist?
46. Did you do anything that put you at risk of harm
   during therapy (like drink too much, or hurt yourself,
   or do other risky things)? Was there anything that
   your therapist did that made it more likely or less
   likely that you would [perform the behavior]?
47. Did you and your therapist ever touch? How? Did
   any touch happen that made you uncomfortable? Did
   your therapist ever refuse to touch you?

48. Did you ever have an instance when you asked your therapist to change some behavior and he or she did so? Did it help or hurt the therapy?
49. Did your therapist ever seem to refuse to self-examine and change his or her ways when you thought you needed therapy to change?
50. Did your therapist ever seem to fail to consider your perspective?

The findings from this interview are discussed throughout the text.

Index

About the Author

Constance J. Dalenberg, PhD, is an associate professor of psychology at the California School of Professional Psychology and is recognized as an international expert on trauma disclosure and trauma therapy. As director of the Trauma Research Institute in La Jolla, California, she has designed and supervised over 50 research studies on the consequences of trauma. Her private practice, centered on the treatment and forensic evaluation of survivors of trauma, is located in La Jolla, California.